W9-BDO-757

Airport

Airport Expressway

■ Holiday Inn Lido
Yanxiang ■
Hotel
■ Grace
Hotel
Jiali Hotel ■

CHAOYANG
DISTRICT

Chaoyang Lu

Ritan
Park

China
Resources
Hotel
Jianguo Lu

Dabei

■
Furong
Hotel

Second Ring Road

Dongsanhuan Nanlu

Longtan
Park

Beijing - Tianjin Expressway

Beijing

0   1   2 km

Beijing
a Lonely Planet city guide

Robert Storey

Beijing
   2nd edition

Published by
   Lonely Planet Publications
   Head Office: PO Box 617, Hawthorn, Vic 3122, Australia
   Branches: 155 Filbert St, Suite 251, Oakland,
                  CA 94607, USA
                  10 Barley Mow Passage, Chiswick,
                  London W4 4PH, UK
                  71 bis rue du Cardinal Lemoine,
                  75005 Paris, France

Printed by
   Colorcraft Ltd, Hong Kong

Photographs by
   Glenn Beanland, Nikki Burns, Jo O'Brien, Robert Storey, Chris Taylor
   Front cover : Game of checkers, Temple of Heaven, Tiantan Park
                  (Glenn Beanland)

First Published
   February 1994

This Edition
   June 1996

National Library of Australia Cataloguing in Publication Data

Storey, Robert
   Beijing

   2nd ed.
   Includes index.
   ISBN 0 86442 377 2.

   1. Peking (China) – Guide-books.
   I. Title. (Series : Lonely Planet city guide).

   915.11560459

text & maps © Lonely Planet 1996
photos © photographers as indicated 1996
climate charts compiled from information supplied by Patrick J Tyson,
© Patrick J Tyson, 1996

Robert Storey

A refugee from the Third World (New York City), Robert escaped to Las Vegas where he became a distinguished slot machine repairman. After graduating from the University of Nevada in Las Vegas with a worthless liberal arts degree, he then went on the road and learned to speak Chinese along the way. Today, he is a successful writer, computer hacker, model citizen and a pillar of his community – though no one is quite sure which community that is. His last known address was in Taipei.

From the Author

I'd like to express my gratitude to a number of visitors to Beijing, both long-termers and transients. Special thanks to Chiu Miaoling, Bruce A Douglass, Lars-Olof Lindgren, Ola Svensson, RJ Berry and Mark Lyseyko. I'm also deeply grateful to a number of Chinese people I met along the way who provided helpful advice, companionship, hospitality and some terrific dumplings.

From the Publisher

This second edition of the *Beijing city guide* was edited at the Lonely Planet office in Melbourne by Ian Ward, with proofing and editing help from Megan Fraser. Sally Woodward drew the maps and designed and laid out the book. Simon Bracken designed the front cover and gatefolds. Dan Levin programmed the pinyin and Chinese script. Thanks go to Alex Tseng of the Bamboo Terrace Restaurant, Melbourne, Australia; for assistance with culinary information.

Warning & Request

A travel writer's job is never done. Before the ink is dry on a new book, things change, and few places change more quickly than Beijing. At Lonely Planet we get a steady stream of mail from travellers and it all helps – whether it's a few lines scribbled on the back of a used paper plate (please, no garlic sauce), an e-mail or a stack of typewritten pages spewing forth from our fax machine. Prices go up, new hotels open, old ones degenerate, some burn down, others get renovated and renamed, bus routes change, bridges collapse and recommended travel agents get indicted for fraud. Remember, this book is meant to be a guide, not the oracle – since things go on changing we can't tell you exactly what to expect all the time. Hopefully this book will point you in the right direction and save you some time and money. If you find that China is not identical to the way it's described herein, don't get upset but write to Lonely Planet. Your input will help make the next edition better. As usual, the writers of useful letters will score a free copy of the next edition, or another Lonely Planet guide if you prefer. We give away lots of books but, unfortunately, not every author of letters and postcards can receive one.

Contents

Maps

Introduction

The capital of the People's Republic of China: home to bureaucrats, generals, nouveau-riche cadres and *lǎobǎixìng* (the common people); host to reporters, disgruntled diplomats and tourists; a labyrinth of doors, walls, tunnels, gates and entrances, temples, pavilions, parks and museums. As far away as Xinjiang they run on Beijing's clock; around the country they chortle in *pūtōnghuà*, the Beijing dialect; in remote Tibet they struggle to interpret the latest half-baked directives from the capital. This is where they move the cogs and wheels of the Chinese universe, or try to slow them down if they're moving in the wrong direction.

Perhaps nowhere else in China is the generation gap more visible. Appalled by the current drive to 'modernisation', many older people still talk of Chairman Mao and the years of sacrifice for the socialist revolution. But most young people disdain socialist sacrifice and are more interested in money, motorbikes, fashion, video games, sex and rock music – not necessarily in that order.

All cities in China are equal, but some are more equal than others. Beijing has the best of everything in China bar the weather: the best food, the best hotels, the best transport, the best temples. But its vast squares and boulevards, its cavernous monoliths, militaristic parades, ubiquitous police, luxury high-rises and armies of tourists may leave you with the impression that Beijing is China's largest theme park. Foreign residents sometimes call it 'the Los Angeles of China' – traffic-choked freeways plus a surreal imitation of Disneyland.

Among the Chinese, Beijing is the promised land. Poor peasants flock to the capital in search of the elusive pot of gold at the end of the rainbow – many wind up camped out on the pavement in front of the railway station. The government tries to encourage them to go home, but the lure of the capital proves too enticing. Meanwhile, down the road by the Friendship Store, smartly attired customers clutching cellular telephones head for the nearest banquet or disco.

Foreigners seem to enjoy Beijing – the city offers plenty to see and do, and you can't beat the food or shopping. Those who have slugged it out in the ramshackle buses and trains through the poverty-stricken interior of China appreciate the creature comforts of the capital. Other foreigners, having passed their time only in Beijing without seeing the rest of China, come away with the impression that everything is fine in the PRC and that the Chinese are living high. The Chinese they encounter may, in truth, be doing so.

But whatever one says about Beijing, it probably won't be true tomorrow – the city is changing so rapidly it makes you dizzy. Colour TVs and washing machines – unimaginable luxuries in the 1980s – are commonplace now. Whereas bicycles and ox carts were the main form of transport a decade ago, both are prohibited on the new freeways and toll roads which now ring the city.

Whatever impression you come away with, Beijing is one of the most fascinating places in China. It may be something of a showcase, but what capital city isn't? And with a bit of effort you can get out of the make-up department – Beijing houses some of China's most stunning sights: the Forbidden City, Summer Palace, Great Wall, Lama Temple, Tiantan, to name just a few. During the Cultural Revolution of the 1960s, these and other historical treasures of China literally took a beating. Now the damage has been repaired, the temples have been restored and everything is being spruced up.

Group tourists are processed through Beijing in much the same way the ducks are force-fed on the outlying farms – the two usually meet on the first night over the dinner table. But individual travellers will have no trouble getting around. For visitors, Beijing is for the most part 'user-friendly'.

Whatever effort you make to get out and see things will be rewarding. The city offers so much of intrinsic interest that the biggest problem encountered by most visitors is that they simply run out of time before seeing it all.

Facts about Beijing

HISTORY

Beijing is a time-setter for China, but it actually has a short history as Chinese timespans go. Although the area south-west of the city was inhabited by cave dwellers some 500,000 years ago, the earliest records of settlements date from around 1000 BC. It developed as a frontier trading town for the Mongols, Koreans and the tribes from Shandong Province and central China. By the Warring States Period (476-221 BC) it had grown to be the capital of the Yan kingdom and was called Ji, a reference to the marshy features of the area. The town underwent a number of changes as it acquired new warlords, the Khitan Mongols and the Manchurian Jurchen tribes among them. What attracted the conquerors was the strategic position of the town on the edge of the North China Plain. During the Liao Dynasty (907-1125 AD) Beijing was referred to as Yanjing (Capital of Yan) – the name now used for Beijing's most popular beer. The city's oldest street, Sanmiao Lu, is believed to date from this epoch.

In 1215 AD, the great Mongol warrior Genghis Khan razed the city. From the ashes emerged Dadu (Great Capital), alias Khanbaliq, the Khan's town. By 1279 Genghis' grandson Kublai had made himself ruler of most of Asia, with Khanbaliq as his capital. Thus was China's Yuan Dynasty (1215-1368) established.

When the Mongol emperor was informed by his astrologers that the old site of Beijing was a breeding ground for rebels, he shifted his capital further north. The great palace he built no longer remains, but was visited by the great Italian traveller, Marco Polo, who later described what he saw to an amazed Europe. Polo was equally dazzled by the innovations of gunpowder and paper money. The latter was not without its drawbacks – in history's first case of paper-currency inflation, the last Mongol emperor flooded the country with worthless bills. This, coupled with a large number of natural disasters, provoked an uprising led by the mercenary Zhu Yanhang, who took Beijing in 1368. During the Ming Dynasty (1368-1644) which followed, the city was renamed Beiping (Northern Peace), though for the next 35 years the imperial capital was sited in Nanjing.

In the early 1400s Zhu's son Yong Le shuffled the court back to Beiping and renamed it Beijing (Northern Capital). Millions of taels of silver were spent on refurbishing the city. Many of Beijing's most famous structures, like the Forbidden City and Tiantan, were first built in Yong Le's reign. In fact, he is credited with being the true architect of the modern city. The Inner City grew to encircle the imperial compound, and a suburban zone was added to the south – a bustle of merchants and street life. The basic grid of present-day Beijing had been laid.

Under the Manchus, who invaded China and established the Qing Dynasty (1644-1911), and particularly during the reigns of the emperors Kangxi and Qianlong, Beijing was expanded and renovated; summer palaces, pagodas and temples were built.

In the last 120 years of the Manchu Dynasty, Beijing and much of China were subject to invaders and rebels: the Anglo-French troops who in 1860 marched in and burnt the Old Summer Palace to the ground; and the disastrous Boxer Rebellion of 1900 against the corrupt regime of Empress Dowager Wu Cixi (1860-1908). The Manchus were finally trounced in the revolution of 1911 when the Kuomintang (Nationalist Party) ostensibly took power and established the Republic of China (ROC) with Sun Yatsen as president. However, real power remained in the hands of warlords. One such warlord, General Yuan Shikai, declared himself emperor in Beijing during 1915.

Yuan died in 1916, but other warlords continued to control most of northern China while the Kuomintang held power in the south. The country was badly splintered by private Chinese armies, while foreigners controlled important economic zones (called Concessions) in major ports like Shanghai and Tianjin.

China's continued poverty, backwardness and control by warlords and foreigners were a recipe for rebellion. Beijing University became a hotbed of intellectual dissent, attracting scholars from all over China. Karl Marx's *The Communist Manifesto*, translated into Chinese, became the basis for countless discussion groups. One of the attendees was a library assistant named Mao Zedong (1893-1976). The Communists, including Mao, later established a power base in Shanghai and entered into an uneasy alliance with the Kuomintang in order to reunify China.

In 1926, the Kuomintang embarked on the Northern Expedition to wrest power from the remaining war-

lords. Chiang Kaishek (1886-1975) was appointed com-
mander-in-chief by the Kuomintang and the
Communists. The following year, Chiang turned on his
Communist allies and slaughtered them en masse in
Shanghai – the survivors carried on a civil war from the
countryside. By the middle of 1928 the Northern Expedition had reached Beijing, and a national government
was established with Chiang holding both military and
political leadership.

In 1937 the Japanese invaded Beijing and by 1939 had
overrun eastern China. The Kuomintang retreated west
to the city of Chongqing, which became China's temporary capital during WW II. After Japan's defeat in 1945
the Kuomintang returned, but their days were num-
bered; by this time the Chinese civil war was in full
swing. The Communists, now under the leadership of
Mao Zedong, achieved victory in 1949 – the Kuomintang
leaders fled to Taiwan, which they control to this day,
and the People's Liberation Army (PLA) entered Beijing
in January 1949. On 1 October of the same year, Mao
Zedong proclaimed the People's Republic of China
(PRC) to an audience of 500,000 in Tiananmen Square.

After the Revolution

After 1949 came a period of urban reconstruction. Down
came the walls and commemorative arches. Blocks of
buildings were reduced to rubble to widen the boulevards and Tiananmen Square. Soviet technicians poured
in and left their mark in the form of Stalinesque architecture.

Progress of all kinds came to a halt in 1966 when Mao
launched what became known as the Cultural Revolution. Seeing his power-base eroding, Mao officially
sanctioned wall posters and criticisms of party members
by university staff and students, and before long students were being issued with red armbands and were
taking to the streets. The Red Guards (hóngwèibīng) had
been born. By August 1966 Mao was reviewing mass
parades of the Red Guards in Tiananmen Square, who
were chanting while fanatically waving copies of his
famous 'little red book'.

There was nothing sacred enough to be spared the
brutal onslaught of the Red Guards. Universities and
secondary schools were shut down; intellectuals,
writers, artists and monks were dismissed, killed, perse-
cuted or sent to labour camps in the countryside; the
publication of scientific, artistic, literary and cultural
periodicals ceased; temples were ransacked and monasteries disbanded; and many physical reminders of

GLENN BEANLAND

GLENN BEANLAND

Top: Comrades in Arms: Monument to the People's
Heroes in Tiananmen Square.
Bottom: The red flag was first raised in Tiananmen Square
when the PRC was founded in 1949.

China's 'feudal', 'exploitative' or 'capitalist' past (including temples, monuments and works of art) were destroyed. Red Guard factions often battled each other, and in the end the Chinese military was forced to bring them under control.

China was to remain in the grip of chaos for the next decade. It wasn't until around 1979 that Deng Xiaoping – a former protégé of Mao who had emerged as a pragmatic leader – launched a 'modernisation' drive. The country opened up and Westerners were finally given a chance to see what the Communists had been up to for the past 30 years.

Beijing saw considerable change during the 1980s – private businesses, once banned by the Communists, were allowed again. Most temples, monuments and libraries wrecked during the Cultural Revolution were repaired. Unfortunately, the decade ended on a tragic note in June 1989, when PLA troops crushed a student-led pro-democracy movement. For a couple of years China was frozen out by the international community.

Nonetheless, by 1994 the Chinese leadership were confident that China had re-established its reputation on the world stage. When cities were being polled to host the 2000 Olympics, the Chinese assumed that Beijing would win. They took the rebuff badly when Sydney was chosen instead.

Nor did the Chinese win many friends in 1995 when Beijing hosted the United Nation's Conference on

NIKKI BURNS

In 1995 Beijing hosted a major UN conference for women. In the best traditions of Chinese hospitality, the delegates were assigned a secluded compound 50 km from the city centre.

Women. Having lobbied the UN hard to get the conference, the Chinese then denied visas to at least several hundred people who wanted to attend because they were regarded as politically incorrect. About 20,000 representatives of non-governmental organisations did in fact attend, but were forced to stay totally isolated in a fenced compound 50 km from the capital because the Chinese deemed their activities potentially subversive.

China's relations with the Asia-Pacific region remain uneasy, with issues such as human rights and questions about China's territorial ambitions in the South China Sea continuing to cause friction. Taiwan's growing independence remains the other possible flashpoint.

GEOGRAPHY

The city limits of Beijing extend some 80 km, including the urban and the suburban areas and the nine counties under its administration. With a total area of 16,800 sq km, Beijing municipality is roughly the size of Belgium.

CLIMATE

Beijing is not blessed with congenial weather. Autumn (September to early November) is the best time to visit: there's little rain, it's not dry or humid, and the city wears a pleasant cloak of foliage.

Winter can be interesting if you don't mind the cold, but avoid the Chinese New Year when everything is chock-a-block. Although the temperature can dip as far as -20°C and the northern winds cut like a knife through bean curd, parts of the capital appear charming in this season. Burning coal to heat buildings produces pollution, but the resulting subdued light renders the capital oddly photogenic, with contrasting blacks and whites and some extra-sooty greys. Winter clothing is readily available – the locals wear about 15 layers.

Spring is short, dry and dusty. From April to May a phenomenon known as 'yellow wind' plagues the capital – fine dust particles blown from the Gobi Desert in the north-west which sandpaper everything in sight, including your face. Beijing women run around with mesh bags over their heads to protect their smooth complexion.

In summer (June to August) the average temperature is 26°C – hot with sticky humidity, plus heavy afternoon thundershowers and mosquitoes in July.

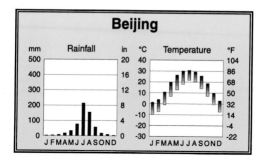

ENVIRONMENT

With 11 million residents and a rapidly growing population of cars, trucks and motorcycles, Beijing's
environment has taken a beating. In the past few years,
the government has made an effort to move polluting
factories out to rural areas in the hope of improving the
city's air quality. To relieve the nightmarish traffic con-
gestion, the municipal government has embarked on a
massive road improvement scheme. The neglected bus
and subway systems are beginning to get some attention, but the short-term prognosis seems to be more
traffic, noise and pollution.

GOVERNMENT

The highest authority in the country rests with the 25-
member Standing Committee of the CCP Politburo.
Below it is the Central Committee, made up of 210
younger Party members and provincial Party leaders. At
grass-roots level the Party forms a parallel system to the
administrations in the army, universities, government
and industries. Real authority is exercised by the Party
representatives at each level in these organisations.
They, in turn, are responsible to the Party officials in the
hierarchy above them, thus ensuring strict central
control.

The basic unit of social organisation outside the
family is the work unit. Every Chinese person is theoretically a member of one. However, many Chinese
nowadays slip through the net by being self-employed
or by working in a private operation. For those who are
members, tight controls are exercised by the leaders of
the unit they belong to.

GLENN BEANLAND

The East is Red: and brown, grey and orange...Smog over Beijing.

Although Beijing is the home of the central government and thus at the apex of the Communist pyramid, it also has a mayor and is an independent municipality, situated within Hubei Province.

However, like many national capitals, Beijing is directly under the control of the central government and subject to factional struggles within the party. When the central government launched an anti-corruption drive in early 1995, and a number of Beijing officials fell from grace, this was seen by many foreigners as part of pre-emptive post-Deng jostling within the CCP. Victims of that particular purge included Beijing's highest official, Communist Party chief Chen Xitong, and treasurer Wan Baosen; the latter committed suicide while under arrest.

ECONOMY

Starting from 1949 when the Communists took over the country, the Chinese could claim to be some of the most devout practitioners of Marxist economic theory. All forms of capitalism were banned and foreign investors were shut out of the country. After 30 years of following this path, China suddenly awoke to find that it had fallen behind almost every other country in the region.

China started experimenting with capitalist-style economic reforms in 1980, initiated by Party leader Deng Xiaoping. The reforms proceeded in fits and starts for nearly a decade, and almost came to a halt with the Tiananmen incident in 1989. But since then, the eco-

nomic shackles of state control have been thrown off and
foreign money and technology have poured in. For the
past decade, economic growth has averaged a dizzying
10% a year. Flush with cash, the Chinese government has
poured money into their capital city, essentially turning
it into a boomtown. This has transformed the face of
Beijing – just 10 years ago it was one of the most austere
capital cities in Asia. Nowadays, it's beginning to look
frighteningly modern.

By some predictions, in another decade China will
have the world's largest economy. Others are not so sure
– the country's messy politics may yet again cause economic grief. Another problem is that the enormous State
sector continues to lose money, but the government is
ideologically opposed to privatisation (it would essentially mean the death of socialism). Inflation, bottlenecks
in the economy and an underdeveloped infrastructure
are other sources of concern. Still, no one is predicting
China's imminent collapse. The pace of economic
liberalisation has gone so far so fast that it has taken on
a momentum of its own. Putting the capitalist toothpaste
back into the tube seems well near impossible.

POPULATION & PEOPLE

The population of Beijing municipality is over 11 million
souls, with perhaps five million in the central city. In
terms of population, it's China's second largest city after
Shanghai. The vast majority of Beijingers (over 95%) are
Han Chinese. The rest of China's 56 official ethnic minorities are scattered about, but a few have established little

GLENN BEANLAND

The one–child policy is still in force: budding musician in the
Old Summer Palace.

enclaves. As China has opened up to the outside world, the capital has acquired a fast-growing foreign community.

The Chinese government still remains committed to a policy of one child per family, at least in urban areas; rural couples may try for a second child if the first is a girl or is disabled. China's ethnic minorities are exempt from this rule. The policy has undoubtedly lowered the country's birthrate, but it is still highly unpopular.

ARTS

Music

Traditional Other than in conservatories, it is becoming rare to hear traditional instrumental Chinese music. More often, opera and other vocal forms tend to predominate. Such recitals as there are usually take the form of soloists or small groups of musicians performing on traditional instruments. These include the flute *(shēng)*, two-stringed fiddle *(èrhú)*, viola *(húqín)*, guitar *(yùeqín)* and lute *(pípá)* – all used in Beijing opera (see boxed aside). Others are the three-stringed lute *(sānxúan)*, vertical flute *(dòngxiāo)*, horizontal flute *(dízi)*, piccolo *(bāngdí)*, zither *(gǔzhēng)*, ceremonial trumpet *(sǔonà)* and ceremonial gongs *(dàlúo)*. Occasionally monks perform music in temples such as the Zhihua temple in Lumicang Hutong (Map 23).

Modern China's music market is heavily influenced by the already well established music industries in Taiwan and Hong Kong. The advent of satellite TV and the popularity of MTV – broadcast via Hong Kong's Star TV network – is also having an impact.

Hip young urban Chinese are into disco. Taiwanese love songs have been enormously successful in China, and Mandarin versions of Hong Kong pop music (the original songs are Cantonese) produced for the Taiwan and China markets are frequently chart hits. While Chinese tastes generally run towards soft melodies, Beijing has a nascent heavy metal and punk scene, often performing impromptu in the shopping malls of Beijing's outer suburbs. In an attempt to show that the geriatric leadership is also hip, government officials authorised a disco version of *The East is Red*, theme song of the Mao generation – though sales figures are not available.

The older generation got a jolt in 1989 with the release of *Rock & Roll for the New Long March*, by Cui Jian, one of China's foremost singers. Despite being put on hold

after Tiananmen, he continues to produce ambiguously
worded lyrics, as well as featuring in *Beijing Bastards,* a
shoestring film by Zhang Yuan about the fringes of the
city's rock scene. More jolts to the system came with
heavy metal sounds by the bands, Tang Dynasty and
Black Panther, though the latter now look and sound like
Bon Jovi. The cassette tape *Rock & Roll Beijing* impressed
many foreigners – the quality of the music could
compete with some of the best offerings in the West. One
feature of the recording was an all-female rock group,
Cobra. Perhaps integral to the growing influence of
Chinese rock as the voice of urban youth is the fact that
it no longer blandly copies foreign models.

There are dance halls in all the major hotels, generally
alternating between jazz, disco, live music and a karaoke
session. For details on venues, see the Entertainment
chapter.

Opera

After decades in the shade of political operas like *Taking
Tiger Mountain by Strategy*, Beijing opera *(píngjù)* has
made a comeback. Although only one of many versions
of the art, it is the most famous, though in fact it's only
got a short history. The year 1790 is the key date given;
in that year a provincial troupe performed before

Beijing Opera

Beijing opera *(jingju)* is usually regarded as the *crème de
la crème* of all the opera styles prevalent in China. Traditionally it's been the opera of the masses. The themes are
usually inspired by disasters, natural calamities, intrigues
or rebellions. Many have their source in the fairy tales and
stock characters and legends of classical literature. Titles
like *The Monkey King, A Drunken Beauty* and *A Fisher-
man's Revenge* are typical.

The music, singing and costumes are products of the
opera's origins. Formerly, opera was performed mostly on
open-air stages in markets, streets, teahouses or temple
courtyards. The orchestra had to play loudly and the
performers had to develop a piercing style of singing
which could be heard over the throng. The costumes are
a garish collection of sharply contrasting colours because
the stages were originally lit by oil lamps.

The movements and techniques of the dance styles of
the Tang Dynasty are similar to those of today's opera.
Provincial opera companies were characterised by their
dialect and style of singing, but when these companies
converged on Beijing they started a style of musical

drama called *kunqu*. This developed during the Ming Dynasty, along with a more popular variety of play-acting with pieces based on legends, historical events and popular novels. These styles gradually merged by the late 18th and early 19th centuries into the opera we see today.

The musicians usually sit on the stage in plain clothes and play without written scores. The *erhu* is a two-stringed fiddle which is tuned to a low register, has a soft tone and generally supports the *huqin*, a two-stringed viola tuned to a high register. The *yueqin*, a sort of moon-shaped four-stringed guitar, has a soft tone and is used to support the erhu. Other instruments are the *sheng* (a reed flute) and the *pipa* (lute), as well as drums, bells and cymbals. Last but not least is the *ban*, a time-clapper which virtually directs the band, beats time for the actors and gives them their cues.

There are four types of actors' roles: the *sheng*, *dan*, *jing* and *chou*. The sheng are the leading male actors and they play scholars, officials, warriors and the like. They are divided into the *laosheng* who wear beards and represent old men, and the *xiaosheng* who represent young men. The *wensheng* are the scholars and the civil servants. The *wusheng* play soldiers and other fighters, and because of this are specially trained in acrobatics.

The dan are the female roles. The *laodan* are the elderly, dignified ladies such as mothers, aunts and widows. The *qingyi* are aristocratic ladies in elegant costumes. The *huadan* are the ladies' maids, usually in brightly coloured costumes. The *daomadan* are the warrior women. The *caidan* are the female comedians. Traditionally, female roles were played by male actors.

The jing are the painted-face roles, and they represent warriors, heroes, statesmen, adventurers and demons. Their counterparts are the *fujing*, ridiculous figures who are anything but heroic.

The chou is basically the clown. The *caidan* is sometimes the female counterpart of this male role.

Apart from the singing and music, the opera also incorporates acrobatics and mime. Few props are used, so each move, gesture or facial expression is symbolic. A whip with silk tassels indicates an actor riding a horse. Lifting a foot means going through a doorway. Language is often archaic Chinese, music is earsplitting (bring some cotton wool), but the costumes and make-up are magnificent. The only action that really catches the Western eye is a swift battle sequence – the female warriors involved are trained acrobats who leap, twirl, twist and somersault into attack.

There are numerous other forms of opera. The Cantonese variety is more 'music hall', often with a 'boy meets girl' theme. Gaojia opera is one of the five local opera forms from Fujian province and is also popular in Taiwan, with songs in the Fujian dialect but influenced by the Beijing opera style. ∎

CHRIS TAYLOR

CHRIS TAYLOR

CHRIS TAYLOR

You've read the book; now see the Beijing opera – *Monkey*.

Emperor Qianlong on his 80th birthday. The form was popularised in the West by the actor Mei Lanfang (1894-1961) who played *dàn* or female roles, and is said to have influenced Charlie Chaplin. There is a museum devoted to Mei Lanfang at 9 Huguosi Lu, in western Beijing (Map 23).

Beijing opera bears little resemblance to its European counterpart. The mixture of singing, dancing, speaking, mime, acrobatics and dancing can go on for five or six hours. The screeching music can be searing to Western ears, but plots are fairly simple and easy to follow.

If you get bored after the first hour or so, and are sick of the high-pitched whining, the local audience will be with you all the way – spitting, eating apples, breast-feeding an urchin on the balcony or plugging into a transistor radio (important sports match?). It's lively prole audience viewing entertainment.

Art

Foreigners struggling to read shop signs might not be so impressed, but calligraphy has traditionally been regarded in China as the highest form of visual art. This derives from the use of ink and brush, which has always been the main mode of Chinese painting. Landscape paintings regularly include calligraphy as part of the composition, and connoisseurs debate the merits of a painting mainly in terms of its brushwork. For over 1500 years, the Chinese have been producing fine ink and watercolour paintings, particularly landscapes, flower paintings and imperial portraits. Although painting as high art was mainly the province of the scholar-gentry, much was also produced for temples and religious sites.

There is also a tradition of incredibly elegant and refined porcelain, which the Chinese first began to produce in the Tang Dynasty. Stoneware was first produced much earlier. Bronze vessels of great sophistication have been discovered dating from around 1200 AD. Silk embroidery, jade jewellery and sculpture in clay, wood and stone are other notable areas of Chinese art.

Acrobatics

Acrobatics *(tèjì biǎoyǎn)* are pure fun. Donating pandas may have soothed international relations but it's the acrobats who are China's true ambassadors. Some people find the animal acts a bit sad, but in general foreigners have reacted to the shows enthusiastically. Sometimes performing tigers and pandas (not together) show up as an added bonus.

Circus acts go back 2000 years in China. Effects are obtained using simple props: sticks, plates, eggs and chairs; and apart from the acrobatics there's magic, vaudeville, drama, clowning, music, conjuring, dance and mime thrown in to complete the performance. Happily it's an art which gained from the Communist takeover and which did not suffer during the Cultural Revolution.

Acts vary from troupe to troupe. Some traditional acts haven't changed over the centuries, while others have incorporated roller skates and motorcycles. A couple of time-proven acts that are hard to follow include the 'balancing in pairs' with one man balanced upside down on the head of another mimicking every movement of the partner below, mirror-image, even drinking a glass of water! Hoop-jumping is another. Four hoops are stacked on top of each other; the human chunk of rubber going through the very top hoop may attempt a backflip with a simultaneous body-twist.

The 'Peacock Displaying its Feathers' act involves an array of people balanced on one bicycle – a Shanghai troupe holds the record at 13. The 'Pagoda of Bowls' is a balancing act where the performer, usually a woman, does everything with her torso except tie it in knots, all the while casually balancing a stack of porcelain bowls on foot, head or both – and perhaps also balancing on a partner.

Cinema

The most dramatic development in Chinese cinema over the last 15 years has been the appearance of films made by the so-called Fifth Generation directors. Although better known abroad than within China, their films, such as *Yellow Earth* (Chen Kaige), *Horse Thief* (Tian Zhuang-zhuang) and *Raise the Red Lantern* (Zhang Yimou), have set a new benchmark for the local film industry after the troughs of socialist propaganda. The popular market however is given over to martial arts and historical epics copied from Hong Kong cinema.

Literature

Fiction Classic works of Chinese literature now available in English translations include *Outlaws of the Marsh*, *The Dream of the Red Chamber* (also translated as *The*

ROBERT STOREY

ROBERT STOREY

Top: Different strokes: calligraphy in China is high art.
Bottom: Flower painting often incorporates the flowers of
the four seasons: the camellia (winter), hibiscus
(spring), lotus (summer), chrysanthemum (autumn).

Dream of Red Mansions and *The Story of the Stone)* and *Journey to the West* (also known as *Monkey*).

The most famous author to have lived in Beijing is Lu Xun (1881-1936). Considered by many Chinese their greatest 20th-century writer, he first achieved fame with *A Madman's Diary*, a paranoiac fable of Confucian society. His most famous work, *The Story of Ah Q*, examines the life of a man who is chronically unable to recognise the setbacks in his life as such, just as China itself seemed unable to accept the desperate urgency of the need to modernise. Because his writing tends to reflect the need for revolution, the Communists have canonised Lu Xun and his house in Beijing has been preserved as a museum.

Lao She, another important novelist of the early 20th century, is most well-known for *The Rickshaw Boy*, a social critique of the living conditions of rickshaw drivers in Beijing.

Since the Communists came to power in 1949, writing has become a particularly dangerous occupation. During the Cultural Revolution, the safest thing a writer could do was to churn out slogans in praise of Chairman Mao. Things have eased up in recent years, but social critics are still kept on a very short leash.

One of the most interesting writers in contemporary China is Zhang Xianliang, whose book *Half of Man is Woman* was extremely controversial in China for its sexual content. His book is available from Penguin.

Blood Red Dusk by Lao Gui (literally 'old devil') is available in English in Panda Books (Beijing). It's a fascinatingly cynical account of the Cultural Revolution years. Feng Jicai is a writer known for his horrific accounts of the same period – his *Voices From the Whirlwind* has been published in English by Pantheon Books. More recently, Wang Shuo's short stories have given a voice to Beijing's growing underclass of unemployed and disaffected youth.

Poetry One of the glories of Chinese culture, poetry has a tradition going back at least three thousand years, starting with the classic *Book of Odes*. The Han, Tang and Song dynasties saw the highpoints of the tradition. Check out the *Three Hundred Tang Poems* anthology for a representative selection. China's two most celebrated poets, Li Bai and Du Fu, have been a major source of inspiration for nearly a millennium.

SOCIETY & CONDUCT

Traditional Practices

Fengshui The ancient Chinese world view included the belief that the earth, like a human body, has 'channels' or veins, along which benevolent and evil influences flowed. This belief, known as *fēngshui*, or geomancy, plays an important role in the choice of sites for buildings or tombs. An example of fengshui in practice is Jingshan. This artificial hill was built specifically to keep evil influences out of the Forbidden City.

Taijiquan The sight of people engaged in slow motion shadow boxing in the park at 6 am is a little startling the first time you see it. Previously spelled 'taichi (chuan)', *tàijí (quán)* has been popular in China for centuries. It is basically a form of exercise designed to improve and maintain health, but it's also an art and is related to Chinese martial arts *(wǔshù)*.

Gongfu One form of the martial arts, *gōngfu* has been popular in the West mostly thanks to Hong Kong-made movies. Previously spelled 'kungfu', gongfu differs from taiji in that the former is performed at much higher speed, can employ weapons and is intended to do bodily harm. While taiji is not a form of self-defence, the movements are similar to gongfu.

Qigong This is another variation on the gongfu theme. *Qì* represents life's vital energy, and *gōng* is from gongfu. Qigong is a form of energy management, and seems to work almost like magic. Practitioners try to project their qi to perform various miracles, including faith healing and driving nails through boards with their fingers. It's a standard feature of Hong Kong gongfu movies – bad guys are blown away without actually being physically touched, while mortally wounded heroes are healed with a few waves of the hands.

Appearance & Conduct

Dress Cynics say that the Communists are the worst-dressed people in the world. Certainly in the days of blue Mao suits, there was a grain of truth to that statement, but these days the Chinese have become increasingly fashion-conscious. Suits and ties for men and flamboyant dresses for women are no longer regarded as unusual.

If wearing sandals outdoors, there is an unwritten rule that the back of the ankle must be covered with a strap – thongs (flip-flops) are not acceptable, and many backpackers run afoul of this unwritten rule. Shorts are OK as long as they remain within a reasonable level of modesty. Short shorts, skimpy bikinis and see-through blouses on women are stretching the definition of 'acceptable'.

Face Face can be loosely considered as status and many Chinese people will go to great lengths to avoid 'losing face'. For example, a foreigner may front up to a hotel desk and have a furious row with the receptionist because the foreigner believes that he is being over-charged (often true) while the receptionist denies it. The receptionist is much less likely to admit the truth (and 'lose face') if the foreigner throws a tantrum.

In such situations, you can accomplish a great deal more with smiles, talking about other things for a while ('Where did you learn such good English?'), showing some of your photos from your trip, etc, before putting forward your case in a quiet manner.

Avoid direct criticisms of people. If you have to complain about something, like the hot water not working, do so in a fairly quiet tone. Confrontation causes loss of face and that leads to trouble. Venting your rage in public and trying to make someone lose face will cause the Chinese to dig in their heels and worsen your situation. Business travellers should especially take note – a lot of Westerners really blow it on this point.

Chopsticks A pair of chopsticks sticking vertically into the rice bowl resembles incense sticks in a bowl of ashes. This is considered a death sign in China and many other countries of the Orient – it's rude and should be avoided. However, younger people care less about this than the old generation.

Red Ink Don't write a note in red ink. If you want to give someone your address or telephone number, write in any colour but red. Red ink conveys a message of unfriendliness. If you're teaching in China it's OK to use red ink to correct students' papers, but if you write extensive comments or suggestions on the back of the paper, use some other colour besides red.

Public Etiquette The Chinese are not nearly as innocent as they pretend to be when it comes to sexual matters. However, the Communist regime is one of the

GLENN BEANLAND

Primary colours in the Old Summer Palace

most prudish in the world. Walking around hand in hand is becoming more common but is still considered risqué. You won't see many people getting passionate with a member of the opposite sex in public; refrain from it yourself. It also goes without saying that any type of public nudity – toplessness at the beach and so on – is asking for big trouble.

RELIGION

While minority religions (mainly Islam and Christianity) exist in large areas of China and even a few pockets in Beijing, Chinese religion is dominated by Confucianism, Taoism and Buddhism. To this mixture could be added ancestor worship, since prayers are addressed to several of these deities for the welfare of the dead in their care.

The three main religions have gradually combined over the centuries. Confucianism, in effect state policy for the last two millennia, advocated loyalty to the emperor and to the patriarchal structure below him as its main tenets. These were originally set out by Confucius in the 5th century BC. Taoism has existed in two forms: firstly in the philosophical outlook advocated by the semi-mythical Laozi (6th century BC) which stresses acceptance of the 'way', of 'going with the flow'; and secondly in a popular form, having many gods and devils in its pantheon. Taoism has also been a strong influence in the Chinese alchemical tradition. Mahayana

ROBERT STOREY

ROBERT STOREY

Top: Laughing Buddha in Beihai Park
Bottom: The symbolic presence of Confucius dominates
Chinese imperial history.

Buddhism, imported from India during the Han Dynasty, has had fluctuating fortunes but by the 10th century was as entrenched as the other two religions in Chinese culture.

The Cultural Revolution had a devastating effect on Chinese religion – it has yet to recover fully. Temples were closed or destroyed, monks were sent to labour in the countryside where they often perished, and believers were prohibited from worship. But slowly the temples are being restored and worshippers are returning. Chinese religion has largely been kept alive in Hong Kong, Macau and Taiwan – donations from Overseas Chinese have become a significant source of funding for temple reconstruction. While freedom of religion is now legally permitted in China, it's worth noting that membership in the Chinese Communist Party is not permitted for anyone found to be actively practising religion.

LANGUAGE

The official language of the PRC is the Beijing dialect, usually referred to in the West as 'Mandarin Chinese'. The word 'Mandarin' derives from the use of the Beijing dialect as a standard language by the scholar class in centuries past. The official name for Mandarin in China is *pǔtōnghuà*, or 'common speech'.

Lonely Planet publishes a *Mandarin Chinese phrasebook*. A small dictionary with English, romanisation and Chinese characters can also be very helpful.

Tones

Chinese is a language with a large number of homonyms (words of different meaning but identical pronunciation), and if it were not for its tonal quality it probably would not work very well as a language. Mandarin has four tones: in the first the voice is pitched quite high; in the second it rises rather like when asking a question; in the third the voice dips and then rises; and in the fourth the voice falls away. The following provides an example of how tones can change the meaning:

(first) high tone	*mā*	mother
(second) rising tone	*má*	hemp or numb
(third) falling-rising tone	*mǎ*	horse
(fourth) falling tone	*mà*	to scold or swear

Pinyin

In 1958 the Chinese officially adopted a system known as *pīnyīn* as a method of writing their language using the Roman alphabet. Pinyin is helpful in that it is often used, at least in major cities, on shop fronts, street signs and advertising billboards. However, don't expect the average Chinese to be able to use it. Unless you speak Chinese you'll need a phrasebook with Chinese characters.

The Pinyin system replaces the old Wade-Giles and Lessing systems of romanising Chinese script. Thus under Pinyin, 'Mao Tse-tung' becomes *Mao Zedong*; 'Chou En-lai' becomes *Zhou Enlai*; and 'Peking' becomes *Beijing*.

Pronunciation

The letter **v** is not used in Pinyin. The trickiest sounds in Pinyin are **c**, **q** and **x**. The following is a description of the sounds produced in spoken Mandarin:

Vowels

a	like the 'a' in 'father'
ai	like the 'i' in 'I'
ao	like the 'ow' in 'cow'
e	like the 'u' in 'blur'
ei	like the 'ei' in 'weigh'
i	like the 'ee' in 'meet'
ian	like in 'yen'
ie	like the English word 'yeah'
o	like the 'o' in 'or'
ou	like the 'oa' in 'boat'
u	like the 'u' in 'flute'
ui	like 'way'
uo	like 'w' followed by an 'o' as in 'or'
yu	like German umlaut 'ü' or French 'u' in 'union'
ü	like German umlaut 'ü'

Consonants

c	like the 'ts' in 'bits'
ch	like in English, but with the tongue curled back
h	like in English, but articulated from the throat
q	like the 'ch' in 'cheese'
r	like the 's' in 'pleasure'
sh	like in English, but with the tongue curled back
x	like the 'sh' in 'shine'
z	like the 'ds' in 'suds'
zh	like the 'j' in 'judge', but with the tongue curled back

With the exception of **n**, **ng**, and **r**, syllables never have a consonant at the end. In Pinyin, apostrophes serve to separate syllables – writing *ping'an* prevents pronunciation as *pin'gan*.

To confuse matters, Beijingers have their own distinct accent sometimes referred to as 'r-hua' because nearly every word ends with an 'r' sound. The word for park (*gongyuan*) becomes *gongyuar*. The Chinese word for tea (*cha*) becomes *char*. And so on.

Gestures

The Chinese have a system for counting on their hands. If you can't speak the language, it would be worth your while to at least learn Chinese finger counting. The symbol for number 10 is to form a cross with the index fingers, but in many locations the Chinese just show a fist.

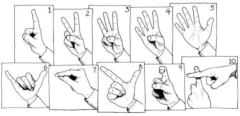

Chinese finger counting

Written Language

Chinese characters look like so many little pictures, and hence are often referred to as a language of 'pictographs'. Many of the basic Chinese characters are in fact highly stylised pictures of what they represent, but often characters give clues to the pronunciation as well.

It is commonly felt that a well-educated contemporary Chinese should know between 6000 and 8000 characters. Students looking at getting through a Chinese newspaper will need to understand around 1200 to 1500 characters to get the gist of what's going on, but will probably need between 2000 and 3000 before the going starts to get easy.

Simplification In the interests of promoting universal literacy, in 1954 the Committee for Reforming the

Chinese Language was set up by the Beijing government. The committee simplified 2238 Chinese
characters, reducing the number of strokes needed by
about half.

The reforms were implemented successfully in the
PRC, but Chinese communities outside China (notably
Taiwan and Hong Kong) continue to use traditional
full-form characters. The last few years have seen a
return of the full-form characters to China, mainly in
advertising (where the traditional characters are considered more attractive) and restaurant, hotel and shop
signs.

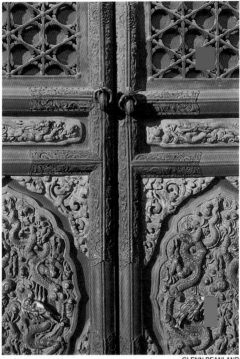

GLENN BEANLAND

Many Chinese characters still retain traces of their original
picture, for example 'door' is 門.

Greetings & Small Talk
Hello.
Nǐ hǎo. 你好!
Goodbye.
Zàijiàn. 再见
Thank you.
Xièxie. 谢谢
You're welcome.
Búkèqi. 不客气
Excuse me/I'm sorry.
Duìbùqǐ. 对不起
May I ask your name?
Nín guìxìng? 您贵性?
My (sur)name is...
Wǒ xìng... 我 性 ...
Where are you from?
Nǐ shī cóng nǎr láide? 你是从哪儿来的?
I am from...
Wǒ shì...láide. 我 是 ... 来的
Are you married?
Nǐ jiéhūnle ma? 你结婚了吗?
Yes.
Yǒu. 有
No.
Méiyǒu. 没有
Wait a moment.
Děng yíxià. 等一下
I want...
Wǒ yào... 我要.....
Do you like...?
Nǐ xǐhuan...ma? 你喜欢...吗?
I (don't) like...
Wǒ (bù) xǐhuan... 我 (不)喜欢 ...
No, I don't have...
Méiyǒu... 没有...
No, not so.
Búshì. 不是

Language Difficulties
I don't understand.
Wǒ tīngbudǒng. 我听不懂.
I understand.
Wǒ tīngdedǒng. 我听得懂.
Do you understand?
Dǒng ma? 懂吗?
Could you speak more slowly please?
Qǐng nǐ shuō màn yídiǎnr hǎo ma?
请 你说 慢一点好儿 ?

Shopping
How much is it?
Duōshǎo qián? 多少钱?

Is there anything cheaper?
  Yǒu piányì yìdiǎn de ma? 有便宜一点的吗?
That's too expensive.
  Tài guìle. 太贵了.
RMB (people's money)
  rénmínbì 人民币
to change money
  huàn qián 换钱
travellers' cheques
  lǚxíng zhīpiào 旅行支票

Post & Communications

post office
  yóujú 邮局
letter
  xìn 信
envelope
  xìnfēng 信封
air mail
  hángkōng xìn 航空信
stamps
  yóupiào 邮票
postcard
  míngxìnpiàn 明信片
aerogramme
  hángkōng xìnjiàn 航空信件
poste restante
  cúnjú hòulǐnglán 存局候领栏
telephone
  diànhuà 电话
telephone card
  diànhuà kǎ 电话卡
international call
  guójì diànhuà 国际电话
collect call
  duìfāng fùqián diànhuà 对方付钱电话
direct-dial call
  zhíbō diànhuà 直播电话
fax
  chuánzhēn (or 'fax' as in English) 传真

Time

What is the time?
  Jǐ diǎnle? 几点了?
When?
  Shénme shíhòu? 什么时候?
now
  xiànzài 现在
today
  jīntiān 今天
tomorrow
  míngtiān 明天

the day after tomorrow
 hòutiān 后天
in the morning
 zǎochén 早晨
afternoon
 xiàwǔ 下午
night, evening
 wǎnshàng 晚上

Places
city centre
 shì zhōngxīn 市中心
embassy
 dàshǐguǎn 大使馆
my hotel
 wǒde lǚguǎn 我的旅馆
Bank of China
 Zhōngguó Yínháng 中国银行
China International Travel Service (CITS)
 Zhōngguó Guójì Lǚxíngshè 中国国际旅行社
China Travel Service (CTS)
 Zhōngguó Lǚxíngshè 中国旅行社
Public Security Bureau (PSB)
 Gōng'ān Jú 公安局
Xinhua Bookstore
 Xīnhuá Shūdiàn 新华书店

Directions
Where is the...?
 ...zài nǎlǐ? ...在哪里？
I'm lost.
 Wǒ mílùle. 我迷路了
Turn right.
 Yòu zhuǎn. 右转
Turn left.
 Zuǒ zhuǎn. 左转
Go straight.
 Yìzhí zǒu. 一直走
Turn around.
 Xiàng huí zǒu. 向回走

Accommodation
hotel
 lǚguǎn 旅馆
tourist hotel
 bīnguǎn/ fàndiàn/ jiǔdiàn 宾馆, 饭店, 酒店
single room
 dānrénfáng 单人房
double room
 shuāngrénfáng 双人房

bed
  chuángwèi 床位
economy room
  jīngjìfáng 经济房
standard room (with bath)
  biāozhǔn fáng 标准房
Can I see the room?
  Wǒ néng kànkàn fángjiān? 我能看看房间?
I don't like this room.
  Wǒ bù xǐhuan zhèjiān fáng. 我不喜欢这间房间
Could I have these clothes washed, please?
  Qǐng bǎ zhèixiē yīfu xǐ gānjìng?
  请把这些衣服洗干净?

Getting Around

I want to go to...
  Wǒ yào qù... 我要去...
Could you buy a ticket for me?
  Kěyǐ tì wǒ mǎi yìzhāng piào mā?
  可以替我买一张票吗?
What time does it depart?
  Jǐdiǎn kāi? 几点开?
What time does it arrive?
  Jǐdiǎn dào? 几点到?
How long does the trip take?
  Zhècì lǚxíng yào duōcháng shíjiān?
  这次旅行要花多长时间?
buy a ticket
  mǎi piào 买票
luggage
  xínglì 行李
left-luggage room
  jìcún chù 寄存处

Air

airport
  fēijīchǎng 飞机场
CAAC
  Zhōngguó Mínháng 中国民航
charter flight
  bāojī 包机
one-way ticket
  dānchéng piào 单程票
return ticket
  láihuí piào 来回票

Bus & Taxi

bus
  gōnggòng qìchē 公共汽车

minibus
xiǎo gōnggòng qìchē, miànbāoche
小公共汽车, 面包车
taxi
chūzū chē 出租车
bus map
jiāotōng dìtú 交通地图
When is the next bus?
Xià yìbān qìchē jǐdiǎn kāi? 下一班汽车几点开?

Train & Subway
train
huǒchē 火车
railway station
huǒchē zhàn 火车站
subway (underground)
dìxiàtiě 地下铁路
subway station
dìtiě zhàn 地铁站
ticket office
shòupiào chù 售票处
platform ticket
zhàntái piào 站台票
Which platform?
Dìjǐhào zhàntái? 第几号站台?

Bicycle
bicycle
zixíngchē 自行车
I want to hire a bicycle.
Wǒ yào zū yíliàng zixíngchē. 我要租一辆自行车
How much is it per day?
Yìtiān duōshǎo qián? 一天多少钱?
How much is it per hour?
Yíge xiǎoshí duōshǎo qián? 一个小时多少钱?
deposit
yājīn 押金

Toilets
toilet, restroom
cèsuǒ 厕所
toilet paper
wèishēng zhǐ 卫生纸
bathroom (washroom)
xǐshǒu jiān 洗手间

Health
I'm sick.
Wǒ shēngbìngle. 我生病了.
I'm injured.
Wǒ shòushāngle. 我受伤了

hospital
  yīyuàn 医院
pharmacy
  yàodiàn 药店

Emergency
police
  jǐngchá 警察
Fire!
  Huǒzāi! 火灾
Help!
  Jiùmìng a! 救命
Thief!
  Xiǎotōu! 小偷

Numbers

0	*líng*	零
1	*yī, yāo*	一
2	*èr, liǎng*	二
3	*sān*	三
4	*sì*	四
5	*wǔ*	五
6	*liù*	六
7	*qī*	七
8	*bā*	八
9	*jiǔ*	九
10	*shí*	十
11	*shíyī*	十一
12	*shí'èr*	十二
20	*èrshí*	二十
21	*èrshíyī*	二十一
100	*yìbǎi*	一百
200	*èrbǎi*	二百
1000	*yìqiān*	一千
2000	*liǎngqiān*	两千
10,000	*yíwàn*	一万
20,000	*liǎngwàn*	两万
100,000	*shíwàn*	十万
200,000	*èrshíwàn*	二十万

Facts for the Visitor

ORIENTATION

Though it may not appear so in the shambles of arrival, Beijing is a place of very orderly design. Long, straight boulevards and avenues are crisscrossed by a network of lanes. Places of interest are either very easy to find if they're on the avenues, or impossible to find if they're buried down the narrow alleys.

This section refers to the chessboard of the central core, once a walled enclosure. The symmetry folds on an ancient north-south axis passing through Qianmen (Front Gate). The major east-west road is Chang'an (Avenue of Eternal Tranquillity), which runs across the north of Tiananmen Square. It is called Fuxing Lu in its western section and Jianguomen in the east.

Key areas are:

Wangfujing – A major shopping street two blocks east of the Forbidden City, running north-south.

Jianguomenwai – The popular shopping area covering the eastern section of Chang'an Dajie.

Xidan – Running north-south, Xidan market is two blocks west of the Forbidden City.

Dazhalan – A narrow street market running south-west from below Qianmen.

As for the street names: Chaoyangmenwai Dajie, for example, means 'the avenue *(dajie)* outside *(wai)* Chaoyang Gate (Chaoyangmen)'; whereas Chaoyangmennei Dajie means 'the avenue inside *(nei)* Chaoyang Gate'. It's an academic exercise since the gate in question no longer exists.

Streets are also split along compass points: either *běi* (north) and *nán* (south), or *dōng* (east) and *xī* (west). For example, Andingmen Dong Dajie is East Andingmen Avenue, and Andingmen Xi Dajie is the western part of the same street. These streets tend to head off from an intersection, usually where a gate – in this case Andingmen – once stood. A major boulevard can change names six or eight times along its length, so intersections become important.

GLENN BEANLAND

GLENN BEANLAND

Top: Looking across Di'anmen from Jingshan: Former
gates *(men)* of the old city remain as major
intersections.
Bottom: Cyclists on Qianmen Dajie

The four main districts are Xicheng and Dongcheng (the eastern and western halves of the city), Xuanwu in the south-west and Chongwen in the south-east.

There are five 'ring roads' around Beijing, circum-navigating the city centre in three concentric circles. The first (innermost) ring road is a mapmaker's fiction – just part of the grid around the Forbidden City. However, the second ring road *(èrhuán)* and third *(sānhuán)* should be taken seriously – they are multi-lane freeways that get you around town quickly. Construction of a fourth ring road *(sìhuán)* is nearly complete and work has just started on a fifth.

MAPS

Welcome to China, Beijing is a freebie handout available at many big hotels. It comes with a basic English map of the city along with a good deal of up-to-date tourist information.

Good bilingual maps of Beijing showing the bus routes are a rare find. There are some still around (try hotel giftshops and the Friendship Store – see Map 21) but they tend to be out of date.

If you can deal with Chinese characters, you'll find a wide variety of up-to-date maps to choose from. New editions printed by different companies are issued every couple of months. Street vendors hawk these maps near the subway stations and park entrances, and at other likely places.

The Foreign Languages Bookstore on Wangfujing (Map 22) sells several excellent atlases of Beijing, but these are entirely in Chinese characters.

TOURIST OFFICES

Beijing doesn't yet have a real walk-in tourist office like you find in Hong Kong or Macau. The closest thing to it is the Beijing Tourism Administration (515-8844), but don't ring them up to get some tourist pamphlets. On the other hand, if you're planning to organise an inter-national Beijing Marathon, they'd be the people to talk to.

Individual travellers would be better served by calling the tourist hotline (513-0828), which is also oper-ated by the Beijing Tourism Administration.

For more information on the two major government-owned travel agencies – China International Travel Service (CITS) and China Travel Service (CTS) – look under Travel Agents in the Getting There & Away chapter. These agencies also have offices overseas.

Individual travel agencies have some useful tourist information, but remember that they are in the business of organising tours in return for cold hard cash. Don't expect them to be very charitable with their time.

DOCUMENTS

Visas

Visas are readily available from Chinese embassies and consulates in most Western and many other countries (see the list under Embassies further on).

One-month single-entry visas are valid from the date of entry that you specify on the visa application. But all other visas are valid from the date of issue, *not* from the date of entry, so there's no point in getting such a visa far in advance of your planned entry date. There are seven types of visas, as follows:

L travel *(lǚxíng)*
F business *(fǎngwèn)*
D resident *(dìngjū)*
G transit *(guòjìng)*
X student *(liúxué)*
Z working *(rènzhí)*
C steward/ess *(chéngwù)*

When you check into a hotel, there is usually a question on the registration form asking what type of visa you have. The letter specifying your visa category is usually stamped on the visa itself.

In Australia The Chinese embassy and consulates in Australia charge $A30 for the standard single-entry visa and $60 for a double-entry visa for 30 days and can usually process an application within a week. You must apply in person or through a CITS office.

In Hong Kong The cheapest visas can be obtained from the Visa Office of the Ministry of Foreign Affairs of the PRC (2585-1794, 2585-1700), 5th Floor, Low Block, China Resources Building, 26 Harbour Rd, Wanchai, Hong Kong Island. You'll have to queue, but you're saving a few dollars. The office is open from Monday to Friday, 9 am to 12.30 pm and 2 to 5 pm, Saturday 9 am to 12.30 pm. You pay in Hong Kong dollars (HK$) here;

GLENN BEANLAND

Soldier in Tiananmen Square

HK$90 for 2½ day service, HK$240 for same day (exchange rate approximately US$1 = HK$8.1).

Numerous travel agencies in Hong Kong also can obtain your Chinese visa. Besides saving you the hassle of visiting the visa office and queueing, a few travel agents can get you more time than the usual 30 days. For a standard single-entry tourist visa of one or two months' validity, issued in two working days, expect to pay around HK$130 (but some agencies ask HK$200!). For a visa issued in 24 hours, HK$200; issued the same day, HK$300. Dual-entry visas cost double.

Multiple-entry business visas are available through most travel agencies. These cost approximately HK$700 and are valid for six months' duration, allowing an unlimited number of border crossings during this time. But there is a catch – you can only stay in China for 30 days at a time and getting this extended is nearly impossible unless you are really working in China and your 'work unit' completes the necessary paperwork.

In Macau You can obtain a Chinese visa the same day from CTS (705506), Xinhua Building, Rua de Nagasaki. Visa applications require one passport-size photo.

In the UK Standard 30-day single-entry visas from the embassy in London take three to five days and cost £25; get an application form in person or by post from there or from the Chinese consulate in Manchester. A visa mailed to you will take three weeks. Your passport must be valid for at least six months after the expiry date of your visa. You might find the embassy discourages independent travellers during the summer.

In the USA The standard 30-day single-entry visa costs US$30 and takes about one week to process at the Chinese embassy and consulates throughout the USA.

Visa Extensions

The Public Security Bureau (PSB) is the name given to China's police force, and visa extensions are handled by the PSB's Foreign Affairs Section. The Beijing PSB (525-5486) is at 85 Beichizi Dajie, the street running north-south at the east side of the Forbidden City (Map 22). It's open from 8.30 to 11.30 am and 1 to 5 pm Monday to Friday; from 8.30 to 11.30 am Saturday; closed on Sunday. Visa extensions cost Y25 for most nationalities, but others pay Y50 while some get it free.

The general rule is that if you entered on a one-month visa you can get one extension of one month's duration. You may be able to wangle more, especially with cogent reasons like illness (except AIDS) or transport delays, but second extensions are usually only granted for one week with the understanding that you are on your way out of China. Similarly, if you entered on a three-month visa, you'll probably only get a one-week extension.

Passport

Carry your old expired passport if you have one. Some hotels also require you to hand over your passport as security, even if you've paid in advance – an expired passport is useful for these situations. Ditto for bicycle renters who want your passport as security, though they will often take a cash deposit.

As for your real passport, if yours is within a few months of expiry, get a new one now – many countries will not issue a visa if your passport has less than six months of validity remaining. Be sure that your passport has at least a few blank pages for visas and entry and exit stamps.

Losing your passport is very bad news indeed. Getting a new one takes time and money. However, if you will be staying in China or any foreign country for a long period of time, it helps tremendously to register your passport with your embassy. This will eliminate the need to send faxes back to your home country to confirm that you really exist.

If you lose your passport, you should certainly have some ID card with your photo. Many embassies require this before issuing a new passport. Some embassies will accept a driver's licence but others will not – again, an old expired passport will often save the day.

Travel Insurance

It's very likely that a health insurance policy which you contribute to in your home country will *not* cover you in China – if unsure, ask your insurance company. If you're not covered, it would be prudent to purchase travel insurance. The best policies will reimburse you for a variety of mishaps such as accidents, illness, theft and even the purchase of an emergency ticket home. The policies are usually available from travel agents, including student travel services. Read the small print: some policies specifically exclude 'dangerous activities', which may include motorcycling, scuba diving and even hiking. Obviously, you'll want a policy that covers you in all the circumstances you're likely to find yourself in.

To make a claim for compensation, you will need documentation (hopefully in English). This can include medical reports, police reports, baggage receipts from airlines, etc.

Driver's Licence

Foreign tourists are not permitted to drive in China without special permission, and getting such permission will cost you dearly. In other words, it's highly unlikely that you'll get much use out of either your home country's licence or an international driver's licence.

It's a different story if you plan to take up residence in Beijing. If you have a Chinese residence certificate, you can obtain a Chinese driver's licence after some bureaucratic wrangling. You'll need to enlist the assistance of a local Chinese to help you sort out the red tape. As a general rule, the Chinese authorities are willing to exchange your original driver's licence for a Chinese one. They will keep your original licence until you depart China, at which time it will be returned to you in exchange for the Chinese one.

Name Cards

Business name cards are essential, even if you don't do business – exchanging name cards with someone you've just met goes down well. It's particularly good if you can get your name translated into Chinese and have that printed just next to your English name. You can get name cards made cheaply in China, but it's better to have some in advance of your arrival.

Marriage Certificate

If married and travelling with your spouse, a copy of your marriage certificate can save some grief if you become involved with the police, hospitals or other bureaucratic authorities.

Credentials

If you're thinking about working or studying in China, photocopies of college or university diplomas, transcripts and letters of recommendation could prove helpful.

Chinese Documents

Foreigners who live, work or study in China will be issued with a number of documents, and some of these can be used to obtain substantial discounts for trains, flights, hotels, museums and tourist sites.

Most common and least useful is the so-called 'white card', a simple student ID card with pasted-on photo which is usually kept in a red plastic holder (some call it a 'red card' for this reason). A white card is easily forged – they can be reproduced with a photocopy machine – and the red plastic holders are on sale everywhere. For this reason, you might be approached by touts wanting to sell you a fake one. The fact is that outside of Beijing and other major cities railway clerks really have no idea what a white card is supposed to look like – fake ones sometimes work when real ones don't! One French student had a knock-down drag-out battle at a railway station with a smug booking clerk who threw her absolutely genuine white card into the rubbish bin and told her it was a fake.

The so-called 'yellow card' (really orange) is not so much a card as a small booklet. The cover is orange and the pages are white. Except for the cover, the book can be easily forged with a photocopier, but there do not seem to be too many fakes around – yet. These do seem to work better than white cards.

The 'green card' is a residence permit, issued to English teachers, foreign experts and students who live in the PRC. It's such a valuable document that you'd better not lose it if you have one, or the PSB will be all over you. Foreigners living in China say that if you lose your green card, you might want to leave the country rather than face the music. A green card will permit you to pay Chinese prices in hotels, on flights, trains and elsewhere. In addition, many hotels offer major discounts to green card holders (even five-star hotels!). The green card is not really a card but resembles a small passport – it would be very difficult to forge without modern printing equipment and special paper. Green cards are issued for one year and must be renewed annually.

Travel Permits Almost all of China is open except for certain remote border areas. You certainly don't need a travel permit *(tōngxíngzhèng)* for Beijing, but if you're contemplating travel in remote spots, inquire at the local PSB to learn the latest regulations.

EMBASSIES

Chinese Embassies Abroad

Some of the addresses of Chinese embassies and consulates in major cities overseas include:

Australia
15 Coronation Drive, Yarralumla, ACT 2600 (☎ (06) 273-4780, 273-4781)
Consulates in Melbourne, Perth, Sydney
Austria
Meternichgasse 4, 1030 Wien (☎ (06) 713-6706)
Belgium
Boulevare General Jacques 19, 1050 Bruxelles (☎ (02) 640 40 06)
Canada
515 St Patrick St, Ottawa, Ontario KIN 5H3 (☎ (613) 234-2706, 234-2682)
Consulates in Toronto, Vancouver
Denmark
Oregards alle 12, 2900 Hellerup, Copenhagen (☎ 31 61 10 13)
France
21 Rue de L'amiral Destaing, 75016 Paris (☎ (01) 47.20.86.82, 47.20.63.95)
Germany
Friedrich-Ebert Strasse 59, 53177 Bonn (☎ (0228) 35 36 54, 35 36 22)
Consulate in Hamburg
India
50-D, Shantipath, Chanakyapuri, New Delhi 110021 (☎ (011) 600-328)
Consulate in Bombay

Italy
    00135 Roma Via Della Camilluccia 613 (☎ (06) 3630-8534,
    3630-3856)
    Consulate in Milan
Japan
    3-4-33 Moto-Azabu, Minato-ku, Tokyo 106 (☎ (03) 3403-
    3380, 3403-3065)
    Consulates in Fukuoka, Osaka, Sapporo
Malaysia
    229 Jalan Ampang, Kuala Lumpur (☎ (03) 242-8495)
    Consulate in Kuching
Myanmar (Burma)
    1 Pyidaungsu Yeiktha Rd, Yangon (☎ (01) 21280)
Netherlands
    Adriaan Goekooplaan 7, 2517 JX The Hague (☎ (070) 355
    15 15, 355 92 09)
New Zealand
    104A Korokoro Rd, Petone, Wellington (☎ (04) 587-0407)
    Consulate in Auckland
Singapore
    70-76 Dalvey Rd, Singapore 1025 (☎ 734-3360, 734-3307)
South Korea
    1-10 Kahoe-Dong, Chongno-gu, Seoul (☎ (02) 743-1491)
    Consulate in Pusan
Spain
    Arturo Soria III, 28043 Madrid (☎ (341) 413-5892, 413-
    2776)
Sweden
    Ringvagen 56, 18134 Lidingo (☎ (08) 767 87 40, 767 40 83)
Switzerland
    7 J V Widmannstrasse, 3074 Muri Bern (☎ (031) 951 14 01,
    951 14 02)
Thailand
    57 Ratchadaphisek Rd, Dindaeng, Bangkok 10310 (☎ (02)
    245-7032)
    Consulate in Songkhla
UK
    Cleveland Court, 1-3 Leinster Gardens, London W2 6DP
    (☎ (0171) 723-8923, 262-0255)
USA
    2300 Connecticut Ave NW, Washington, DC 20008
    (☎ (202) 328-2500, 328-2517)
    Consulates in Chicago, Houston, Los Angeles, New York,
    San Francisco
Vietnam
    46-52 Pho Hoang Dieu, Hanoi (☎ (04) 232-845)
    Consulate in Ho Chi Minh City

Foreign Embassies in Beijing

A visit to Beijing's embassyland is a trip in itself – sentry
boxes with Chinese soldiers, fancy residences for the
diplomats and fancy stores, restaurants, discos and
nightclubs for entertainment. There are two main

embassy compounds – Jianguomenwai and Sanlitun. Map 21 at the back of the book gives details of the location of the embassies in these two areas.

The following embassies are in Jianguomenwai:

Austria
    5 Xiushui Nanjie (☎ 532-2061; fax 532-4605)
Brazil
    27 Guanghua Lu (☎ 532-2881)
Bulgaria
    4 Xiushui Beijie (☎ 532-1946; fax 532-2826)
Czech & Slovak
    Ritan Lu (☎ 532-1531; fax 532-5653)
India
    1 Ritan Donglu (☎ 532-1908; fax 532-4684)
Ireland
    3 Ritan Donglu (☎ 532-2691; fax 532-2168)
Israel
    Room 405, West Wing, China World Trade Centre, 1 Jianguomenwai Dajie (☎ 505-0328)
Japan
    7 Ritan Lu (☎ 532-2361)
Mongolia
    2 Xiushui Beijie (☎ 532-1203; fax 532-5045)
New Zealand
    1 Ritan Dong 2-Jie (☎ 532-2731; fax 532-4317)
North Korea
    Ritan Beilu (☎ 532-1186)
Philippines
    23 Xiushui Beijie (☎ 532-2794)
Poland
    1 Ritan Lu (☎ 532-1235; fax 532-5364)
Romania
    Corner of Ritan Dong 2-Jie and Ritan Donglu (☎ 532-3442; fax 532-5758)
Singapore
    1 Xiushui Beijie (☎ 532-3926; fax 532-2215)
South Korea
    4th Floor, China World Trade Centre, 1 Jianguomenwai Dajie (☎ 505-3171)
Sri Lanka
    3 Jianhua Lu (☎ 532-1861; fax 532-5426)
Thailand
    40 Guanghua Lu (☎ 532-1903; fax 532-1748)
UK
    11 Guanghua Lu (☎ 532-1961; fax 532-1939)
USA
    Embassy: 3 Xiushui Beijie (☎ 532-3831 ext 274; fax 532-6057);
    Consulate: Bruce Building, 2 Xiushui Dongjie (☎ 532-3431 ext 225)
Vietnam
    32 Guanghua Lu (☎ 532-1155; fax 532-5720)

The Sanlitun compound in Beijing is home to the following embassies:

Australia
    21 Dongzhimenwai Dajie (☎ 532-2331; fax 532-4605)
Belgium
    6 Sanlitun Lu (☎ 532-1736; fax 532-5097)
Cambodia
    9 Dongzhimenwai Dajie (☎ 532-1889; fax 532-3507)
Canada
    19 Dongzhimenwai Dajie (☎ 532-3536; fax 532-4072)
Chile
    1 Dongsi Jie (☎ 532-2074)
Denmark
    1 Sanlitun Dong 5-Jie (☎ 532-2431; fax 532-2439)
Finland
    Tayuan Diplomatic Building, 14 Liangmahe Nanlu
    (☎ 532-1817; fax 532-1884)
France
    3 Sanlitun Dong 3-Jie (☎ 532-1331; fax 532-4841)
Germany
    5 Dongzhimenwai Dajie (☎ 532-2161; fax 532-5336)
Hungary
    10 Dongzhimenwai Dajie (☎ 532-1431; fax 532-5053)
Italy
    2 Sanlitun Dong 2-Jie (☎ 532-2131; fax 532-4676)
Malaysia
    13 Dongzhimenwai Dajie (☎ 532-2531; fax 532-5032)
Myanmar
    6 Dongzhimenwai Dajie (☎ 532-1584; fax 532-1344)
Nepal
    1 Sanlitun Xi 6-Jie (☎ 532-1795; fax 532-3251)
Netherlands
    1-15-2 Tayuan Building, 14 Liangmahe Nanlu (☎ 532-
    1131; fax 532-4689)
Norway
    1 Sanlitun Dong 1-Jie (☎ 532-2261; fax 532-2392)
Pakistan
    1 Dongzhimenwai Dajie (☎ 532-2504)
Russia
    4 Dongzhimenbei Zhongjie, west of the Sanlitun Compound in a separate compound – see Map 23 (☎ 532-2051; fax 532-4853)
Spain
    9 Sanlitun Lu (☎ 532-1986; fax 532-3401)
Sweden
    3 Dongzhimenwai Dajie (☎ 532-3331; fax 532-5008)
Switzerland
    3 Sanlitun Dong 5-Jie (☎ 532-2736; fax 532-4353)

CUSTOMS

Chinese border crossings have gone from being severely traumatic to exceedingly easy. There are clearly marked 'green channels' and 'red channels', the latter reserved for those with such everyday travel items as refrigerators and colour TV sets.

Antiques or things which look antique could cause hassles with Customs:

If you plan to take antiques out of China, you need a certificate or red seal to clear Customs. I bought a bronze Buddha head (Customs found it when they x-rayed my baggage). I spent US$600 on it, and had it confiscated by Customs upon leaving China. At this point, I may or may not be able to recover it, but it will require a trip back to China to get it. To add insult to injury, I will be required to pay Customs for storage. If I am not able to recover the Buddha, Customs will sell it and keep the money they receive!

Nancy Parshall

You're allowed to import 600 cigarettes or the equivalent in tobacco products, two litres of alcoholic drink and one *pint* of perfume. Importation of fresh fruit is prohibited.

It's illegal to import any printed material, film, tapes, etc which are 'detrimental to China's politics, economy, culture and ethics'. But don't be too concerned about what you take to read. As you leave China, any tapes, manuscripts, books, etc 'which contain state secrets or are otherwise prohibited for export' can be seized. Mainly, the authorities are interested in things written in Chinese – they seldom pay much attention to anything written in English.

MONEY

Cash

Australian, Canadian, US, UK, Hong Kong, Japanese and most West European currencies are acceptable in China, but US dollars are still the easiest to change.

Travellers' Cheques

Besides the advantage of safety, travellers' cheques are useful to carry in China because the exchange rate is actually more favourable than the rate you get for cash. Cheques from most of the world's leading banks and issuing agencies are acceptable in Beijing – stick to the major companies such as Thomas Cook, American Express and Bank of America, and you'll be OK.

The American Express office in Beijing, due to government regulations, cannot provide the emergency cheque cashing service, but this is provided by four Chinese banks. For inquiries, contact American Express (☎ 505-2888; fax 505-4972) in Beijing at room L115D, Shopping Arcade, China World Trade Centre, 1 Jianguomenwai Dajie (Map 21).

ATMs

There is currently no way to use a foreign-issued ATM card in Beijing, though this may change soon. On the other hand, foreigners can indeed open bank accounts in China and apply for a local ATM card. Accounts can be opened in both Chinese yuan and US dollars (the latter only at special foreign-exchange banks), but the ATMs only pay in Chinese yuan. You do not need to have resident status – a tourist visa is sufficient. Virtually every foreigner working in Beijing will tell you that CITIC (China International Trust & Investment Corporation; Map 21) is far better to do business with than the Bank of China.

Credit Cards

Plastic is gaining more acceptance in Beijing. Useful cards include Visa, MasterCard, American Express, JCB and Diners Club. It's even possible to get a cash advance against your card.

International Transfers

Interbank money transfers sent or received through China's wobbly banking system can take weeks. Fortunately, a new money transfer service which opened in 1995 can reduce the procedure to a mere few hours.

The money transfer service is a cooperative venture between Western Union Financial Services in the USA and China Courier Service Corporation. China Courier (☎ 318-4313) is at 173 Yong'an St in Beijing. There are also branches at the National Olympic Sports Centre post office and Jianguomennei Dajie post office. At the moment, the only currency handled by this service is US dollars.

Currency

The basic unit of Chinese currency is the *yuan* – designated in this book by a capital 'Y'. In spoken Chinese, the word *kuai* or *kuaiqian* is often substituted for *yuan*. Ten *jiao* – in spoken Chinese, it's pronounced *mao* – make up one *yuan*. Ten *fen* make up one *jiao*, but these days *fen* are becoming rare because they are worth so little.

Renminbi (RMB), or 'people's money', is issued by the Bank of China. Paper notes are issued in denominations of one, two, five, 10, 50 and 100 yuan; one, two and five jiao; and one, two and five fen. Coins are in denominations of one yuan; five jiao; and one, two and five fen. The one-fen note is small and yellow, the two-fen note is blue, and the five-fen note is small and green – all are next to worthless.

Exchange Rates

Exchange rates include the following:

Australia	A$1	=	Y6.18
Belgium	Bfr1	=	Y0.27
Canada	C$1	=	Y6.03
France	Ffr1	=	Y1.67
Germany	DM1	=	Y5.70
Hong Kong	HK$1	=	Y1.06
Japan	¥100	=	Y7.70
Netherlands	G1	=	Y5.08
New Zealand	NZ$1	=	Y5.43
Singapore	S$1	=	Y5.75
Sweden	Kr1	=	Y1.24
Switzerland	Sfr1	=	Y7.01
UK	UK£1	=	Y12.7
USA	US$1	=	Y8.18

Changing Money

Foreign currency and travellers' cheques can be changed at main branches of the Bank of China, CITIC, tourist hotels, the Friendship Store and some other big department stores. Hotels usually give the official rate, but some will add a small commission. A bigger problem is that a few upmarket hotels only change money for their own guests.

Hong Kong dollars, Japanese yen and most West European currencies can be exchanged at major banks, but US dollars are still the easiest to change.

Whenever you change foreign currency into Chinese currency you'll be given a money-exchange voucher recording the transaction. Theoretically you need to show this to change Chinese yuan back to foreign currency – in practice, there is no problem. It's easier to buy and sell Chinese yuan in Hong Kong and Macau.

At Beijing's Capital Airport there is only a single moneychanger on duty, and when several large international flights arrive at once you may have to queue for an hour or more! People have complained about this for years, to no avail. The best bet is to have several hundred yuan before arrival – you can then change money at a bank or your hotel though this may not work if you arrive late in the evening.

Black Market Forget it – black-market money-changers are nothing but thieves. Don't even bother talking to them unless you enjoy getting ripped off.

As for bringing things to Beijing to sell, you'll probably find that the Chinese strike too much of a hard bargain to make it worth the trouble.

Costs

Costs in Beijing are rising, and no matter what you do, it's not going to be as cheap as Jakarta or Bangkok. How much it actually costs you largely depends on the degree of comfort you desire. Hotels are going to be the biggest expense, but food and transport can add up quickly too. Excluding the cost of getting to Beijing, you can survive on US$15 per day. This means you must stay in dormitories, travel by bus or bicycle rather than taxi, eat from street stalls or small cafes and refrain from buying anything.

Travelling, however, is something to be enjoyed. Staying in some dump and slugging it out on Beijing's hopelessly overcrowded buses can make your trip not worth the trouble.

On the opposite end of the spectrum, rooms at five-star hotels can be over US$200 per day and meals at upmarket restaurants can be US$50. And there are an increasing number of classy department stores charging Western prices. If you're looking for ways to blow a lot of money, Beijing can accommodate you.

Foreigners will inevitably be charged more for most things in Beijing. This situation certainly exists in many other developing countries, but the big difference is that in China, it's official policy. All businesses, from the airlines and railways to museums and parks, are told *by the government* that foreigners are to be milked for all they are worth. With such official support, many Chinese view ripping off foreigners as their patriotic duty. Sometimes the charge is just a little bit more than a local would pay, but at other times it's 30 times more than the Chinese price.

Being treated like cash cows has caused more than a few foreigners to become very cynical about China and hop on the first flight out of the country. Indeed, China's own tourism statistics show that while more foreigners

GLENN BEANLAND

Just the ticket: admission fees for foreigners are often sky-high.

are visiting the country, the average length of stay has dropped sharply in the past few years. But sometimes, the opposite happens – some total stranger in a restaurant pays for your meal; a passenger you met on the bus offers you a free place for the night and lets you borrow the family bicycle; a young student works as your personal tour guide for the entire day and wants nothing in return but a chance to practise English. Such moments are especially touching in China, because most Chinese are still poor and can hardly afford to be so generous.

Admission Fees Beijing officials have antagonised foreigners further with a double-standard policy regarding the admission fees charged to parks, museums and historical sites. The prices foreigners must pay can be from two to 30 times what a local Chinese pays. ID cards are not checked, so it comes off very much as a discriminatory policy – if you have a Chinese face you pay local prices, but a foreign face pays more. Japanese travellers, who can usually pass for Chinese, often take advantage of this policy.

By way of compensation, foreigners' tickets *(tàopiào)* often include admission to some sites within the park compounds that would normally cost extra. However, this is not guaranteed – in many cases you'll have to pay additional fees for each temple, garden, pavilion, etc, despite having paid more for your general admission ticket.

A new policy being instituted at more and more sites is to check your ticket at the entrance and exit. If you lose or throw away your ticket after entering – they are waiting for that – pay again!

Consumer Taxes Although big hotels and fancy restaurants may add a tax or 'service charge' of 15%, all other consumer taxes are included in the price tag.

Tipping & Bargaining

As some compensation for being frequently over-charged, Beijing is at least one of those wonderful cities where tipping is not done and almost no one asks for it. This applies throughout China. Porters at upmarket hotels will, of course, expect a tip.

Bargaining is something else. As it is government policy to charge foreigners at least double for everything, many private businesses pitch in by charging three or four times the Chinese rate; this may or may not leave room to make a saving.

In large stores where prices are clearly marked, there is usually no latitude for bargaining. In small shops, bargaining is sometimes possible, especially when no price tags exist. At street stalls, it is expected. In all cases, there is one important rule to follow – be polite. There is nothing wrong with asking for a 'discount', if you do so with a smile. The worst they can say is 'no'. Some foreigners seem to think that bargaining is a battle of wits, involving bluff, screams and threats. This is not only unpleasant for all concerned, it seldom results in you getting a lower price – indeed, in 'face-conscious' China, intimidation is likely to make the vendor more recalcitrant and you'll be overcharged.

You should keep in mind that entrepreneurs are in business to make money; they aren't going to sell anything to you at a loss. Your goal should be to pay the Chinese price, as opposed to the foreigners' price – if you can do that, you've done well.

Discounts

Especially at hotels, there is some latitude when it comes to price. Foreigners are usually charged twice as much as Chinese for the exact same room. However, these rules are house rules, and the management can offer discounts if so inclined. During the off-season (winter, except Chinese New Year) discounting is common, and you may be able to negotiate a better rate for a longer stay, especially at better hotels. On the other hand there's not much discounting at the few budget backpackers' dormitories; prices are low but firmly fixed.

If you have a residence permit to live or work in China, you can often pay the Chinese price for many things (transport, hotel rooms, admission fees, etc).

It's also worth knowing that government-owned travel agencies (CITS, CTS, etc) can get you sizable discounts at the top-end hotels. See under Travel Agents in the Getting There & Away chapter.

BUSINESS SERVICES

Business Centres

Most major hotels have business centres and a few are open 24 hours. Services typically include photocopying, postal service, international direct dial (IDD) phone, fax and telex. Many business centres have typewriters, and a few even have personal computers with attached laser printers. Needless to say, you should enquire about the cost before you use any of the services. Prices are generally high and sometimes nothing short of outrageous.

Doing Business

In bureaucratic China, even simple things can be made difficult. Renting property, getting a telephone installed, hiring employees, paying taxes, etc, can generate mind-boggling quantities of red tape. Many foreign business people working in Beijing and elsewhere say that success is usually the result of dogged persistence and finding cooperative officials.

If you have any intention of doing business in Beijing, be it buying, selling or investing, it's worth knowing that most urban districts *(shìqū)* have a Commerce Office *(shāngyè jú)*. If you approach one of these offices for assistance, the reaction you get can vary from enthusiastic welcome to bureaucratic inertia. In the case of a dispute (the goods you ordered are not what was delivered, etc), the Commerce Office could assist you, provided that they are willing.

Buying is simple, selling is more difficult, but setting up a business in Beijing is a whole different can of worms.

If yours is a high-technology company, you can go into certain economic zones and register as a wholly foreign-owned enterprise. In that case you can hire people yourself without going through the government, enjoy a three-year tax holiday, obtain long-term income tax advantages and import duty-free personal items for corporate and expat use (including a car!). The alternative is listing your company as a representative office, which does not allow you to sign any contracts in China – these must be signed by the parent company.

It's easier to register as a representative office. First find out where you want to set up (the city or a special economic zone), then go through local authorities (there are no national authorities for this). Go to the local Commerce Office, Economic Ministry, Foreign Ministry, or any ministry that deals with foreign economic trade promotion. In Beijing, the Haidian High-Technology Zone is recommended if you can qualify, but where you register depends on what type of business you're doing. Contact your embassy first – they can advise you.

The most important thing to remember when you go to register a company is not to turn away when you run into a bureaucratic barrier. Bureaucrats will tell you that everything is 'impossible'. In fact, anything is possible – it all depends on your *guānxi* (relationships). Whatever you have in mind is negotiable, and all the rules are not necessarily rules at all.

Tax rates vary from zone to zone, authority to authority. It seems to be negotiable but 15% is fairly standard in economic zones. Every economic zone has a fairly comprehensive investment guide, available in English and Chinese – ask at the economic or trade section of your embassy, which might have copies of these. These investment guides are getting to be very clear, although even all their printed 'rules' are negotiable!

The Foreign Enterprise Service Corporation (FESCO) is where you hire employees (its address is given under Useful Organisations further on). FESCO currently demands around US$325 per month per employee, 75% of which goes to the government. Bits of the bureaucracy

ROBERT STOREY

It's the real thing: but many products aren't.

which foreign business people should become familiar with are listed under the same heading as FESCO.

Printing

One place which offers professional typesetting and printing of namecards, envelopes and stationery is Alphagraphics. You'll find it in the basement of the West Wing Office Tower, China World Trade Centre, 1 Jianguomenwai Dajie (Map 21). This place also allows you to use their personal computers for a fee.

POST & COMMUNICATIONS

Post

All letters and parcels marked 'Poste Restante, Beijing Main Post Office' will wind up at the International Post Office on Jianguomenbei Dajie, not far from the Friendship Store (Map 21). Hours are from 8 am to 7 pm. The staff even file poste restante letters in alphabetical order, a rare occurrence in China, but you pay for all this efficiency – there is a Y1.50 fee charged for each letter received!

Some major tourist hotels will hold mail for their guests, but this doesn't always work.

Officially, the PRC forbids several items from being mailed to it – the regulations specifically prohibit 'reactionary books, magazines and propaganda materials, obscene or immoral articles'. You also cannot mail Chinese currency abroad, or receive it by post. Like elsewhere, mail-order hashish and other recreational chemicals will not amuse the authorities.

The international postal service seems efficient, and air-mailed letters and postcards will probably take around five to 10 days to reach their destinations. If possible, write the country of destination in Chinese as well as English, as this should speed up the delivery. Domestic post is amazingly fast, perhaps one day from Beijing to Shanghai. Within Beijing it may be delivered the same day that it's sent.

You can post letters at the reception desks of all major hotels. Even at cheap hotels you can do this – reliability varies but in general it's OK. There is a small but convenient post office in the CITIC building. Another useful post office is in the basement of the China World Trade Centre.

Overseas parcels must be posted from the International Post & Telecommunications Building on Jianguomen Bei Dajie. A counter inside sells wrapping paper, string, tape and glue. All post offices are very picky about how you pack things; don't finalise your packing until the thing has got its last Customs clearance. Most countries impose a maximum weight limitation (10 kg is typical) on packages received. This rate varies from country to country but Chinese post offices should be able to tell you what the limitation is. If you have a receipt for the goods, then put it in the box when you're mailing it, since it may be opened again by Customs further down the line.

With China's rapid inflation, postal rates can escalate suddenly so use the following only as a general guide. Rates are of course cheaper for printed matter, small packets and parcels:

Letters Up to 20 g: local city Y0.10; elsewhere in China Y0.20; Hong Kong, Macau & Taiwan surface mail Y0.60; Hong Kong, Macau & Taiwan airmail Y0.80; international surface mail Y2.20; international airmail Y2.90.

Postcards Local city Y0.10; elsewhere in China Y0.15; Hong Kong, Macau & Taiwan surface mail Y0.40; Hong Kong, Macau & Taiwan airmail Y0.60; international surface mail Y1.60; international airmail Y2.30.

Aerogrammes Hong Kong, Macau and Taiwan Y0.60; other countries Y2.80.

EMS Domestic EMS parcels up to 200 g cost Y12; each additional 200 g costs Y3. For international EMS, rates vary according to country. For nearby Asian countries (Japan, Korea, etc) it's Y105 for up to 500 g, plus Y30 for each additional 500 g.

Registration Fees The registration fee for letters, printed matter and packets posted to Hong Kong, Macau and Taiwan is Y2.20. Elsewhere in the world it costs Y4.50.

Private Carriers There are a number of private couriers in Beijing which offer international express posting of documents and parcels. None of these private carriers are cheap, but they're fast and secure. Some companies to try include: United Parcel Service (☎ 465-1565; fax 465-1897), Room 120A, Lufthansa Centre, 50 Liangmaqiao Lu; DHL (☎ 466-2211; fax 467-7826), 45 Xinyuan Jie, Chaoyang District; and TNT Skypak (☎ 467-7877; fax 467-7894), Building 14, Shuguangxili, Chaoyang District.

Telephone

China's creaky phone service is steadily improving. Reverse-charge calls to other countries are often cheaper than calls paid for in China.

If you're planning to take up residence in Beijing, consider subscribing to one of the many private callback services which allow you to pay foreign rates plus a small surcharge. However, bear in mind that such services have been declared illegal by the Chinese government. Even though they seem to be going strong at the moment, it's possible that the government will suddenly shut them down.

Many hotel rooms are equipped with phones from which local calls are free. Local calls can be made from public pay phones (there are some around but not many). Beijing's budding entrepreneurs try to fill the gap – people with private phones run a long cord out the window and stand on street corners with them, allowing you to use their phone to place local calls for around Y1 each. Long-distance domestic and international calls are not always possible on these phones, but ask. A few restaurants and hotels use the same system – free calls for guests, Y1 for non-guests, and long-distance calls are charged by the minute.

You can place both domestic and international long-distance phone calls from main telecommunications offices, but it's more trouble than it's worth. Domestic long-distance rates in China vary according to distance, but are cheap. By contrast, international calls are expensive. At the International Post & Telecommunications Building, phone and fax service cost the same: domestic Y50, international Y200, for three minutes (there is a three-minute minimum).

If you are expecting a call, try to advise the caller beforehand of your hotel room number. The operators frequently have difficulty understanding Western names, and the hotel receptionist may not be able to locate you. If this can't be done, then try to inform the operator that you are expecting the call and write down your name and room number – this increases your chances of success.

Direct Dialling Domestic direct dialling (DDD) and international direct dialling (IDD) calls are cheapest if you can find a phone which accepts magnetic cards. These phones are usually available in the lobbies of major hotels, and the hotel's front desk should also sell the phone cards. These cards come in three denominations, Y20, Y50 and Y100; for an international call, you'll need the Y100 card.

You can also dial direct from the phones found in hotel business centres, but this will cost more than using a magnetic phone card. Business centres usually charge a three-minute minimum regardless of how briefly you talk.

If your hotel lacks card phones or a business centre, you should be able to dial direct from your hotel room. You'll have to ask the staff at your hotel what's the dial-out code for a direct line (usually a '7' on most switchboards, or sometimes a combination like '78'). Once you have the outside line, dial 00 (the international access code – the same throughout China) followed by the country code, area code and the number you want to reach. If the area code begins with zero (like '03' for Melbourne, Australia) omit the first zero.

There are a few things to be careful about. The equipment used on most hotel switchboards is not very sophisticated. It's often a simple timer and it begins charging you starting from 30 seconds after you dial '7' (or '78' or whatever). The timer does not know if your call succeeds or not so you get charged if you stay on the line over 30 seconds, even if you just let the phone ring repeatedly or get a busy signal! On the other hand, if you complete your conversation within 30 seconds and hang up, you don't get charged at all. The hotel switchboard timer keeps running until you hang up, not when the other party hangs up, so replace the receiver as soon as the conversation ends. Many business centres use this same system, so be careful.

ROBERT STOREY

Talking shop: Chinese public phones are often very public.

The usual procedure is that you make the call and someone comes to your room five or 10 minutes later to collect the cash. If the hotel does not have IDD, you can usually book calls from your room through the switchboard and the operator calls you back, but this procedure will be more expensive.

To make a reverse-charge call, dial 108 followed by the country code. An operator in the country you are calling will answer.

With domestic direct dialling, it's useful to know the area codes of China's cities. These all begin with zero, but if you're dialling into China from abroad, omit the first zero from each code. China's country code is 86. Some significant area codes to know include Beijing (010), Guangzhou (020), Shanghai (021), Shenzhen (0755) and Tianjin (022).

International Country Codes

Country	Direct Dial Home	Country Direct
Australia	00-61	108-61
Canada	00-1	108-1
Hong Kong	00-852	108-852
Japan	00-81	108-81
Netherlands	00-31	108-31
New Zealand	00-64	108-64
UK	00-44	108-44
USA	00-1	108-1*

* For the USA you can dial 108-11 (AT&T), 108-12 (MCI) or 108-13 (Sprint)

Useful Phone Numbers There's at least a 50% chance that the person answering the phone will not speak English, in which case you get to practise Chinese. With that warning in mind, the following might prove useful:

Ambulance hotline	☎ 120
Car accident hotline	☎ 122
Fire hotline	☎ 119
HK & Macau directory assistance	☎ 115
Local directory assistance	☎ 114
Long-distance directory assistance	☎ 113, ☎ 173
Phone repair	☎ 112
Police hotline	☎ 110
Post code check	☎ 303-7131
Time	☎ 117
Tourist hotline	☎ 513-0828
Weather	☎ 121

Your Own Phone Getting a private telephone line installed in your hotel room or apartment is possible. There are no more waiting lists for installation, especially if you drop some RMB into the right pocket. To get your own phone line, a residence permit is required. Foreigners are charged 50% more than Chinese for phone service.

Cellular telephones are all the rage with cadres and other status-conscious urban Chinese with money to burn. Previously, the Ministry of Post & Telecommunications had a monopoly on cellular phone service in China, but in 1995 China United Telecommunications Corporation joined the marketing fray.

For a Chinese, a nationwide cellular phone costs a steep Y16,000 initially, but foreigners are charged more.

The cost per minute to both make and receive a local call is Y0.8. Dialling long-distance of course costs extra.

Pagers Those living on a budget, such as foreign students, may well find pagers a more realistic option than having a phone installed. Though considered a luxury in the West, pagers are far more common in China than telephones. China is the world's second largest pager market after the USA and will probably soon be the largest. This is due to the fact that the number of telephone lines available is inadequate to meet demand, but no such problem exists with pagers. Those with a residence permit can obtain a pager in just a couple of weeks.

Pagers for use in Beijing only cost Y15 a month. For a pager usable throughout China, the price rises to Y80 per month. The paging market was opened to free competition in 1993 – there are now more than 1700 paging operators in China so it's difficult to say which company is best.

The leading manufacturers of cellular phones and pagers are America's Motorola and Sweden's Ericsson. The Chinese don't yet manufacture cellular phones, but they do make pagers which even the locals will tell you are junk.

Fax, Telegraph, E-mail & Telex

All but the most rock-bottom hotels offer international telephone and fax services. Since you are charged a three-minute minimum at most places, sending a one-page fax works out to be absurdly expensive.

International telegram rates are usually around Y4 per word, and more for the express service. Rates to Hong Kong, Macau and Taiwan are charged somewhere half way between international and domestic rates.

If you're into computers at all then you are most likely familiar with E-mail. Unfortunately, only a few hotels have computers and modems for the use of their guests. If you're travelling with a portable computer and modem, all you need is an IDD line with an RJ-11 phone jack to call to your favourite E-mail service abroad – many business centres are so equipped. It is *not* advisable to attach your modem to the phone in your hotel room and dial out through the switchboard, unless you've got a device called an 'online handset coupler'. Otherwise, you risk frying your modem. It will be cheapest to call to Hong Kong, provided that your E-mail service has a node in Hong Kong. Otherwise, it will be an expensive international call.

If you are a foreign resident of Beijing, you can surf the Internet with China Online (☎ 849-8603). For more details you can send an E-mail message to: info@chinaonline.com.cn.net.

The telephone companies' bid in this market comes in three flavours. One is Chinapac (CNPAC), a very expensive packet-switching network. Somewhat more economical is Chinamail, the nation's government-owned E-mail service. Finally, there is Chinanet, which offers full access to the Internet. All three services are available from the Beijing Telegraph Office (☎ 601-0757; fax 601-0717), 11 Xichang'an Jie, or the Beijing Telecom Business Centre (☎ 505-1000, 532-1000), B1, China World Trade Centre, 1 Jianguomenwai Dajie.

Telex is old technology, rapidly dying out in the West as well as China. However, you can still find telex machines in the business centres of major hotels.

BOOKS

There is enough literature on China to keep you reading for the next 5000 years of their history, but relatively little dealing with Beijing exclusively. Another irony is that Beijing itself is not a good place to look for books about Beijing – the widest selection is in Hong Kong.

Guidebooks

In Search of Old Peking by Arlington and Lewisohn is one of the great classic guidebooks of the city.

Beijing – Old & New New World Press (1984) is a travel guide of sorts. It provides infinite details of nearly every pagoda, park, pavilion, brick and stone in China's capital, but it's rather dry reading. *Places of Interest in Beijing* (China Travel & Tourism Press) is far more readable than the former. The guide includes all the major and minor attractions, but also some unusual 'sights' such as the Changping Highway, China-Japan Friendship Hospital and Beijing No 3 Cotton Textile Mill.

Biking Beijing by Diana Kingsbury has a useful selection of self-guided tours around the thoroughfares and hutongs.

The *Beijing Official Guide* is published four times a year by the Chinese government. Though the information is far from complete, it's at least up to date. You can find free copies around the lobbies of various tourist hotels.

The government toots its own horn in *Beijing – A Magnificent City* and the *Beijing Investment Guide*. If you can't find copies at the Friendship Store, try calling the

GLENN BEANLAND

Despite the shopping malls, historical Beijing survives in hutongs like this one off Dazhalan.

Beijing Foreign Cultural Exchange Service Centre (☎ 512-3388 ext 2338).

An invaluable resource for business people is *The China Phone Book & Business Directory* (Far Eastern Economic Review), which contains essential phone and fax contact numbers in Beijing.

History

Twilight in the Forbidden City by Reginald F Johnston (Oxford University Press) was written by a British colonial official who tutored China's last emperor from 1919 to 1924. A fascinating read.

Of the many general books on the history of modern China, one that stands out is Jonathan Spence's *The Search for Modern China* (Norton, 1991).

An interesting sidelight on current intellectual history is provided by Perry Link in his *Evening Chats in Beijing*.

General

Peking (Pan Books) by Anthony Grey is your standard blockbuster by the author of *Saigon*. Not bad. The foregoing should not be confused with *Peking* by Juliet Bredon, another great book.

See also under Literature in the Arts section of the Facts about Beijing chapter.

MEDIA

Newspapers & Magazines

Chinese-Language Publications The *Renmin Ribao* (People's Daily) is the main newspaper for the masses. At the other end of the scale there is China's version of the gutter press – several hundred 'unhealthy papers' and magazines hawked on street corners and at bus stations in major cities with nude or violent photos and stories about sex, crime, witchcraft, miracle cures and UFOs. There are also about 40 newspapers for the minority nationalities.

Foreign-Language Publications China publishes various newspapers, books and magazines in a number of European and Asian languages. The government's English-language mouthpiece is the *China Daily*. First published in June 1981, it now has two overseas editions (Hong Kong and USA). Overseas subscriptions can be obtained from the following sources: Wen Wei Po (☎ 2572-2211; fax 2572-0441), 197 Wanchai Rd, Hong Kong; and China Daily Distribution Corporation (☎ (212) 219-0130; fax 210-0108), Suite 401, 15 Mercer St, New York, NY 10013, USA.

Surely the most interesting English-language publication in China is the *Beijing Scene* which is published twice monthly. Free copies pop up around hotels and expat bars, but it's also available by subscription. Try contacting Wins Industries, Ltd (☎ 532-6706; E-mail scene@well.com), 2-2-11 Qijiayuan, Beijing 100600.

Although you might stumble across some of the English-language magazines in luxury hotels and the Friendship Store, they are most readily available by subscription. These can be posted to you overseas. The

---

Recycled Rubbish

When a Communist Party committee of Beijing investigated the bustling black market for foreign books, magazines and newspapers, they discovered that hotel staff and garbage collectors are well-placed intermediaries for this business. Foreign hotel guests regularly leave behind several tonnes of foreign publications every month, but resident foreigners throw out nearly 20 tonnes.

The Beijing committee analysed printed matter left behind at the Xinqiao Hotel and was pleased to discover that nearly half of the publications had good or relatively good contents. The remaining items contained 'partly erroneous' or 'problematic' material such as 'half-naked advertisements'. When the courageous committee delved into diplomatic dustbins, they discovered that 15% of their haul was 'anti-communist, anti-Chinese, obscene and pornographic' – definitely bottom of the barrel. ■

---

place to contact is the Beijing Foreign Cultural Exchange Service Centre (☎ 512-3388 ext 2338; fax 512-3415), 3rd floor, CVIK Hotel, 22 Jianguomenwai Dajie, Beijing 100004 (Map 21). This outfit produces the *Beijing Official Guide*, *Beijing This Month*, *Business Beijing*, *Beijing Investment Guide* and *Beijing – A Magnificent City*.

China also produces a number of other magazines not dealing exclusively with Beijing. If interested in subscribing, contact Peace Book Company (☎ 2896-7382; fax 2897-6251), 17th Floor, Paramount Building, 12 Ka Yip St, Chai Wan, Hong Kong. You can write, fax or call in at the office for their catalogue.

In Beijing, it's easy to score copies of popular imported English-language magazines including *Time*, *Newsweek*, *Far Eastern Economic Review* and *The Economist*. Occasionally you might find European magazines in French or German. Foreign newspapers like the *Asian Wall Street Journal* and *International Herald-Tribune* are available. Hong Kong's *South China Morning Post* produces a whitewashed China edition which is not worth reading. Imported magazines are most readily available from the big tourist hotels and the Friendship Store.

Radio & TV

Domestic radio broadcasting is controlled by the Central People's Broadcasting Station (CPBS). Broadcasts are made in pǔtōnghuà, the standard Chinese speech, as well as in local Chinese dialects and minority languages.

Music buffs can listen to Chinese classical, opera, foreign violin concertos, piano solos, etc on AM radio at 640 kHz and 720 kHz, or FM stereo at 94.5 MHz and 98.2 MHz.

If you want to hear world news broadcasts in English, a short-wave radio receiver would be worth bringing with you. You can buy these in China, but Japanese-made ones are more compact and better quality.

The Chinese Central Television (CCTV) began broadcasting in 1958, and colour transmission began in 1973. Beijing boasts a second local channel, Beijing Television (BTV). Unless you want to practise your Chinese, you'll probably find most of the local stuff boring.

But the situation is not hopeless – satellite TV is all the rage in China. Hong Kong's Star TV has taken the country by storm because it broadcasts in Chinese and does not require a decoder (advertising revenues pay the bill) to receive it. Star TV also has an English channel, available in your hotel room (if you've got the right kind of room). The news, of course, has been sanitised so as to not offend the Chinese government. Some upmarket hotels also offer in-house video. If you can't live without TV shows, you should inquire at a hotel before checking in to see just what's available.

PHOTOGRAPHY & VIDEO

Beijing is a very photogenic city, and there are 11 million potential human portraits as well. Some Chinese shy away from having their photo taken, and even duck for cover. Others are proud to pose and will ham it up for the camera – and they're especially proud if you're taking a shot of their kid. Nobody expects any payment for photos, so don't give any or you'll set a precedent. What the Chinese would go for is a copy of a colour photo, which you could mail to them.

There are three basic approaches to photographing people. One is the polite 'ask for permission and pose it' shot, which is sometimes rejected. Another is the 'no-holds barred and upset everyone' approach. The third is surreptitious – standing half a km away with a metre-long telephoto lens. Many Chinese will disagree with you on what constitutes good subject matter; they don't really see why anyone would want to take a street scene, a picture of a beggar or a shot of an old man driving a donkeycart.

The Chinese are obsessed with photos of themselves standing in front of something. A temple, waterfall, heroic statue or important vintages of calligraphy are considered suitable backgrounds. At amusement parks,

GLENN BEANLAND

GLENN BEANLAND

Beijing offers a wide variety of photo opportunities.

GLENN BEANLAND

GLENN BEANLAND

Mickey Mouse and Donald Duck get into nearly every photo, while Ronald McDonald and the Colonel of Kentucky Fried fame are favourite photo companions in Beijing. If you hang around these places you can sometimes clip off a few portrait photos for yourself, but don't be surprised if your photo subjects suddenly drag you into the picture as an exotic prop!

Big-name colour print film (Kodak, Fuji, etc) is available almost everywhere, but is almost exclusively 100 ASA (21 DIN). Black and white film can be found at a few select photo shops, but its use is not common as colour photos are now the big thing. Colour slide film is seldom used by the Chinese, but can be bought in Beijing at speciality shops. It's cheapest at the Friendship Store and photo shops on Wangfujing Dajie. Major hotels also sell it, but at a significant mark-up.

Genuine Chinese brands of film are a rarity. Polaroid film is rumoured to exist, but if you know you'll need it, bring your own supply. Lithium batteries can generally be found at photo shops, but it doesn't hurt to carry a spare.

Many of the scenic spots in Beijing (Summer Palace, Forbidden City, etc) impose special fees on video cameras or ban them outright. It's not clear if this is to prevent you from stealing State secrets, or from filming a sequel to *The Last Emperor* without paying fees to the Chinese government.

Big hotels and stores along Wangfujing are equipped with the latest Japanese photoprocessing machines. Quality colour prints can be turned out in one or two hours for a reasonable cost.

It's a different situation with colour slides. Ektachrome and Fujichrome can be processed in Beijing, but this is normally slow and expensive and quality is not assured. There is no place in China to develop Kodachrome.

Undeveloped film can be sent out of China and, going by personal experience only, the dreaded X-ray machines do not appear to be a problem.

Prohibited Subjects

Religious reasons for avoiding photographs are absent among the Han Chinese. Some guy isn't going to stick a spear through you for taking a picture of his wife and stealing part of her soul. On the other hand, photographing monks and the interiors of temples is generally prohibited.

Photography from planes and photographs of airports, military installations, harbour facilities, train terminals and bridges can be a touchy subject. Of course, these rules only get enforced if the enforcers happen to be around.

Taking photos is not permitted in most museums, at archaeological sites and in many temples, mainly to protect the postcard and colour slide industry. It prevents Westerners from publishing their own books about these sites and taking business away from the Chinese-published books. It also prevents valuable works of art from being damaged by countless flash photos, but in most cases you're not allowed to take even harmless natural light photos or time exposures. The Chinese are not alone in imposing such restrictions, which can be frustrating at times.

TIME

All of China runs on Beijing's clock, which is set eight hours ahead of Greenwich Mean Time and daylight-saving time was abandoned in 1992. When it's noon in Beijing, it's 4 am in London, 5 am in Frankfurt, 5 am in Paris, 5 am in Rome, noon in Hong Kong, 2 pm in Melbourne, 4 pm in Wellington, 8 pm in Los Angeles, 11 pm in Montreal and 11 pm in New York.

ELECTRICITY

Electricity is 220 volts, 50 cycles AC. Plugs come in at least four designs – three-pronged angled pins (like in Australia), three-pronged round pins (like in Hong Kong), two flat pins (American-style but without the ground wire) or two narrow round pins (European-style). Conversion plugs are easily purchased in Hong Kong but are damn near impossible to find in Beijing. Battery chargers are widely available, but these are generally the bulky style which are not suitable for travelling – buy a small one in Hong Kong or elsewhere.

LAUNDRY

Each floor of just about every hotel in China has a service desk. The attendant's job is to clean the rooms, make the beds and collect and deliver laundry. Almost all tourist hotels have a laundry service, and if you hand in clothes one day you should get them back a day or two later. If the hotel doesn't have a laundry, the staff can usually direct you to one. Hotel laundry services tend to be expensive and if you're on a tight budget you might wind up doing what many travellers do – hand-washing

ROBERT STOREY

Local corner stores offer a wide range of services.

your own clothes. If you plan on doing this, dark clothes are better since the dirt doesn't show up so clearly.

WEIGHTS & MEASURES

China officially subscribes to the international metric system. However, ancient Chinese weights and measures still persist. The most likely ones that tourists will encounter are the *tael (liǎng)* and the *catty (jīn)*.

One catty is 0.6 kg (1.32 pounds). There are 16 taels to the catty, so one tael is 37.5 grams (1.32 ounces). Most fruits and vegetables in China are sold by the jin, while tea and herbal medicine are sold by the liang.

The other unit of measure that you might encounter is the *ping*. Pings are used to measure area, and one ping is approximately 1.82 metres square (5.97 feet square). When you buy cloth or carpet, the price will be determined by the number of pings. Ditto for leasing or purchasing an apartment or house.

HEALTH

Beijing is a reasonably healthy city – the cold climate means you needn't fear tropical bugs like malaria. Water supplies are fairly good, but it's still recommended that you only drink boiled or bottled water. Tea and coffee should pose no problem.

Some basic precautions are advisable. It is worth having your own health kit, for example. This need contain only Panadol, Band-aids, sunscreen and anti-diarrhoea tablets. Other items you might like to include are laxatives, contraceptives and, if you are travelling in spring, a gauze face-mask for protection against the dusty northern winds. If you wear spectacles, take a prescription with you in case they get broken. If you require a particular medication, take an adequate supply as it may not be available locally. Take the prescription with the generic rather than the brand name, which may be unavailable, as it will make getting replacements easier.

The most likely illness to befall you in Beijing is influenza. China is notorious for outbreaks of nasty strains of flu, especially during winter and spring. Pneumonia is a possible complication. The situation is exacerbated by the Chinese habit of spitting anywhere and everywhere, which spreads respiratory illnesses. You can protect yourself up to a limited extent with a flu vaccine, but 100% protection would require that you live in total quarantine or give up breathing.

Sexually Transmitted Diseases

The Cultural Revolution may be over but the sexual revolution is booming in China, and STDs are spreading rapidly. Therefore it pays to be cautious in sexual activity, particularly as you could be unlucky enough to catch herpes or, worse still, AIDS, for neither of which is there any cure. Apart from sexual abstinence, condoms provide the most effective protection and they are available in China. The word for condom is *bǎoxiǎn tào* which literally translates as 'insurance glove'.

As most people know by now, AIDS can also be spread through infected blood transfusions, and by dirty needles – vaccinations, acupuncture, ear piercing and tattooing can potentially be as dangerous as intravenous drug use if the equipment is not clean. You may choose to buy your own acupuncture needles, which are widely available in Beijing, if you're intending having that form of treatment. Medical clinics which cater to foreigners all use disposable needles and syringes.

Toilets
There are hygienic facilities in modern hotels, but public toilets are – perhaps luckily – few and far between. The average public convenience is a squat-down affair with only a low screen between it and the next 'cubicle', and usually lacks a flushing mechanism. Take toilet paper and a clothes peg. There are no toilets in the subway. ■

Medical Facilities

The International Medical Centre (☎ 465-1561; fax 465-1984) is in the Lufthansa Centre at 50 Liangmaqiao Lu (Map 21). Emergency service is available 24 hours a day, but there are regular office hours and it's a good idea to call first for an appointment. Vaccinations and dental service are available.

Another place gaining popularity with expats is the Hong Kong International Medical Clinic (☎ 501-2288 ext 2346) *(guójì yīliáo zhōngxīn)*, 3rd Floor, Hong Kong-Macau Centre, 2 Chaoyangmenbei Dajie (Map 23). There are staff on duty 24 hours.

Also good is the Sino-German Policlinic (☎ 501-1983) *(zhōngdé zhěnsuǒ)*. The clinic is in the basement of Landmark Tower B-1, adjacent to the Great Wall Sheraton Hotel (Map 21).

Asia Emergency Assistance (☎ 462-9100 fax 462-9111) operates a 24-hour alarm centre. Contact their office for information about their health care plan. AEA is in the Tayuan Diplomatic Building, 14 Liangmahe Nanlu, in the Sanlitun embassy compound (Map 21).

The Sino-Japanese Friendship Hospital (☎ 422-1122) *(zhōngrì yǒuhǎo yīyuàn)* is at Yinghua Donglu, Hepingli (Hepingli Beijie and Hepingli Dongjie) in the north-east (Map 21).

Beijing Union Hospital *(xiéhé yīyuàn)* has a 24-hour emergency room *(jízhěn shì)* (☎ 512-7733 ext 251) and a foreigners' clinic *(wàishìbàn gōng shì)*. The address is 1 Shifuyuan, Wangfujing (Map 22).

There is a foreigners' clinic at the Friendship Hospital (☎ 301-4411) *(yǒuyí yīyuàn)*, 95 Yongan Lu. The hospital is on the west side of Tiantan Park in the Tianqiao area (Map 20). Normal outpatient business hours are from 8 to 11.30 am and 2.30 to 5 pm.

Another Chinese clinic serving foreigners is Tongren Hospital (☎ 512-9911) *(tóngrén yīyuàn)* at 2 Chong-wenmennei Dajie (Map 22).

WOMEN TRAVELLERS

In general, foreign women are unlikely to suffer serious sexual harassment in China. There have been reports of foreign women being harassed by Chinese men in Beijing's parks or while cycling alone at night, but rape (of foreign women) is not common. This doesn't mean it cannot happen, but most Chinese rapists appear to prefer Chinese victims. The police tend to investigate crimes against foreigners much more closely and more severe penalties (like execution) are imposed if the perpetrator is caught. This provides foreign women with a small but important aura of protection.

DISABLED TRAVELLERS

While Beijing is not particularly user-friendly to disabled travellers, it's not the worst offender in this regard. Compared to the narrow lanes of other Asian cities, Beijing's wide boulevards and pedestrian footbaths make it easier to maneuver wheelchairs or for blind people to avoid being run over. On the downside, there are a number of places where the only way to cross the street is via an underground walkway with many steps. Uneven pavements can be a hazard too. Another drawback is that the city is very spread out. And Beijing's bus system is such a horror that it's liable to leave you disabled even if you weren't previously. (The good news is that air-conditioned tourist buses are gradually being introduced.)

Travel agents such as CITS and CTS may be able to make special arrangement for disabled persons with a little advance notice.

SENIOR TRAVELLERS

As already noted in the Health section of this book, China is one vast reservoir of the influenza virus. The elderly are particularly prone, and pneumonia can be a fatal complication. Older travellers should be sure that their influenza vaccines are up to date and should not hesitate to seek medical care or leave the country if problems arise.

Aside from this, Beijing poses no particular problem for seniors.

BEIJING FOR CHILDREN

Beijing is a city notable for its history and architecture. Many children do enjoy running around atop the Great Wall, but most kids are not much impressed by architectural and historical masterpieces such as the Forbidden City and Lama Temple.

In short, if you want to bring the kids, you may have trouble keeping them happy. Salvation lies in some of Beijing's theme parks (see the Entertainment chapter). Other places offering children-oriented entertainment include the rides at Badachu and the Kangxi Grasslands (see the Excursions chapter).

GLENN BEANLAND

Some of Beijing's large-scale sights can be daunting for younger visitors.

USEFUL ORGANISATIONS

The Beijing ISS International School (☎ 428-3151; fax 428-3156), No 17, Area 4, Anzhenxili, Chaoyang District, provides education for expat children from kindergarten through to the eighth grade.

Other important addresses for expats and business people include:

Foreign Enterprise Service Corporation (FESCO), 14 Chaoyangmen Nanjie (☎ 512-0547)

Foreign Investment Service Centre, 3A Jianguomenwai Dajie (☎ 701-7766 ext 2048), and 7K Kaiqi Building, 21 Beisanhuan Zhong Lu (third ring road) (☎ 202-3332 ext 2707)

Industry & Commerce Office, 360B Caihuying Dongjie (☎ 346-9955)

Investment Information Advisory Service Centre, 2A Baiwanzhuang Dajie (☎ 831-5349; fax 831-5583)

Tax Bureau, 13B Xin Zhongjie, Gongti Beijie (☎ 466-0568)

LIBRARIES

The National Library *(běijīng túshūguǎn)* holds around five million books and four million periodicals and newspapers, over a third of which are in foreign languages. Access to books is limited and access to rare books is even more limited, though you might be shown a microfilm copy if you're lucky. The large collection of rare books includes surviving imperial works such as the *Yong Le Encyclopedia* and selections from the old Jesuit library. Of interest to Ming-Qing scholars is the special collection, the *Shanbenbu*. The library is across Baishiqiao Lu west of the zoo (Map 23).

The old Beijing Library is near Beihai Park on the south-west corner.

CAMPUSES

Beijing University *(běidà)* and Qinghua University *(qīnghuá dàxué)* are the most prestigious institutes in China. Beida was founded at the turn of the century; it was then called Yanjing University and was administered by the Americans. Its students figured prominently in the 4 May 1919 demonstrations and the later resistance to the Japanese. In 1953 the university moved from Jingshan to its present location. In the 1960s the Red Guards first appeared here and the place witnessed some scenes of utter mayhem as the battles of the Cultural Revolution took place.

NIKKI BURNS

Beijing University: the radical young Mao studied Marxism here but intellectual discussion is now strictly controlled.

Beijing University students were leaders in the pro-democracy protests of 1989, and the government is still paranoid about the place. Foreigners poking around and asking too many questions will sooner or later attract the attention of plain-clothes police who keep a lid on dissent.

Beijing has about 50 colleges and universities. An intriguing one is the Central Nationalities Institute *(zhōngyāng mínzú xuéyuàn)*, just north of the zoo. This college trains cadres for the regions where ethnic minorities live. Beijing University is on the bus No 332 route from the zoo (Map 1).

DANGERS & ANNOYANCES

Theft

Some would say that the ridiculous overcharging of foreigners is the most common form of theft in China, but that happens to be legal. As for illegal crime, pickpocketing is a problem you need to carefully guard against. In back alleys, a thief might try to grab your bag and run away, but far more common is the razoring of bags and pockets in crowded places like buses and railway stations. If you want to avoid opening wallets or bags on the bus, keep a few coins or small notes ready in an accessible pocket before launching yourself into the crowd.

Hotels are usually safe places to leave your stuff; each floor has an attendant watching who goes in and out. If anything is missing from your room then they're going to be obvious suspects since they've got keys to the rooms. Don't expect them to watch over your room like a hawk, though, because they won't.

Dormitories could be a problem; there have been a few reports of thefts by staff, but the culprits are more likely to be other foreigners! There are at least a few people who subsidise their journey by ripping off their fellow travellers. Most hotels have storage rooms where you check your bags in; some insist that you do. Don't leave your valuables (passport, travellers' cheques, money, air tickets) lying around anywhere.

A money belt is the safest way to carry valuables, particularly when travelling on buses and trains. During the cooler weather, it's more comfortable to wear a vest (waistcoat) with numerous pockets, but you should wear this under a light jacket or coat since visible pockets invite wandering hands even if sealed with zips.

Perhaps the best way to avoid getting ripped off is to not bring a lot of junk you don't need – Walkmans, video cameras, expensive watches and jewellery all invite theft.

Spitting

The national sport, spitting, is practised by everyone regardless of how well-dressed or sophisticated they look. All venues are possible – on board buses and trains, in restaurants, etc. Never walk too closely alongside a stationary bus full of passengers, and try not to get caught in the crossfire elsewhere!

In Beijing, it is technically illegal. Anti-spitting campaigns with fines for violators are periodically launched, usually to coincide with a visit by an important foreign dignitary. Out in the countryside, it's a free-for-all.

Queues

Basically, there are none. People tend to 'huddle' rather than queue, resembling American-style football but without the protective gear. You're most likely to encounter the situation when trying to board a bus or buy a train ticket. Good luck.

Sex Vigilantes

For all the Communists' talk of the equality of women in Chinese society, the fact remains that China is a bastion of male chauvinism. There seems to be nothing as upsetting to the average Chinese male as seeing a Western male being accompanied by a Chinese woman. In the opposite scenario (where a Chinese male is being accompanied by a Western woman), the male is likely to receive knowing winks and snide remarks congratulating him on his sexual prowess.

The reason why all this is important is because it can occasionally lead to trouble. Racially mixed couples often receive verbal abuse, and occasionally find themselves being followed by gangs of semi-drunk males looking for trouble. If you're caught in this situation, don't expect much help from the police. The Beijing police have been known to arrest foreigners for 'insulting Chinese women', while the women being 'insulted' may be arrested for prostitution (even though they are not prostitutes).

Beijing has far more police than you at first realise, since most are dressed in plain clothes. There are also civilian 'snitch squads' who watch foreigners and report suspicious activities to the police. This has led to some spectacular blunders:

The police receive a tip – a Western man has a Chinese woman in his hotel room. At 3 am the hotel staff unlock the door of the Westerner's room without knocking and the police barge in. Acting with as much diplomacy as a bull in a China shop, the cops drag the naked couple out of bed – the man is totally bewildered and the woman is screaming hysterically while trying to cover her nude body. Then the police discover she's Japanese, not Chinese – they leave without offering any explanation or apology. As it turns out, the two are married.

Mixed couples should at least take the precaution of carrying a photocopy of their marriage certificate. Showing this is usually all you need to do to stop any hassles by inquisitive police or overzealous hotel staff.

BUSINESS HOURS

Banks, offices, government departments and PSB offices are open from Monday to Friday. As a rough guide only, they open at around 8 to 9 am, close for two hours in the middle of the day, then re-open until 5 or 6 pm. Saturday and Sunday are both public holidays.

Many museums, parks, zoos and monuments have similar opening hours, and are also open on Saturday and Sunday but close on Monday and Tuesday to compensate.

Out in the free market, business hours are long – you can grab breakfast at 7 am or dinner at 8 pm with no problem. Around the railway station, you can find people peddling food nearly 24 hours a day, seven days a week.

PUBLIC HOLIDAYS

Weekends and holidays are *not* good times to go sightseeing in Beijing. All places from the Great Wall to the shopping malls look like a phone-booth stuffing contest. Crowds are thinner on Monday, but many museums are closed at that time.

Aside from Saturday and Sunday, the PRC has nine national holidays during the year:

New Year's Day
    1 January
Spring Festival
    Otherwise known as Chinese New Year, it starts on the first day of the first moon according to the traditional lunar calendar. Although officially lasting only three days, many people take a week off work. This is a bad time for a visit – hotels are booked solid, many places shut

down totally and those that remain open may double their rates.

International Working Women's Day
> 8 March

International Labour Day
> 1 May

Youth Day
> 4 May – commemorates the student demonstrations in Beijing on 4 May 1919, when the Versailles Conference decided to give Germany's 'rights' in the city of Tianjin to Japan

Children's Day
> 1 June

Anniversary of the Founding of the Communist Party of China
> 1 July

Anniversary of the Founding of the PLA
> 1 August

National Day
> 1 October – celebrates the founding of the PRC on 1 October 1949

FESTIVALS

Beijing is probably at its prettiest on May Day (1 May), a religious holiday for Communists officially known as International Labour Day. During this time, the whole city (especially Tiananmen Square) is decorated with flowers.

Beijing also rolls out its marching bands and militaristic displays on National Day (1 October).

Special prayers are held at Buddhist and Taoist temples on days when the moon is either full or just the thinnest sliver. According to the Chinese lunar calendar, these days fall on the 14th and 15th days of the lunar month and on the last (29th or 30th) day of the month just ending and the first day of the new month.

The Lantern Festival *(yuánxiāo jié)* is not a public holiday, but it's a relatively colourful time to visit Beijing. It falls on the 15th day of the 1st moon according to the lunar calendar. People take the time to walk the streets at night carrying colourful paper lanterns.

Guanyin is the goddess of mercy. Her birthday falls on the 19th day of the 2nd moon and is a good time to visit Taoist temples.

Tomb Sweep Day *(qīng míng jié)* is a day for worshipping ancestors; people visit the graves of their departed relatives and clean the site. They often place flowers on the tomb and burn ghost money for the departed. It falls on 5 April in the Gregorian calendar in most years, and on 4 April in leap years.

Festival Dates to the Year 2000				
Festival	*1996*	*1997*	*1998*	*1999*
Spring Festival	19 Feb	7 Feb	28 Jan	16 Feb
Lantern Festival	4 Mar	21 Feb	11 Feb	2 Mar
Guanyin's Birthday	6 Apr	27 Mar	17 Mar	5 Apr
Mid-Autumn Festival	27 Sept	16 Sept	5 Oct	24 Sept

The Mid-Autumn Festival *(zhōngqiū jié)*, also called the Moon Festival, takes place on the 15th day of the 8th moon. Romantic gazing at the moon with one's lover is a popular pastime, and this is also the time to eat tasty moon cakes.

WORK

As Chairman Mao used to say, 'We all must be happy in our work'. Foreigners seeking happiness in Beijing usually wind up teaching English or foreign languages. Teaching in China is not a way to get rich – pay is roughly Y2000 a month. This is about four times what the average urban Chinese worker earns. There are usually some fringe benefits like free or low-cost housing and sub-sidised medical care. If you possess certain technical skills much in demand, you could possibly land a good-paying job with a foreign company in Beijing but such plum jobs are not easy to come by. Most foreign profes-sionals working in Beijing are overwhelmingly recruited from overseas; many have spent years employed in the company in their home countries.

The main reason to work in China is to experience the country at a level not generally available to travellers. Unfortunately, just how close you will be able to get to the Chinese people depends on what the PSB allows. In Beijing, where the local PSB is almost hysterical about controlling evil foreign 'spiritual pollution', your stu-dents may be prohibited from having any contact with you beyond the classroom, though you may secretly meet them far away from the campus. Foreign teachers are usually forced to live in separate apartments or dormitories. Chinese students wishing to visit you at your room may be turned away at the reception desk; otherwise they may be required to register their name, ID number and purpose of visit. Since many people are reluctant to draw attention to themselves like this (and they could be questioned by the PSB later), they may be unwilling to visit you at all.

In other words, teaching in Beijing can be a lonely experience, unless you spend all your free time in the company of other expats, but this deprives you of the 'foreign experience' you may be seeking.

Two topics which cannot be discussed in the classroom are politics and religion. Foreigners teaching in Beijing have reported spies being placed in their classrooms. Other teachers have found microphones hidden in their dormitory rooms (one fellow took revenge by attaching his Walkman to the microphone wires and blasting the snoops with punk music!).

Rules change – Beijing is becoming more liberal than in years past. However, just because the Chinese can now listen to rock music and wear miniskirts does not mean that it is a free society.

If you are interested in working in Beijing, contact a Chinese embassy or the universities directly.

Getting There & Away

AIR

If you're only planning to visit Beijing and nowhere else in China, the cheapest option is to purchase a return-trip ticket in your own country that goes directly to Beijing. Tickets to Hong Kong are generally cheaper than tickets directly to the capital, but a Hong Kong to Beijing flight will probably eat up the savings. And if you go to Beijing on a one-way ticket you will find it expensive to fly out. While Hong Kong is a great place to find cheap air fares, Beijing is not – this reflects the lack of free-market competition. A London to Beijing ticket is likely to be less than half the price of a Beijing to London ticket, for example.

Another possibility that may be more suitable if you want to travel around China is an 'open-jaw' ticket. This allows you to fly into a particular destination and exit by another route. For example, you could fly London to Beijing and fly from Hong Kong back to London. The advantage is that you get to do some overland touring in China without having to backtrack.

Discount Tickets

When you're looking for cheapie fares you have to go to a travel agent rather than directly to the airline which can only sell fares at full list price.

There are numerous discount tickets which are valid for 12 months, allowing multiple stopovers with open dates. These tickets allow for a great deal of flexibility. Just be sure that you check the ticket carefully – some are only valid for six months or even 60 days.

Off-season discounts are available. The 'low season' is winter, except during the Chinese New Year. The 'shoulder season' is spring and autumn. Summer is the 'peak season', when peak prices are charged and seat availability can be a problem, but there are still ways to get discounts even at this time. If you're flying from the southern hemisphere, seasons are reversed. Some off-season round-trip discount tickets require that you both arrive at and depart from your destination during low season, so that if you arrive in China during low season and later change the departure date to peak season, you might have to pay a penalty.

APEX (Advance Purchase Excursion) tickets are sold at a discount but will lock you into a rigid schedule. Such tickets must be purchased two or three weeks ahead of departure, do not permit stopovers and may have minimum and maximum stays as well as fixed departure and return dates. Unless you definitely must return at a certain time, it's best to purchase APEX tickets on a one-way basis only. There are stiff cancellation fees if you decide not to use your APEX ticket.

Some airlines offer student discounts on their tickets to student card holders, of up to 25%. Besides an International Student Identity Card (ISIC), an official-looking letter from the college is also required by some airlines. Many airlines also require you to be aged 26 or younger to qualify for a discount.

Frequent flyer deals are common. The way it works is that you fly frequently with one airline, and eventually you accumulate enough mileage to qualify for a free ticket or other prizes. You must first apply to the airline for a frequent flyer account number. Every time you buy an air ticket and/or check in for your flight, you must inform the clerk of your frequent flyer account number, or you won't get credit. Save your tickets and boarding passes, since it's not uncommon for the airlines to fail to give proper credit. You should receive monthly statements by post informing you how much mileage you've accumulated. Once you've accumulated sufficient mileage to qualify for freebies, you're supposed to receive vouchers by mail. Many airlines have 'black-out periods', or times when you cannot fly for free (Christmas and the Chinese New Year for example). The worst thing about frequent flyer programmes is that these tend to lock you into one airline while another airline might be offering a cheaper fare or a more convenient flight schedule.

Airlines usually carry babies up to two years of age at 10% of the relevant adult fare; a few may carry them free of charge. For children aged four to 12 years the fare on international flights is usually 50% of the full fare or 67% of a discounted fare.

To/From Australia

Australia is not a cheap place to fly out of. Among the cheapest regular tickets available in Australia are the APEX fares. The cost of these tickets depends on your departure date from Australia. Peak season in Australia is from December to January.

It's possible to get reductions on the cost of APEX and other fares by going to the student travel offices and/or some of the travel agents in Australia that specialise in cheap air tickets.

The cheapest way into China is via Hong Kong. A one-way fare from Melbourne to Hong Kong in the low season is likely to cost from about A$800 (A$1130 return) in the low season, A$950 (A$1300) in the high season.

Malaysia Airlines flies from Melbourne and Sydney to Beijing for A$1300/1450 return low/high season, but you will probably have to stay overnight at your own expense in Kuala Lumpur (if you're lucky you might get a through connection).

CAAC (the China Aviation Administration of China or *zhōngguó mínháng*; the country's official flag carrier) flies direct from Sydney to Beijing for A$1100/1320 return low/high season. Qantas has similar fares: single, A$1080/1170 low/high season; return, A$1200/1499.

Travel agents advertise in the travel sections of the Saturday papers, such as the Melbourne *Age* and the *Sydney Morning Herald*. Well worth trying is the Flight Centre, which has dozens of offices throughout Australia. Some good deals are also available from STA Travel and you don't have to be a student to use their services. They have offices in all the major Australian cities.

Departure tax from Australia is A$27 for passengers 12 years of age and over. Usually it's incorporated into the price of the ticket.

To/From Canada

Travel CUTS is Canada's national student travel agency and has offices in Vancouver, Victoria, Edmonton, Saskatoon, Toronto, Ottawa, Montreal and Halifax. You don't have to be a student to use their services.

Getting discount tickets in Canada is much the same as in the USA. Go to the travel agents and shop around until you find a good deal. In Vancouver try Kowloon Travel, Westcan Treks and Travel CUTS.

In general, air fares from Vancouver to Hong Kong or China will cost about 5% to 10% more than tickets from the US west coast.

Besides numerous flights to Hong Kong, CAAC has two flights weekly which originate in Toronto, then fly onward to Vancouver, Shanghai and Beijing (in that order).

In Canada, departure taxes are included in the original price of the ticket and there is no additional charge at the airport.

To/From Europe

Western Europe Fares similar to those from London
(see the To/From the UK section) are available from
other European cities.

Austrian Airlines offers an open-jaw ticket that allows
you to fly to Ürümqi (in China's Xinjiang Province),
travel overland and fly back from Beijing.

The Netherlands, Belgium and Switzerland are good
places for buying discount air fares. In Antwerp, WATS
has been recommended. In Zurich try SOF Travel and
Sindbad. In Geneva try Stohl Travel. In the Netherlands,
NBBS is a reputable agency.

CAAC has flights between Beijing and Berlin, Frankfurt, London, Milan, Moscow, Paris, Rome, Stockholm
and Zurich. Other international airlines operate flights
out of Beijing but there are very few, if any, cut-rate fares
from the Chinese end.

Russia Any air ticket you buy in Russia is likely to be
expensive. You're not paying for fine service – you're
paying for the lack of competition. Aeroflot is the only
Russian airline, and within Russia it's expensive. Ironically, if you purchase an Aeroflot ticket in some other
country (like the UK), it can be very cheap. No matter
what you pay for the ticket, be forewarned that Aeroflot
has a reputation for frequent cancellations, high prices,
poor safety and lost or stolen luggage.

A direct Moscow to Beijing flight costs US$1200, and
foreigners are required to pay in dollars even for domestic flights within Russia – forget any rumours you've
heard about cheap rouble-denominated tickets.

Both CAAC and Aeroflot offer a once-weekly flight
between Ürümqi (in China's Xinjiang Province) and
Moscow (via Novosibirsk) for US$260 – a tremendous
saving! Another relatively cheap option is to take a
domestic flight from Moscow to the Siberian city of
Irkutsk, then fly internationally from Irkutsk to
Shenyang in north-east China. The combined Moscow-
Irkutsk-Shenyang ticket costs US$495. From Shenyang,
you can take a domestic flight to Beijing on CAAC for
Y220. Taking this route may be slower and less convenient, but the saving of over US$700 is a powerful
incentive.

To/From Hong Kong

Although China makes it clear that Hong Kong is a part
of China, flights between Hong Kong and the rest of the
country are treated as international flights. You must go

through immigration and customs, and pay international departure taxes.

CAAC and Dragonair have the Beijing-Hong Kong route sewn up. Many foreign airlines would like to fly on this lucrative route, but the Chinese government won't allow them in.

In Hong Kong, travel agents cannot book you into a CAAC flight; for this, you need to go directly to the airline office. There are two such offices in Hong Kong, as follows: Ground Floor, 17 Queen's Rd, Central (☎ 2840-1199) and Ground Floor, Mirador Mansion, 54-64B Nathan Rd, Tsimshatsui (☎ 2739-0022).

Dragonair (*gǎnglóng hángkōng*) is a joint-venture airline between Hong Kong's Cathay Pacific and CAAC. If you fly on Dragonair, you can book through Cathay Pacific's offices around the world. If you're a member of Cathay's frequent flyer programme (known as the 'Marco Polo Club'), flights on Dragonair can be credited to your mileage total.

In Hong Kong, any travel agent with a computer can book you onto a Dragonair flight but you can also directly contact the ticketing office at Dragonair (☎ 2868-6777), World Wide House, 19 Des Voeux Rd, Central.

Hong Kong is a good place to pick up cheap air tickets to almost anywhere in the world. Remember that prices of cheap tickets change and bargains come and go rapidly, and that some travel agents are more reliable than others. Travel agents advertise in the classified sections of the newspapers. Some agents with good recommendations in the Kowloon area include:

Phoenix Services, Room B, 6th Floor, Milton Mansion, 96 Nathan Rd, Tsimshatsui (☎ 2722-7378; fax 2369-8884)

Shoestring Travel, Flat A, 4th Floor, Alpha House, 27-33 Nathan Rd, Tsimshatsui (☎ 2723-2306; fax 2721-2085)

Traveller Services, Room 1012, Silvercord Tower 1, 30 Canton Rd, Tsimshatsui (☎ 2375-2222; fax 2375-2233)

To/From Japan

CAAC has several flights a week from Beijing to Tokyo, Osaka, Fukuoka and Sendai. Some of these flights are via Shanghai. Japan Airlines flies from Beijing and Shanghai to Tokyo, Osaka and Nagasaki. There are flights between Dalian and Fukuoka/Tokyo on All Nippon Airways.

Chinese visas obtained in Japan are outrageously expensive – US$80 to US$120 depending on which agent you use.

To/From Korea (South)

Asiana Airlines, Korean Air and CAAC operate routes between Seoul and Beijing. The fare is US$270/540 single/return.

Seoul is a reasonably good place to get discounted air tickets. Recommended agents include:

Joy Travel Service, 10th Floor, 24-2 Mukyo-dong, Chung-gu (directly behind City Hall) (☎ (02) 776-9871; fax 756-5342)
Korean International Student Exchange Society (KISES), Room 505, 5th Floor, YMCA building on Chongno 2-ga (next to Chonggak subway station) (☎ (02)733-9494; fax 732-9568)
Top Travel, Room 506, 5th Floor, YMCA building on Chongno 2-ga (☎ (02)739-5231; fax 736-9078)

To/From Korea (North)

If you can get a visa for North Korea (a big *if*), both Koryo Airlines and CAAC fly Beijing-Pyongyang once weekly for US$120.

To/From Macau

As with Hong Kong, flights between Macau and the rest of China are regarded as international flights even though Macau is officially part of China.

The recently completed new airport at Macau now offers Beijing-Macau flights with CAAC and Air Macau.

To/From Malaysia

CAAC has direct Beijing-Kuala Lumpur flights four times weekly, but it's certainly easier to find an empty seat if you fly via Hong Kong.

To/From New Zealand

Singapore Airlines and Malaysia Airlines offer low-season return fares to Hong Kong for NZ$1345, and Qantas and Cathay Pacific offer fares from NZ$1400. At the time of writing, Garuda Airlines was offering the cheapest fare to Beijing – NZ$1360 round-trip during low season.

The departure tax from New Zealand is NZ$20. Children under the age of two are exempt.

To/From the Philippines

CAAC has a twice-weekly flight from Beijing to Manila.

To/From Singapore

Any airline worth its wings flies between Singapore and Hong Kong, but you'll have to change to a CAAC or Dragonair flight to Beijing. CAAC does direct flights between Singapore and Beijing five times weekly.

Good places for buying cheap air tickets in Singapore are Airmaster Travel Centre and STA Travel. Other agents advertise in the *Straits Times* classifieds.

To/From Thailand

Bangkok is one of Asia's hot spots when it comes to finding bargain basement prices on air tickets.

There are five flights weekly from Beijing to Bangkok via Guangzhou (you can pick up the flight in Guangzhou too). There is also a very popular flight from Bangkok to Kunming via Chiang Mai on Thai Airways, and from there you can pick up a domestic flight to Beijing.

To/From the UK

Air-ticket discounting is a long-running business in the UK and there's nothing under-the-counter about it at all. To find out what's available, there are a number of magazines in Britain which have good information about flights and agents. These include: *Trailfinder*, free from the Trailfinders Travel Centre in Earls Court; and *Time Out*, the London weekly entertainment guide widely available in the UK.

Discount tickets are almost exclusively available in London. The danger with discounted tickets in Britain is that some of the 'bucket shops' are unsound. Sometimes the backstairs over-the-shop travel agents fold up and disappear after you've handed over the money and before you've got the tickets, so make sure you get the tickets before you hand over your cash.

Two reliable London bucket shops are Trailfinders in Earls Court and STA Travel with several offices.

A standard-price one-way ticket with CAAC from London to Beijing will cost £275 (£450 return). Flights to Hong Kong are almost the same price.

To/From the USA

There are some very good open tickets which remain valid for six months or one year (opt for the latter unless you're sure) without locking you into any fixed dates of departure. For example, there are cheap tickets between the US west coast and Hong Kong with stopovers in

Japan, Korea and Taiwan for very little extra money –
the departure dates can be changed and you have one
year to complete the journey. However, be careful during
the peak season (summer and Chinese New Year)
because seats will be hard to come by unless reserved
months in advance.

Usually, and not surprisingly, the cheapest fares to
China are offered by ethnic Chinese. San Francisco is the
budget ticket capital of America, though some good
deals can be found in Los Angeles, New York and other
cities. Discount travel agents can be found through the
yellow pages or the major daily newspapers. Those
listed in both Roman and Chinese scripts are usually
discounters. A more direct way is to wander around San
Francisco's Chinatown where most of the shops are –
especially in the Clay St and Waverly Place area. Many
of these are staffed by recent arrivals from Hong Kong
and Taiwan who speak little English. Inquiries are best
made in person and be sure to compare prices – cheating
is not unknown.

It's not advisable to send money (even cheques)
through the post unless the agent is very well-established. Some travellers have reported being ripped off
by fly-by-night mail-order ticket agents.

Council Travel is the largest student travel organisation, and though you don't have to be a student to use
it, it does have specially discounted student tickets.
Council Travel has an extensive network in all major US
cities and is listed in the telephone book.

One of the cheapest and most reliable travel agents on
the west coast is Overseas Tours (☎ (800) 323-8777 in
California, (800) 227-5988 elsewhere), 475 El Camino
Real, Room 206, Millbrae, CA 94030. Another good agent
is Gateway Travel (☎ (214) 960-2000, (800) 441-1183),
4201 Spring Valley Rd, Suite 104, Dallas, TX 75244; they
seem to be reliable for mail-order tickets.

Northwest and United airlines both fly to Beijing, and
both offer more generous frequent flyer programmes
than the Asian airlines. It's worth knowing that both
Northwest and United sell open return tickets that are
valid for only six months rather than one year – no
problem for most travellers, but be sure to get one that
suits your schedule.

One-way trips usually cost 35% less than a round trip.
From Hong Kong, one-way fares to the American west
coast start from about US$365 (with APEX restrictions).
Return APEX tickets begin at US$575. APEX fares to
New York start from US$493 one way, US$883 return.

For direct flights from the USA to China the general
route is from San Francisco (with connections from New

York, Los Angeles and Vancouver in Canada) to Tokyo, then Beijing, Shanghai or several other cities in China. It's entirely possible to go through to Beijing and then pick up the return flight in Shanghai. Tickets from the USA directly to Beijing will cost around US$200 to US$300 more than tickets to Hong Kong, even though the flying distance to Beijing is actually shorter.

To/From Vietnam

China Southern Airlines and Vietnam Airlines fly the China-Vietnam route using fuel-guzzling Soviet-built Tupolev 134 aircraft. The Beijing-Hanoi flight on China Southern Airlines stops at Nanning (capital of China's Guangxi Province) en route – you can board or exit the plane there.

Chinese Carriers

The China Aviation Administration of China (*zhōngguó mínháng*), also known as CAAC, is the official flag carrier of the PRC. Officially CAAC has been broken up into some 30 domestic and international airlines. This doesn't mean that CAAC is out of business, but it now assumes the role of 'umbrella organisation' for its numerous subsidiaries which include Air China (its major international carrier), China Eastern, China Southern, China Northern, China Southwest, China Northwest, etc.

In its role as 'umbrella organisation', CAAC publishes a comprehensive international and domestic timetable in both English and Chinese, which comes out in April and November each year. These can be bought at some CAAC offices in China, but are easiest to get from the CAAC office in Hong Kong.

Domestic Flights The CAAC aerial web spreads out in every conceivable direction, with daily flights to major cities and quite a few minor ones. For the most current information, get a CAAC timetable.

Foreigners must pay a surcharge of 200% on top of the fare charged to local Chinese people. A student or foreign expert with a legitimate residence permit might get a discount on the surcharge. If you do somehow happen to score the Chinese price and it's discovered, your ticket will be confiscated and no refund given. Children over 12 years are charged the adult fare.

On domestic flights, if you cancel 24 hours before departure you lose 10% of the fare; if you cancel between two and 24 hours before the flight you lose 20%; and if you cancel less than two hours before the flight you lose 30%. If you don't show up for a domestic flight, you are entitled to a refund of 50%.

Generally domestic airline tickets in China must be paid for in cash. Bear this in mind if you envisage travelling elsewhere in China.

In theory, you can reserve seats without paying for them. In practice, this often leads to disappointment. The staff at some booking offices will hold a seat for more than a week, while other offices will only hold a seat for a few hours so you can run to the bank and change money. Until you've actually paid for and received your ticket, nothing can be guaranteed. On some routes, competition for seats is keen and people with connections can often jump the queue. Stand-by tickets do exist, a fact worth knowing about if you're desperate.

Airline Offices in Beijing

CAAC goes by a variety of aliases (Air China, China Eastern Airlines, etc), but you can buy tickets for all of them at the Aviation Building (domestic ☎ 601-3336; international ☎ 601-6667) (*mínháng dàshà*), 15 Xichang'an Jie, Xidan District (Map 23). You can purchase the same tickets at the CAAC office in the China World Trade Centre (Map 21) or from the numerous other CAAC service counters like the one in the Beijing Hotel or the CITS counter in the International Hotel.

Inquiries for all airlines can be made at Beijing's Capital Airport (☎ 456-3604).

The individual offices of other international airlines are:

Aeroflot
  Hotel Beijing-Toronto, 3 Jianguomenwai Dajie (☎ 500-2412)
Air France
  Room 2716, China World Trade Centre, 1 Jianguomenwai (☎ 505-1818)
Alitalia
  Rooms 139 & 140, Jianguo Hotel, 5 Jianguomenwai (☎ 500-2871, 500-2233 ext 139 or 140)
All Nippon Airways
  Room 1510, China World Trade Centre, 1 Jianguomenwai (☎ 505-3311)
American Airlines
  c/o Beijing Tradewinds, 114 International Club, 11 Ritan Lu (☎ 502-5997)
Asiana Airlines
  Room 134, Jianguo Hotel, 5 Jianguomenwai (☎ 506-1118)

Austrian Airlines
> Jianguo Hotel, 5 Jianguomenwai (☎ 500-2233 ext 8038; 591-7861)

British Airways
> Room 210, 2nd Floor, SCITE (CVIK) Tower, 22 Jianguomenwai (☎ 512-4070)

Canadian Airlines
> Unit S104, Lufthansa Centre, 50 Liangmaqiao Lu (☎ 463-7901)

Dragonair
> 1st Floor, L107, China World Trade Centre, 1 Jianguomenwai (☎ 505-4343)

Ethiopian Airlines
> Room 0506, China World Trade Centre, 1 Jianguomenwai (☎ 505-0134)

Finnair
> SCITE (CVIK) Tower, 22 Jianguomenwai (☎ 512-7180)

Garuda Indonesia
> Unit L116A, West Wing, China World Trade Centre, 1 Jianguomenwai (☎ 505-2901)

Japan Airlines
> Ground Floor, Changfugong Office Building, Hotel New Otani, 26A Jianguomenwai (☎ 513-0888)

JAT (Yugoslav) Airlines
> Room 414, Kunlun Hotel, 2 Xinyuan Nanlu (☎ 500-3388 ext 414)

Koryo Airlines
> Hong Kong-Macau Centre, 2 Chaoyangmenbei Dajie (☎ 501-1557)

LOT Polish Airlines
> Chains City Hotel, 4 Gongren Tiyuchang Donglu (☎ 500-7215, 500-7799 ext 2002)

Lufthansa
> Lufthansa Centre, 50 Liangmaqiao Lu (☎ 465-4488)

Malaysia Airlines
> Lot 115A/B Level One, West Wing Office Block, China World Trade Centre, 1 Jianguomenwai (☎ 505-2681)

MIAT Mongolian Airlines
> Room 8-05, CITIC Building, 19 Jianguomenwai (☎ 507-9297, 500-2255 ext 3850)

Northwest Airlines Room 104, China World Trade Centre, 1 Jianguomenwai (☎ 505-3505, 505-2288 ext 8104)

Pakistan International
> Room 106A, China World Trade Centre, 1 Jianguomenwai (☎ 505-1681)

Qantas
> Suite S120B, East Wing Office Building, Kempinski Hotel, Lufthansa Centre, 50 Liangmaqiao Lu (☎ 467-4794)

Scandinavian Airlines
> 18th Floor, SCITE (CVIK) Tower, 22 Jianguomenwai (☎ 512-0575)

Singapore Airlines
> Room 109, China World Trade Centre, 1 Jianguomenwai (☎ 505-2233)

Swissair
    Room 201, SCITE (CVIK) Tower, 22 Jianguomenwai
    (☎ 512-3555)
Thai Airways International
    Room 207, SCITE (CVIK) Tower, 22 Jianguomenwai
    (☎ 512-3881)
United Airlines
    Lufthansa Centre, 50 Liangmaqiao Lu (☎ 463-1111)

Departure Tax

If leaving China by air, the departure tax is Y90. Domestic departure tax is Y15. On both international and domestic flights in China the free-baggage allowance for an adult passenger is 20 kg in economy class and 30 kg in 1st class. You are also allowed five kg of hand luggage, though this is rarely weighed.

BUS

There are no international buses serving Beijing, but there are plenty of long-distance domestic buses. The advantage buses have over the train (besides cost) is that it's easier to get a seat on buses. In general, arriving in Beijing by bus is easier than departing mainly because it's very confusing figuring out which bus station has the bus you need.

The basic rule is that long-distance bus stations are on the perimeter of the city in the direction you want to go. The four major ones are at Dongzhimen (north-east), Haihutun (south), Beijiao (north – also called Deshengmen) and Majuan (east). In addition, there is a tiny bus station in the car park in front of the main Beijing railway station, and this is where you catch buses to Tianjin and the Great Wall at Badaling. Another tiny bus station is in the car park of the Workers' Stadium; this is mainly geared towards buses for destinations within Beijing municipality (like Miyun Reservoir).

TRAIN

International Trains

The Trans-Siberian Railway connects Europe to Asia. Its popularity has declined in recent years due to the general state of chaos in Russia plus rising prices. Nevertheless, it's an option worth considering.

There is some confusion of terms here since there are, in fact, three railways. The 'true' Trans-Siberian line runs from Moscow to the eastern Siberian port of Nakhodka, from where one can catch a boat to Japan. This route does not go through either China or Mongolia. Only the other two lines enter China itself. The Trans-Manchurian line crosses the Russia-China border at Zabaikalsk-Manzhouli, completely bypassing Mongolia. The Trans-Mongolian line connects Beijing to Moscow, passing through the Mongolian capital city, Ulaan Baatar.

Which direction you go makes a difference in cost and travelling time. The trains from Beijing take 1½ days to reach Ulaan Baatar. The journey from Moscow to Ulaan Baatar is four days. There are delays (three to six hours) at both the China-Mongolia and Russia-Mongolia borders.

A popular book about this journey is the *Trans-Siberian Handbook* by Bryn Thomas, Trailblazer Publications.

From Europe Travel Service Asia (☎ (07) 371-4963; fax 371-4769), Kirchberg 15, 7948 Dürmentingen, Germany, is recommended for low prices and good service.

In the UK, one of the experts in budget rail travel is Regent Holidays (UK) Ltd (☎ (0117) 921-1711; fax 925-4866), 15 John St, Bristol BS1 2HR. Another agency geared towards budget travellers is Progressive Tours (☎ (0181) 262-1676), 12 Porchester Place, Connaught Square, London W2 2BS.

Several travellers have recommended Scandinavian Student Travel Service (SSTS), 117 Hauchsvej, 1825 Copenhagen V, Denmark. This organisation has branch offices in Europe and the USA, and provides a range of basic tours for student or budget travellers, mostly during summer.

From China & Hong Kong In theory, the cheapest place to buy a ticket is at the CITS office (☎ 515-8570; fax 515-8603), Beijing Tourist Building, 28 Jianguomenwai Dajie, buried behind the New Otani Hotel. A straight Beijing-Moscow economy/deluxe ticket costs US$191/303. All tickets bought from CITS are straight through to Moscow (or Ulaan Baatar in Mongolia) – no stopovers are permitted. And contrary to what CITS brochures say, train tickets bought from CITS are nonrefundable.

Your other alternative is to buy from a private travel agent. This will always be more expensive than CITS because the private companies are forced to purchase their tickets from CITS too. However, some travel agents can offer stopover tours. If you're planning this trip far ahead, it's better to get a ticket in Hong Kong. The best organised of the Trans-Manchurian or Mongolian tour agents is Monkey Business, officially known as Moonsky Star (☎ 2723-1376; fax 2723-6653), 4th Floor, Block E, Flat 6, Chungking Mansions, 30 Nathan Rd, Tsimshatsui, Kowloon. Monkey Business also maintains an information office in Beijing at Beijing Commercial Business Complex (☎ 6329-2244 ext 4406), Room 406, No 1 Building, Yu Lin Li. However, it's best to book through their Hong Kong office, and as far in advance as possible. A booking can be done by telephone or fax and a deposit can be wired to them. One advantage of booking through them is that they keep all their passengers in a group (for mutual protection against theft). Furthermore, they can arrange visas and stopover tours to Mongolia and Irkutsk (Siberia).

You can also organise tickets and visas in Hong Kong through Wallem Travel (☎ 2528-6514), 46th Floor, Hopewell Centre, 183 Queen's Rd East, Wanchai. This place does organise tours, but is expensive.

Russian Visas The burning question that many travellers ask is 'can I stop off along the way?'. The answer is essentially 'no'. You can get a few days in Moscow on a transit visa, but stopping off elsewhere requires a tourist visa. The same problem applies to Mongolia.

Transit visas are valid for a maximum of 10 days and tourist visas are required if the journey is broken. In practice, you can stay in Moscow for three days on a transit visa and apply for an extension when you arrive. This only really works if you're going from Beijing to Moscow rather than the other way otherwise you'll miss your train to Beijing. Trying to extend a tourist visa is much more expensive – the hotel 'service bureau' will do it for you through Intourist, but only with expensive hotel bookings.

Before you can get a transit visa, you must have a ticket in hand or a ticket voucher. A transit visa can be issued in three working days for US$40; in two working days for US$60; or on the same day for the same price as the two-day service!

Then there is also the bizarre 'consular fee' for certain nationalities. There is no logic here – Belgians pay a consular fee of US$12 for transit visas and US$33 for tourist visas, while the French pay US$12 for both kinds of visas. The Swiss pay US$18 for a transit visa but get the tourist visa for free. These fees go up and down like a toilet seat – we can't make any predictions how much you'll actually have to pay.

Russian embassies are closed during all Russian public holidays: New Year's Day (1 January), Women's Day (8 March), Labour Day (1 & 2 May), Victory Day (9 May), Constitution Day (7 October) and October Revolution (7 & 8 November).

In Beijing, the Russian embassy (☎ 532-2051, 532-1267) is at Beizhongjie 4, just off Dongzhimen and west of the Sanlitun embassy compound. Opening hours are Monday to Friday from 9 am to noon.

Mongolian Visas The Mongolian embassy in Beijing is open all day, but the visa section keeps short hours only on Monday, Tuesday, Thursday and Friday from 8.30 to 11.30 am. They close for all Mongolian holidays, and they shut down completely for the entire week of National Day *(Naadam)*, which officially falls on 11-13 July. In the UK, the Mongolian embassy (☎ (0171) 937-0150, 937-5235) is at 7 Kensington Court, London W85 DL. One photo is required.

Needs, Problems & Precautions If you are approached in either Moscow or Beijing by people plugging black-market tickets on the Trans-Siberian, chances are 90% certain that you will be ripped off. Most likely, you will be sold a rouble-denominated ticket which only Russian nationals can use.

Bring plenty of US dollars cash in small denominations for the journey – only in China can you readily use the local currency. In China, food is plentiful and readily available from both the train's dining car and vendors in railway stations. In both Russia and Mongolia, food quality is poorer, but meals are available on the train. Once you get off the train it's a different story – food can be difficult to buy in both Russia and Mongolia, especially once you get away from the capital cities. Bring plenty of munchies like biscuits, instant noodles, chocolate and fruit.

Showers are only available in the deluxe carriages. In economy class, there is a washroom.

There is much theft on the train, so never leave your luggage unattended, even if the compartment is locked. Make sure at least one person stays in the compartment while the others go to the dining car. A lot of theft is committed by Russian gangs who have master keys to the compartments, so don't assume that a 'foreign face' means honesty.

The luggage limit is 35 kg per passenger and there is now some attempt being made to enforce this.

Domestic Trains

China's extensive rail network covers every province except Tibet. The main problem is ticketing hassles, particularly if you want something more comfortable than the lowest class known as 'hard-seat'.

Just about all railway stations have left-luggage rooms *(jìcún chù)* where you can safely dump your bags for a few yuan.

Hard-Seat Except on the trains which serve some of the branch or more obscure lines, hard-seat is not in fact hard but is padded. But it's hard on your sanity – the hard-seat section tends to be spectacularly dirty, noisy and smokey, and you'll get little sleep in the upright seats.

Since hard-seat is the only thing the locals can afford it's packed to the gills. If you're lucky, you'll get a ticket with an assigned seat number, but in many cases you'll have no seat reservation and will have to battle for a seat or piece of floor space with 5000 other hopefuls.

Hard-seat is survivable for a day trip; some foreigners can't take more than five hours of it, while others have a threshold of 12 hours or even longer. A few brave, penniless souls have even been known to travel *long-distance* this way – some roll out a mat on the floor under the seats and go to sleep on top of the peanut shells, chicken bones and spittle.

You may have to travel hard-seat even if you're willing to pay more for a higher class. The reason is that hard-seat tickets are relatively easy to obtain.

Hard-Sleeper The carriage is made up of doorless compartments with half a dozen bunks in three tiers, and sheets, pillows and blankets are provided. It does very nicely as an overnight hotel. The best bunk to get is a middle one since the lower one is invaded by all and sundry who use it as a seat during the day, while the top one has little headroom and loudspeakers which spew forth an indecipherable cacophony of military music and pleas in Chinese not to spit and throw beer bottles out the windows. Lights and speakers in hard-sleeper go out at around 9.30 to 10 pm.

Hard-sleeper tickets are the most difficult of all to buy; you almost always need to buy these far in advance.

Soft-Seat On shorter journeys (such as Beijing to Tianjin) some trains have soft-seat carriages. The seats are comfortable and overcrowding is not permitted.

Smoking is prohibited, a significant advantage unless you enjoy asphyxiation. If you want to smoke in the soft-seat section, you can do so only by going out into the corridor between cars. Soft-seats cost about the same as hard-sleeper and are well worth it. Unfortunately, soft-seat cars are a rarity.

Soft-Sleeper Luxury. Softies get the works with four comfortable bunks in a closed compartment – complete with straps to stop the top fatso from falling off in the middle of the night, wood panelling, potted plants, lace curtains, teacup sets, clean washrooms, carpets (so no spitting), and often air-conditioning. As for those speakers, not only do you have a volume control, you can turn the bloody things off! Soft-sleeper costs twice as much as hard-sleeper, and almost the same price as flying (on some routes even *more* than flying!). Soft-sleeper tickets are easier to come by than hard-sleeper simply because of the high price. However, with China growing more affluent, even soft-sleeper tickets are becoming difficult to obtain on short notice.

Dining Car For the desperate, you may be allowed to sleep in the dining car after it closes for meals. There is usually a charge for this – Y15 is typical. It's not terribly comfortable but is less horrible than hard-seat.

Platform Tickets An alternative to all the above is not to bother with a ticket at all and simply walk on to the train. To do this, you need to buy a platform ticket *(zhàntái piào)*. These are available from the station's information booth for a few jiao. You then buy your ticket on the train. This method is usually more hassle than it's worth, but may be necessary if you arrive at the station without enough time to get your ticket.

Upgrading If you get on the train with an unreserved seating ticket, you can seek out the conductor and upgrade *(bǔpiào)* yourself to a hard-sleeper, soft-seat or soft-sleeper if there are any available. This is sometimes the only way to get a sleeper or even a seat, but there are no guarantees that you won't be left standing.

If the sleeper carriages are full then you may have to wait until someone gets off. That sleeper may only be available to you until the next major station which is allowed to issue sleepers, but you may be able to get several hours of sleep. The sleeper price will be calculated for the distance that you used it for.

Over 95% of foreigners arriving or departing by train do so at the main Beijing railway station *(běijīng huǒchē zhàn)*. Within the lifespan of this book, the shiny new Beijing West railway station *(běijīng xī huǒchē zhàn)* will open – this will be the largest railway station in China. There are also two other stations of significance in the city, Yongdingmen (the south railway station) and Xizhimen (the north railway station).

There is a foreigners' ticketing office at the main Beijing railway station. Enter the station and it's to the rear and left side; you'll see a small sign in English saying 'International Passenger Booking Office'. The ticketing office is inside the foreigners' waiting room. It's open daily, from 5.30 to 7.30 am, 8 am to 5.30 pm. At least those are the official times, but foreigners have often found the staff unwilling to sell tickets in the early morning. Before you can buy a ticket, you must first fill out a reservation slip *(dēngjì dān)* which you get from the staff at window No 1. Return to window No 1 with the filled-in form, and if anything is available, you'll be given a confirmation slip which you take to window Nos 2 or 3 to pick up the ticket.

Whether or not you get a ticket here is pot luck. Sometimes the staff are friendly and helpful, at other times downright hostile. Tickets can be booked several days in advance. Your chances of getting a sleeper (hard or soft) are good so long as you book ahead.

Lockers are available in the comfortable foreigners' waiting room. If the lockers are full, you'll have to use the left-luggage rooms outside the station (head out of the station and car park, then to the right).

Outside Beijing, obtaining tickets is not so straightforward. Shanghai and a few other cities also have booking offices for foreigners, but in many cases your only hope of obtaining a sleeper is to seek the assistance of a travel agent. Most hotels employ an in-house travel agent to book train tickets, so inquire at the reception desk. You must give your passport to the travel agents when they go to buy your ticket, but an old expired passport will do just fine. Again, be aware that these agencies may rip you off by selling you a Chinese-priced ticket while charging foreigners' prices. If the agencies can't help you out, go to the railway station and fight it out yourself.

If you have a sleeper ticket the carriage attendant will take it from you and give you a metal or plastic chit, then when your destination is close he or she will swap it back and give you the original ticket. Keep your ticket until you get through the barriers at the other end, as you'll need to show it there.

Timetables There are paperback railway timetables available in Chinese only. Unfortunately, the timetables are so excruciatingly detailed that it's a drag working your way through them. Even the Chinese complain about this. Thinner versions listing the major trains can sometimes be bought from hawkers outside the railway stations.

Costs Foreigners are often required to pay three times more than PRC nationals for their train tickets, and these tickets look completely different from the standard Chinese ones. Foreign students and foreign experts can pay the Chinese price with the proper credentials.

Travel Times & Train Fares from Beijing

Destination	Hard-Sleeper	Hard-Seat	Soft-Sleeper	Soft-Seat	Approx. Time (hrs)
Beidaihe	105	65	200	99	6
Chengde	-	66	-	99	5
Chengdu	398	245	761	-	34
Dalian	256	158	488	-	19
Fuzhou	503	309	957	-	43
Guangzhou	512	-	973	-	30
Guilin	412	254	782	-	31
Hangzhou	317	183	630	-	24
Harbin	297	183	568	-	20
Kunming	589	362	1120	-	59
Luoyang	194	119	369	-	14
Nanjing	264	162	502	-	20
Qingdao	210	129	401	-	17
Shanghai	363	223	689	-	17
Shenyang	203	125	386	192	11
Shijiazhuang	-	51	-	77	4
Tianjin	-	35	-	54	2
Xi'an	273	168	521	-	22
Yantai	221	128	437	-	18

* Foreigners' price fares in RMB

Warning: Black-Market Tickets Black-market train tickets have become something of a cottage industry in China. You simply order a ticket (at the Chinese price plus a commission) from one of the touts standing around the railway station or operating through a cafe or hotel. This works fine in rural China, but it does *not* work in Beijing unless you have a Chinese face. The main Beijing railway station now has guards at both the entrance and exits – anyone with a big nose and a Chinese-priced ticket will be arrested and fined!

Even more disgusting is the fact that travellers have unknowingly purchased black-market tickets from CITS, CTS and other government-owned travel agencies. In other words, these agencies charge you the foreigners' price and sell you a Chinese-priced ticket, pocketing the difference for themselves. Then when the hapless travellers show up at Beijing railway station, they get busted. Even if you have an official receipt from CITS for the ticket, the railway staff do not care. You have a foreign face and a Chinese-priced ticket, so you're busted – end of discussion. Even a fake student card will not get you out of this one – you also need a student visa in your passport plus a residence certificate.

BOAT

While Beijing is not on the ocean, there is a seaport 2½ hours away by train at Tianjin's port district (Tanggu).

To/From Japan

Kobe-Tianjin Passenger ships ply the route from Kobe to Tanggu. Departures from Kobe are every Thursday at noon, arriving in Tanggu the next day. Economy/1st-class tickets cost US$253/343, or pay US$1355 for your very own stateroom. The food on this boat gets poor reviews so bring a few emergency munchies. Tickets can be bought in Tianjin from the shipping office (☎ 331-2283) at 89 Munan Dao, Hepingqu, or right at the port in Tanggu (☎ 938-3961). In Kobe, the office is at the port (☎ (078) 321-5791; fax 321-5793).

To/From South Korea

Inch'ŏn-Tianjin This popular but irregular ferry runs once every four or five days and the journey takes a minimum of 28 hours. Departures from Tianjin are at 10 am. The boat departs Inch'ŏn at 1 pm. The fares are: 3B class US$120, 3A class US$140, 2B class US$150, 2A class US$160, 1st class US$180 and VIP class US$230.

The boat doesn't dock at Tianjin proper but at the nearby port of Tanggu. Unlike Tianjin, Tanggu has at least one reasonable place to stay, the Seaman's Hotel. There are trains and buses directly to Beijing. Third class on the boat is a huge vault with around 80 beds and horrid toilets.

TRAVEL AGENTS

China has two major government-owned travel agencies and numerous smaller ones. Private agencies also exist, but they have a difficult time competing without the proper connections and state subsidies.

The main government-owned travel agencies in Beijing are as follows:

China International Travel Service (CITS), main branch at the Beijing Tourist Building, 28 Jianguomenwai Dajie, behind the New Otani Hotel (☎ 515-8570; fax 515-8603) – other branches at various hotels around town

China Travel Service (CTS), main office at 8 Dongjiaomin Xiang, Dongcheng District (☎ 512-9933; fax 512-9008)

It's pot luck what kind of reception you'll get when you show up. Some of the staff can be extremely courteous and helpful, but there have been complaints from travellers in the past about lousy service at high prices.

Branches Abroad

CITS The main office of China International Travel Service in Hong Kong can book air tickets to Beijing and elsewhere in China, and has a good collection of English-language pamphlets.

Outside of China and Hong Kong, CITS is usually known as the China National Tourist Office.

Australia
    China National Tourist Office, 11th Floor, 55 Clarence St, Sydney, NSW 2000 (☎ (02) 9299-4057; fax 9290-1958)
France
    China National Tourist Office, 51 Rue Saint-Anne, 75002, Paris (☎ (01) 42 96 95 48; fax 42 61 54 68)
Germany
    China National Tourist Office, Eschenheimer Anlage 28, D-6000 Frankfurt am Main-1
    (☎ (069) 55 52 92; fax 597 34 12)
Hong Kong
    Main Office, 6th Floor, Tower Two, South Seas Centre, 75 Mody Rd, Tsimshatsui East (☎ 2732-5888; fax 2721-7154)
    Central Branch, Room 1018, Swire House, 11 Chater Rd, Central (☎ 2810-4282)
Japan
    China National Tourist Office, 6F Hachidai Hamamatsu-cho Building, 1-27-13 Hamamatsu-cho, Minato-ku, Tokyo (☎ (03) 3433-1461; fax 3433-8653)
UK
    China National Tourist Office, 4 Glentworth St, London NW1 (☎ (0171) 935-9427; fax 487-5842)

USA
>   China National Tourist Office, Los Angeles Branch, 333 West Broadway, Suite 201, Glendale CA 91204 (☎ (818) 545-7505; fax 545-7506)
>   New York Branch, Lincoln Building, 60E, 42nd St, Suite 3126, New York, NY 10165 (☎ (212) 867-0271; fax 599-2892)

CTS China Travel Service in Hong Kong and Macau is one of the best places to arrange visas and book trains, planes, boats and other transport to the rest of China. CTS can sometimes get you a better deal on hotels booked through their office than you could obtain on your own:

Australia
>   Ground Floor, 757-759 George St, Sydney, NSW 2000 (☎ (02) 9211-2633; fax 9281-3595)
Canada
>   556 West Broadway, Vancouver, BC V5Z 1E9 (☎ (604) 872-8787; fax 873-2823)
France
>   32 Rue Vignon, 75009, Paris (☎ (01) 44 51 55 66; fax 44 51 55 60)
Germany
>   Düsseldorfer Strasse 14 6000, Frankfurt am Main-1 (☎ (069) 25 05 15; fax 23 23 24)
Hong Kong
>   Central Branch, 2nd Floor, China Travel Building, 77 Queen's Road, Central (☎ 2525-2284; fax 2868-4970)
>   Kowloon Branch, 1st Floor, Alpha House, 27-33 Nathan Rd, Tsimshatsui (☎ 2721-1331; fax 2721-7757)
Indonesia
>   PT Cempaka Travelindo Service, Jalan Hayam Wuruk 97, Jakarta-Barat (☎ (021) 629-4252; fax 629-4836)
Japan
>   Nihombashi-Settsu Building, 2-2-4 Nihombashi, Chuo-ku, Tokyo (☎ (03) 3273-5512; fax 3273-2667)
Macau
>   Xinhua Building, Rua de Nagasaki (☎ 705 506; fax 706 611)
Malaysia
>   112-114 Jalan Pudu, 55100, Kuala Lumpur (☎ (03) 201-8888; fax 201-3268)
Philippines
>   801-803 Gandara St (corner Espeleta St), Santa Cruz, Manila (☎ (02) 48-3717; fax 530-0463)
Singapore
>   1 Park Rd, No 03-49 to 52, People's Complex, Singapore, 0105 (☎ 532-9988; fax 538-6068)
Thailand
>   559 Yaowaraj Rd, Sampuntawong, Bangkok 10100 (☎ (02) 226-0041; fax 226-4712)

UK
  24 Cambridge Circus, London WC2H 8HD
  (☎ (0171) 836-9911; fax 836-3121)
USA
  San Francisco Branch, 2nd Floor, 212 Sutter St, San Francisco, CA 94108 (☎ (800) 332-2831, (415) 398-6627; fax 398-6669)
  Los Angeles Branch, 119 South Atlantic Blvd, Suite 303, Monterey Park, CA 91754 (☎ (818) 457-8668; fax 457-8955)

ORGANISED TOURS

Are tours worth it to you? Perhaps, but apart from the expense, they tend to screen you from some of the basic realities of China travel. Most people who come back with glowing reports of the PRC never had to travel proletariat class on the trains or battle their way on board a local bus for the whole three days of their stay.

Tours do make everything easy, but that assumes your tour operator gives a damn. There have been negative comments from travellers who have booked through CITS and CTS, but service is *slowly* improving.

A number of travel agents in the West do China tours, but most are forced into some sort of cooperative joint-venture with CITS or other government bodies, which means high prices.

WARNING

Prices are volatile, and anything quoted today is sure to be obsolete tomorrow. That includes all of the prices quoted in this book. In the past few years China has experienced rates of inflation in the vicinity of 20% to 30%.

Getting Around

THE AIRPORT

Beijing's Capital Airport is 25 km from the centre (Forbidden City area) but add another 10 km if you're going to the southern end of town.

At the airport, you catch the shuttle bus in front of the terminal building, and you have to buy the bus ticket from the counter inside the terminal building, not on the bus itself. The bus terminates at the Aviation Building (see below), but makes several stops en route. Get off at the Swissôtel/Hong Kong-Macau Centre if you want to take the subway (Dongsishitiao station).

To get to the airport from the city, you can catch the airport shuttle bus (Y12) from the Aviation Building *(mínháng dàshà)* on Xi Chang'an Jie, Xidan District (Map 23) – this is the location of Air China and China Northwest Airlines, but *not* the same place as the CAAC office. The bus departs on the opposite side of the street (south side of Xichang'an Jie), not from the car park of the Aviation Building.

Airport taxi drivers ask ridiculous amounts of money for a ride to town (Y200 or more). Going the other way, a taxi (using its meter) from the Forbidden City area would cost only about Y75, though drivers may ask for Y20 extra because they are not assured of getting a return passenger. They will also expect you to pay the Y10 toll if you take the airport expressway. Avoid the taxi drivers who hang around the Aviation Building, as they also charge rip-off prices to take you to the airport.

Beijing's Capital Airport is an overcrowded mess and you can expect long queues at both the domestic and international departure areas. It can take an awfully long time to clear security – you'd best arrive at the airport early if you don't want to miss your flight. Keep a lookout too; not all departures are announced, and sometimes departures are not from the area you expect.

In the domestic section of the airport there are a couple of pathetic restaurants, but in the international section there is nothing but an overpriced coffee bar serving drinks only. If you're hungry, bring some food from outside or be satisfied pigging out on expensive chocolate-covered macadamia nuts from the duty-free shop.

BUS

Sharpen your elbows, chain your wallet to your under-wear and muster all the patience you can because you'll need it. Overstuffed buses are in vogue in Beijing, and should be avoided during rush hours and holidays at all costs. Given the crowds and lack of air-conditioning, you can expect the buses to be unbearably hot during summer. They're cosy in winter if you haven't frozen at the bus stop by the time the trolley arrives, but difficult to exit from – try the nearest window. Fares are typically two jiao depending on distance, but often it's free because you can't see (let alone reach) the conductor.

There are about 140 bus and electric trolley routes, which make navigation rather confusing, especially if you can't see out of the window in the first place. Bus maps save the day.

One or two-digit bus numbers are city core, 100-series buses are trolleys, and 300-series are suburban lines. Buses run from around 5 am to 11 pm.

Minibus

These are much more comfortable than the buses and definitely faster, but figuring out where the minibuses go is tricky. Many simply follow the busiest bus routes and even display the same bus numbers, while others have only a sign in Chinese indicating the final destination. Fares are about Y2.

ROBERT STOREY

Beijing has a variety of buses serving the centre and outer suburbs.

Double Decker Bus

A special two-tiered bus for tourists and upper-crust locals, the double deckers run in a circle around the city centre. These cost Y2 but you are spared the traumas of normal public buses – passengers are guaranteed a seat! Useful stops along the route include Tiananmen Square, Lufthansa Centre and the National Olympic Sports Centre.

SUBWAY

The Underground Dragon is definitely the best way of travelling around. Unlike most other subways the crime rate is low (there is the odd pickpocket), graffiti is non-existent and messy suicides are said to be rare. Trains can move at up to 70 km/h, which is the speed of a jaguar compared to the lumbering buses. The subway is also less crowded per sq cm than the buses, and trains run at a frequency of one every few minutes during peak times. The carriages have seats for 60 and standing room for 200. Platform signs are in Chinese and Pinyin. The trains are *not* air-conditioned, so you suffer in summer but can enjoy a toasty ride in winter. The fare is a flat Y2 regardless of distance; like other subways around the world, it loses money. Trains run from 5 am to 11 pm. The subway map (Map 2) is a useful guide to the routes and stations.

At the time of writing, the East-West Line was being expanded further east, but no word yet on just when this new route will open.

Circle Line

This 16-km line presently has 18 stations: Beijing Zhan (the main railway station), Jianguomen, Chaoyangmen, Dongsishitiao, Dongzhimen, Yonghegong, Andingmen, Gulou Dajie, Jishuitan, Xizhimen (the north railway station and zoo), Chegongzhuang, Fuchengmen, Fuxingmen, Changchun Jie, Xuanwumen, Hepingmen, Qianmen and Chongwenmen.

East-West Line

This line has 13 stops and runs from Xidan to Pingguoyuan which is – no, not the capital of North Korea – but a western suburb of Beijing whose name translates as 'Apple Orchard' (unfortunately, the apple trees have long since vanished). It takes 40 minutes to traverse the length of the line. The stops are: Xidan, Fuxingmen, Nanlishilu, Muxidi, Junshibowuguan

MAP 2

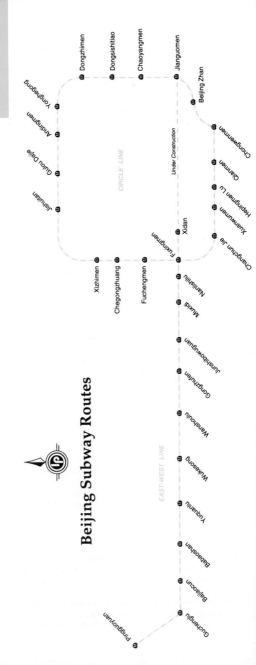

Beijing Subway Routes

(Military Museum), Gongzhufen, Wanshoulu, Wukesong, Yuquanlu, Babaoshan, Bajiaocun, Guchenglu and Pingguoyuan. Fuximen is where the Circle Line meets the East-West Line and there is no additional fare to make the transfer. When completed, the East-West Line will reach eastwards towards Jianguomenwai and beyond.

CAR & MOTORCYCLE

The use of private vehicles by foreigners is tightly controlled. Resident expats with a Chinese driver's licence are allowed to drive their own cars anywhere within the environs of Beijing, Tianjin and their suburbs. They are not permitted to drive further afield without special permission. Expats in Beijing say that the rule can be stretched a bit, but the further from the capital you go the greater the risk of trouble with the local authorities. Those foreigners who have been busted for this particular offence have mostly been caught when checking into hotels far from Beijing.

A small economy car rents for about Y250 to Y300 per day, or Y5500 to Y7000 per month. Several companies have plunged into the car rental business, but they either serve the domestic market exclusively or can rent vehicles only to foreigners who have a Chinese driver's licence. One of the first car rental companies to open in Beijing is called First Car Rental Company (☎ 422-3950), but none of the staff seem to speak English.

Resident foreigners can also purchase a motorbike, either with or without a sidecar. Bikes are liable to be left around unused during Beijing's fierce winters, but they can be fun when the weather cooperates. In China, it's required that both driver and passenger wear a safety helmet.

Rather than drive yourself, it's simpler to hire a chauffeur-driven car. This can be arranged at major hotels, CITS or other travel agencies. Of course, it would be significantly cheaper to hire a microbus taxi by the day.

TAXI

In 1986 there were fewer than 1000 taxis available in the capital, so if you wanted one, it had to be booked hours in advance. By 1995, the number of taxis exceeded 60,000 and is still increasing.

In other words, finding a cab is seldom a problem, though surging demand means that during rush hours you may have to battle it out with the other 10 million plus residents of Beijing. One government brochure claims that 80% of Beijing taxi drivers can speak English. Perhaps they meant 80 drivers, since out of the total 60,000 that would be just about the right percentage. If you don't speak Chinese, bring a map or have your destination written down in characters.

It helps if you know the way to your destination; sit in the front with a map, or you will almost certainly be taken for quite a long ride.

The vehicles usually have a sticker on the window indicating their per-km charge, which varies all the way from Y1 to Y2 with a Y10 minimum. If you don't get one with a meter, be sure to negotiate the fare for the trip in advance. Cabs can be hired for distance (use the meter), by the hour or by the day. When negotiating, you can usually get a cheaper rate if you say in advance, 'I don't need an official receipt' *(wǒ bùbì fāpiào)*. The small yellow microbuses – affectionately called 'bread taxis' by the Chinese because they resemble a loaf of bread – are cheapest.

Taxis can be hailed in the street or summoned by phone. For telephone booking, you can try Beijing Taxi (☎ 831-2288), Capital Taxi (☎ 513-8893), Beijing Tourism Taxi (☎ 515-8605) or Beixin Taxi (☎ 842-0546). There is also a number for taxi complaints (☎ 601-2620, 701-6181, 834-4238).

PEDICAB

Three-wheeled bicycles can accommodate one or two passengers in the back plus the driver up front. These look like a charming and aesthetic way to enjoy travelling around Beijing, but sadly they are not. What ruins it is that the drivers are almost universally dishonest. Whatever fare you've agreed on in advance always gets multiplied by 10 when you arrive at your destination and the final price is usually several times what a taxi would cost. Unless you enjoy vociferous arguments and near-violent confrontations, this mode of transport is not recommended.

BICYCLE

The scale of Beijing is suddenly much reduced on a bike, which can also give you a great deal of freedom. Beijing's rush hour can be rather astounding, consisting of a roving population of three million plus bicycles – a fact explained by the agony of bus rides.

GLENN BEANLAND

ROBERT STOREY

Top : Don't get taken for a ride: Beijing taxis like to go
the long way round.
Bottom: Flying Pigeons at rest

Hotels often have bike hire, especially budget hotels. Bike hire agencies tend to congregate around hotels and tourist spots – look for signs in English. Prices vary wildly (Y20 per day at the Peace Hotel versus Y80 at the neighbouring Palace Hotel – see Map 22). The Rainbow Hotel (Map 20) charges Y30. The renter may demand you leave your passport, but a deposit of about Y100 will usually do.

If you have the money, you could even buy a standard bike for around Y450.

Beware of a scam some unscrupulous renters will try. They rent you a bike which includes a lock and key. But the renter's brother or cousin has a key to the same lock. He follows you and at the first opportunity, steals the bike. You then have to pay for a new bike to replace the 'stolen' one, or forfeit your deposit (or passport!). The solution – always use your own cable lock, and make sure it's a good one (preferably foreign-made). Bike theft is a major problem anyway; a cable lock, available from department stores, increases security.

Several shopping areas are closed to cyclists from 6 am to 6 pm; Wangfujing is an important one. Bike parks are everywhere and cost peanuts – compulsory peanuts since your trusty steed can otherwise be towed away. Roadside puncture repair kits cost around Y5.

It's not hard to find picture displays around Beijing exhibiting the gory remains of cyclists who didn't look where they were going and wound up looking like Y3 worth of fried noodles. These displays also give tips on how to avoid accidents and show 're-education classes' for offenders who have had several accidents. To avoid becoming a feature in the next billboard display, take care when you're riding.

Beijing in winter presents special problems, like slippery roads (black ice) and frostbite. The fierce winds during springtime present another challenge – not exactly optimum cycling conditions but if you follow the example of the locals, nothing will deter you.

Dogs – bane of cyclists the world over – are less of a problem in China than elsewhere. This is because Fido is more likely to be stir-fried than menacing cyclists on street corners.

Bringing your own bike to China is not particularly recommended, because local ones are cheap and good enough for all but very long-distance tours. If you plan a long-distance bike tour, this presents special problems, in particular those faceless, cold-hearted figures collectively known as 'the authorities'. Although no law actually prohibits foreigners from riding in the countryside, local PSB officials pretty much make up their own law because they can't stand to see foreigners getting away so cheaply. After all, 'respectable' foreigners only travel by tour bus, taxi or limousine.

ORGANISED TOURS

CITS, CTS and numerous other travel agencies operate high-priced tours to destinations in and around Beijing (eg, Great Wall and Ming Tombs, Y130, including guide and lunch). You can dispense with the guide and food and go for the Chinese tour-bus operators who offer the same tour for Y25.

Typical tours take in the Great Wall and Ming Tombs; Western Hills and Summer Palace; Old Summer Palace and Sleeping Buddha Temple; Tanzhe Temple; Yunshui Caves; Peking Man Site; and Zunhua (Eastern Qing Tombs). Tours further afield to Chengde (three days) and Beidaihe (five days) are possible.

Things to See & Do

HIGHLIGHTS

Beijing has so much worth seeing that it's difficult to
know where to begin. Many start with Qianmen, Tiananmen Square and the Forbidden City, followed by a jaunt
through nearby Jingshan and Beihai parks. Another
busy day could be spent at the Summer Palace and
Fragrant Hills. A major excursion out of town is the
journey to the Great Wall and nearby Ming Tombs.
Those with an extra day may wish to explore Tianjin.
(For the last three, see the Excursions chapter.)

SQUARES, GATES & HALLS

Tiananmen Square 天安门广场

Though it was a gathering place and the location of
government offices in the imperial days, Tiananmen
Square (tiān'ānmén guǎngchǎng) is Mao's creation, as is
Chang'an Jie leading onto it. This is the heart of Beijing, a
vast desert of paving and photo booths. Major rallies
took place here during the Cultural Revolution when
Mao, wearing a Red Guard armband, reviewed parades
of up to a million people. In 1976 another million people
jammed the square to pay their last respects. In 1989,
army tanks and soldiers cut down pro-democracy dem-
onstrators here. Today the square is a place for people to
wander and fly decorated kites or balloons for the
kiddies.

Surrounding or studding the square are a strange
mish-mash of monuments past and present: Tiananmen
(Gate of Heavenly Peace), the Chinese Revolution
History Museum (see the Museums section for details),
the Great Hall of the People, Qianmen (Front Gate), the
Mao Mausoleum and the Monument to the People's
Heroes (Map 20).

If you get up early you can watch the flag-raising
ceremony at sunrise, performed by a troop of PLA soldiers drilled to march at precisely 108 paces per minute,
75 cm per pace. The same ceremony in reverse gets
performed at sunset, but you can hardly see the soldiers
from the throngs gathered to watch. Most foreigners
don't find it all that inspiring, but the Chinese queue for
hours to get a front-row view.

GLENN BEANLAND

GLENN BEANLAND

GLENN BEANLAND

Tiananmen Square has seen huge rallies for and against
the Party leadership.

Tiananmen Gate 天安门

Tiananmen (*tiān'ānmén*; Gate of Heavenly Peace) is a national symbol which pops up on everything from airline tickets to policemen's caps. The gate was built in the 15th century and restored in the 17th. From imperial days it functioned as a rostrum for dealing with or proclaiming to the assembled masses. There are five doors to the gate, and in front of it are seven bridges spanning a stream. Each of these bridges was restricted in its use, and only the emperor could use the central door and bridge. The dominating feature is now the gigantic portrait of Mao, the required backdrop for any photo the Chinese take of themselves at the gate. To the left of the portrait is a slogan in Chinese, 'Long Live the People's Republic of China' and to the right is another, 'Long Live the Unity of the Peoples of the World'.

You pass through Tiananmen Gate on your way into the Forbidden City (assuming you enter from the south side). There is no fee for walking through the gate, but to go upstairs and look down on the square costs a whopping Y40 for foreigners, Y10 for Chinese. It's hardly worth it, since you can get a similar view of the square from inside Qianmen for a quarter of the price.

Qianmen 前门

Qianmen (*qiánmén*; Front Gate) sits on the south side of Tiananmen Square. Qianmen guarded the wall division between the ancient Inner City and the outer suburban zone, and dates back to the reign of Emperor Yong Le in the 15th century. With the disappearance of the city walls, the gate has had its context removed, but it's still an impressive sight.

There are actually two gates – the southern one is called Arrow Tower (*jiàn lóu*) and the rear one is Zhongyang Gate (*zhōngyángmén*, also called *chéng lóu*). You can go upstairs into Zhongyang Gate. There are plans to open the Arrow Tower to visitors, but at the time of writing this it still hadn't happened.

Great Hall of the People 人民大会堂

The Great Hall of the People (*rénmín dàhuì táng*) is the venue of the rubber-stamp legislature, the National People's Congress. It's open to the public when the Congress is not sitting, and to earn some hard currency it's even rented out occasionally to foreigners for conventions! You tramp through the halls of power, many of them named after provinces and regions of China and decorated appropriately. You can see the 5000-seat banquet room and the 10,000-seat auditorium with the familiar red star embedded in a galaxy of lights in the ceiling. The hall was completed over a 10-month period, from 1958 to 1959.

The hall is on the west side of Tiananmen Square and admission costs Y40.

MONUMENTS & MAUSOLEUMS

Monument to the People's Heroes
人民英雄纪念碑

On the site of the old Outer Palace Gate at the southern end of Tiananmen Square, the Monument to the People's Heroes (rénmín yīngxíong jìnìan běi) was completed in 1958 (Map 20). The 36-metre obelisk, made of Qingdao granite, bears bas-relief carvings of key revolutionary events (one relief shows the Chinese destroying opium in the 19th century) as well as appropriate calligraphy from Mao Zedong and Zhou Enlai.

Mao Zedong Mausoleum 毛主席纪念堂

Chairman Mao died in September 1976, and his mausoleum (máo zhǔxí jìnìan běi) was constructed shortly thereafter. Known to Beijing expats as the 'Maosoleum', this enormous building is located just behind the Monument to the People's Heroes.

However history will judge Mao, his impact on its course was enormous. Easy as it now is to vilify his deeds and excesses, many Chinese show deep respect when confronted with the physical presence of the man. CITS guides freely quote the old 7:3 ratio on Mao that first surfaced in 1976 – Mao was 70% right and 30% wrong (what, one wonders, are the figures for CITS itself?) and this is now the official Party line.

The atmosphere in the inner sanctum is one of hushed reverence. Foreigners are advised to avoid loud talk, not to crack jokes ('Is he dead?') nor indulge in other behaviour that will get you arrested.

The mausoleum is open daily from 8.30 to 11.30 am and occasionally from 2 pm to around 4 pm; entry is Y10. Join the enormous queue of Chinese sightseers, but don't expect more than a quick glimpse of the body as you file past the sarcophagus. At certain times of year, the body requires maintenance and is not on view.

Whatever Mao might have done to the Chinese economy while he was alive, sales of Mao memorabilia are certainly giving the free market a boost these days.

At the souvenir stalls near the mausoleum you can pick up Chairman Mao key rings, thermometers, face towels, handkerchiefs, sun visors, address books and cartons of cigarettes (a comment on his chain-smoking habit?).

PALACES

Being the capital of China for a number of centuries, Beijing has acquired a substantial number of upmarket residences for various emperors and empresses. In addition, the royal families required housing for their various servants, consorts, concubines, eunuchs and so on. It should not be forgotten that this is still the capital, and the construction of 'palaces' is an ongoing process.

Forbidden City 紫禁城

The Forbidden City (*zǐjìn chéng*), so called because it was off limits for 500 years, is the largest and best-preserved cluster of ancient buildings in China. It was home to two dynasties of emperors, the Ming and the Qing, who didn't stray from this pleasure-dome unless they absolutely had to.

GLENN BEANLAND

Checkers game near the moat.

GLENN BEANLAND

GLENN BEANLAND

GLENN BEANLAND

Forbidden City: two hundred years ago the admission price
would have been instant death, but this has dropped considerably to Y85 for foreigners and Y20 for Chinese.

The Beijing authorities insist on calling this place the
Palace Museum *(gùgōng)*. Whatever its official name, it's
open daily from 8.30 am to 5 pm – last admission tickets
are sold at 3.30 pm. The foreigners' ticket allows admission to all the special exhibition halls, but if you pay
Chinese price these cost extra, although it would still
work out much cheaper if you could get Chinese price.
Your Y85 includes rental of a cassette tape for a self-
guided tour, though you can enter for Y60 without the
tape. Tape players are available free but require a refund-
able Y100 deposit – you can use your own Walkman
instead. For the tape to make sense you must enter the
Forbidden City from the south gate and exit from the
north. The tape is available in a myriad of languages.

On approaching the Forbidden City unscrupulous characters
approach visitors pretending to be an official guide and trying
to convince them that the palace can only be visited with a
guide. This is not true as these people are only after tourists'
money.

Marc Proksch

It's worth mentioning that many foreigners get Tiananmen Gate confused with the Forbidden City entrance
because the two are physically attached and there are no
signs in English. As a result, some people wind up
purchasing the Tiananmen Gate admission ticket by
mistake, not realising that this only gains you admission
to the upstairs portion of the gate. To find the Forbidden
City ticket booths, keep walking north until you can't
walk any further without paying.

History The basic layout of the city was established
between 1406 and 1420 by Emperor Yong Le, command-
ing battalions of labourers and craftspeople – some
estimate up to a million of them. From this palace the
emperors governed China, often rather erratically as
they tended to become lost in this self-contained little
world and allocate real power to the court eunuchs.

The buildings now seen are mostly post-18th century,
as with a lot of restored or rebuilt structures around
Beijing. The palace was constantly going up in flames –
a lantern festival combined with a sudden gust of Gobi
wind would easily do the trick, as would a fireworks
display. There were also deliberate fires lit by court
eunuchs and officials who could get rich off the repair
bills. In 1664, the Manchus stormed in and burned the
palace to the ground.

It was not just the buildings that went up in smoke,
but rare books, paintings, calligraphy and anything else

which was flammable. In this century there have been two major lootings of the palace: first by the Japanese forces, and second by the Kuomintang, who on the eve of the Communist takeover in 1949 removed thousands of crates of relics to Taiwan, where they are now on display in Taipei's National Palace Museum (worth seeing). Perhaps just as well, since the Cultural Revolution turned much of China's precious artwork into confetti. The gaps have been filled by bringing treasures, old and newly remanufactured, from other parts of China.

The palace is so large (720,000 sq metres, 800 buildings, 9000 rooms) that a permanent restoration squad moves around repainting and repairing. It's estimated to take about 10 years to do a full renovation, by which time the beginning is due for repairs again. The complex was opened to the public in 1949.

Layout The palace was built on a monumental scale, one that should not be taken lightly. Allow yourself a full day for exploration, or perhaps several separate trips if you're an enthusiast. The information given here can only be a skeleton guide; if you want more detail then tag along with a tour group for explanations of individual artefacts.

There are plenty of Western tour groups around – the Forbidden City has 10,000 visitors a day. Tour buses drop their groups off at Tiananmen and pick them up again at the north gate; you can also enter the palace from the east or west gates. Even if you had a separate guidebook on the Forbidden City, it would be rather time-consuming to match up and identify every individual object, building and a spoken guide has more immediacy.

On the north-south axis of the Forbidden City, from Tiananmen at the south to Shenwumen at the north, lie the palace's ceremonial buildings.

Restored in the 17th century, **Meridian Gate** *(wǔmén)* is a massive portal which in former times was reserved for the use of the emperor. Gongs and bells would be sounded upon royal comings and goings. Lesser mortals would use lesser gates – the military used the west gate, civilians used the east gate. The emperor also reviewed his armies from here, passed judgement on prisoners, announced the new year calendar and surveyed the flogging of troublesome ministers.

Across Golden Stream, which is shaped to resemble a Tartar bow and is spanned by five marble bridges, is **Supreme Harmony Gate** *(tàihémén)*. It overlooks a massive courtyard that could hold an imperial audience of up to 100,000.

MAP 3

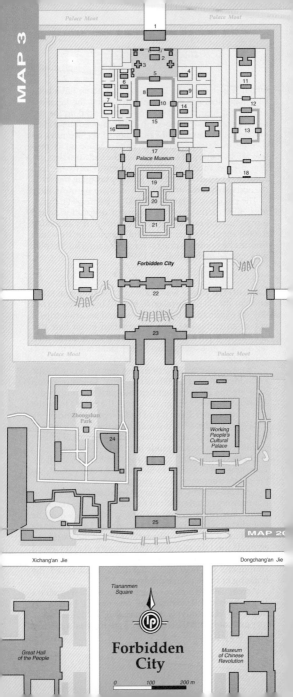

Palace Moat

Palace Moat

1

3
2

5
4

6
11

7
12

8
9
10

14
13

15

16

17
18

Palace Museum

19

20

21

Forbidden City

22

23

Palace Moat

Palace Moat

Zhongshan
Park

24

Working
People's
Cultural
Palace

25

MAP 2

Xichang'an Jie

Dongchang'an Jie

Tiananmen
Square

Great Hall
of the People

Forbidden
City

0   100   200 m

Museum
of Chinese
Revolution

MAP 3 Forbidden City 紫禁城

1 Divine Military Genius Gate
神武门
2 Imperial Peace Hall
钦安殿
3 Thousand Autumns Pavilion
千秋亭
4 Ming & Qing Dynasty Arts & Crafts Exhibition
明清工艺美术馆
5 Imperial Garden
御花园
6 Western Palaces Nos 16, 17 & 18
宫廷史迹陈列
7 Eternal Spring Palace
长春宫
8 Earthly Tranquillity Palace
坤宁宫
9 Ceramics Exhibition
陶瓷馆
10 Union Hall
交泰殿
11 Jewellery Exhibition (Character Cultivation Hall)
珍馆
12 Character Cultivation Hall
养性殿

13 Paintings Exhibition (Imperial Supremacy Hall)
绘画馆
14 Bronzes Exhibition
青铜器馆
15 Heavenly Purity Palace
乾清宫
16 Mental Cultivation Hall
养心殿
17 Heavenly Purity Gate
乾清门
18 Nine Dragon Screen
九龙壁
19 Preserving Harmony Hall
保和殿
20 Middle Harmony Hall
中和殿
21 Supreme Harmony Hall
太和殿
22 Supreme Harmony Gate
太和门
23 Meridian Gate
午门
24 Beijing Music Hall
北京音乐厅
25 Tiananmen Gate
天安门

GLENN BEANLAND

Raised terrace, Hall of Supreme Harmony.

Behind the Wall

If ceremonial and administrative duties occupied most of the emperor's working hours, then behind the high walls of the Forbidden City it was the pursuit of pleasure which occupied much of his attention during the evenings. One of the imperial bedtime systems was to keep the names of royal wives, consorts and favourites on jade tablets near the emperor's chambers – sometimes as many as 50 of them.

By turning the tablet over the emperor made his request for the evening, and the eunuch on duty would rush off to find the lucky lady. Stripped naked and therefore weaponless, she was gift-wrapped in a yellow cloth, and the little bound-footed creature was piggybacked over to the royal boudoir and dumped at the feet of the emperor; the eunuch recorded the date and time to verify legitimacy of a possible child.

Financing the affairs of state probably cost less than financing the affairs of the emperor; keeping the pleasure dome functioning drew heavily on the resources of the empire. During the Ming Dynasty there were an estimated 9000 maids of honour and 70,000 eunuchs serving the court. Apart from the servants and the prize concubines, there were also the royal elephants to maintain. These were gifts from Myanmar (Burma) and were stabled south-west of the Forbidden City. Accorded rank by the emperor, when one died a period of mourning was declared. Periodically the elephant keepers embezzled the funds intended for elephant chow. When this occurred, the ravenous pachyderms went on a rampage.

While pocketing this cash was illegal, selling elephant dung for use as shampoo was not – it was believed to give the hair that extra sheen. Back in the harem the cosmetic bills piled up to 400,000 taels of silver. Then, of course, the concubines who had grown old and were no longer in active service were still supposed to be cared for. Rather than cut back on expenditure, the emperor sent out eunuchs to collect emergency taxes whenever money ran short.

As for the palace eunuchs, the royal chop was administered at the Eunuch Clinic near the Forbidden City, using a swift knife and a special chair with a hole in the seat. The candidates sought to better their lives in the service of the court but half of them died after the operation. Mutilation of any kind was considered grounds for exclusion from the next life, so many eunuchs carried their appendages around in pouches, believing that at the time of death the spirits might be deceived into thinking of them as whole. ■

Raised on a marble terrace with balustrades are the **Three Great Halls**, the heart of the Forbidden City. The **Hall of Supreme Harmony** *(tàihédiàn)* is the most important and the largest structure in the Forbidden City. Built in the 15th century and restored in the 17th century, it was used for ceremonial occasions such as the emperor's birthday, the nomination of military leaders, and coronations. Flanking the entrance to the hall are bronze incense burners. The large bronze turtle in the front is a symbol of longevity and stability – it has a removable lid and on special occasions incense was lit inside so that smoke billowed from the mouth.

To the west side of the terrace is a small pavilion with a bronze grain-measure and to the east is a sundial; both are symbolic of imperial justice. On the corners of the roof, as with some other buildings in the city, you'll see a mounted figure with his retreat cut off by mythical and real animals, a story that relates to a cruel tyrant hung from one such eave.

Inside the hall is a richly decorated Dragon Throne where the emperor would preside (decisions final, no correspondence entered into) over trembling officials. The entire court had to hit the floor nine times with their foreheads; combined with the thick veils of incense and the battering of gongs, it would be enough to make anyone dizzy. At the back of the throne is a carved Xumishan, the Buddhist paradise, signifying the throne's supremacy.

Behind Taihedian is the smaller **Hall of Middle Harmony** *(zhōnghédiàn)* which was used as a transit lounge for the emperor. Here he would make last-minute preparations, rehearse speeches and receive close ministers. On display are two Qing Dynasty sedan chairs, the emperors' mode of transport around the Forbidden City. The last of the Qing emperors, Puyi, used a bicycle and altered a few features of the palace grounds to make it easier to get around.

The third hall is the **Hall of Preserving Harmony** *(bǎohédiàn)* used for banquets and later for imperial examinations. It now houses archaeological finds. The Baohedian has no support pillars, and behind it is a 250-tonne marble block carved with dragons and clouds which was moved into Beijing on an ice path. The outer housing surrounding the Three Great Halls was used for storing gold, silver, silks, carpets and other treasures.

The basic configuration of the Three Great Halls is echoed by the next group of buildings, smaller in scale but more important in terms of real power. In China, real power traditionally lies at the back door, or in this case, the back gate.

GLENN BEANLAND

GLENN BEANLAND

Lighting effects, Palace of Heavenly Purity

GLENN BEANLAND

GLENN BEANLAND

There are plenty of quiet corners in the Forbidden City to sit and relax.

The first structure is the **Palace of Heavenly Purity** (*qiánqīng gōng*), a residence of Ming and early Qing emperors, and later an audience hall for receiving foreign envoys and high officials.

Immediately behind it is the **Hall of Union**, which contains a clepsydra – a water clock with five bronze vessels and a calibrated scale. Water clocks date back several thousand years but this one was made in 1745. There's also a mechanical clock on display, built in 1797, and a collection of imperial jade seals.

At the northern end of the Forbidden City is the **Imperial Garden**, a classical Chinese garden of 7000 sq metres of fine landscaping with rockeries, walkways and pavilions. This is a good place to take a breather, with snack bars, WCs and souvenir shops. Two more gates lead out through the large **Divine Military Genius Gate** (*shénwǔmén*).

The western and eastern sides of the Forbidden City are the palatial former living quarters, once containing libraries, temples, theatres, gardens, even the tennis court of the last emperor. These buildings now function as museums requiring extra admission fees, but the foreigners' all-inclusive ticket covers them. Opening hours are irregular and no photos are allowed without prior permission. Special exhibits sometimes appear in the palace museum halls, so check the *China Daily* for details.

Zhongshan Park (*zhōngshān gōngyuán*), otherwise known as Sun Yatsen Park, is in the south-west of the Forbidden City and was laid out at the same time as the palace. Here you'll find the Altar of Land and Grain, which is divided into five sections, each filled with earth of a different colour (red, green, black, yellow and white) to symbolise all the earth belonging to the emperor. You can also rent boats here to paddle around the moat.

The **Workers' Cultural Palace** (*láodòng rénmín wénhuà gōng*), in the south-east sector of the Forbidden City, is a park with halls dating from 1462 which were used as ancestral temples under the Ming and Qing; they come complete with marble balustrades, terraces and detailed gargoyles. The park is now used for movies, temporary exhibits, cultural performances and the odd mass wedding.

Zhongnanhai 中南海

Just west of the Forbidden City is China's new forbidden city, Zhongnanhai (*zhōngnánhǎi*; Map 23). The interior is off-limits to tourists, but you can gawk at the entrance. The name means 'the central and south seas', in this case called after the two large lakes in the compound. The southern entrance is via Xinhuamen (Gate of New China) which you'll see on Chang'an Jie; it's guarded by two PLA soldiers and fronted by a flagpole with the red flag flying. The gate was built in 1758 and was then known as the Tower of the Treasured Moon.

The compound was first built between the 10th and 13th centuries as a sort of playground for the emperors and their retinues. It was expanded during Ming times but most of the present buildings only date from the Qing Dynasty. Empress Dowager Cixi once lived here; after the failure of the 1898 reform movement she imprisoned Emperor Guangxu in the Hall of Impregnating Vitality where, ironically, he later died. Yuan Shikai used Zhongnanhai for ceremonial occasions during his brief presidency of the Chinese Republic, after the overthrow of the imperial government; his vice-president moved into Guangxu's death-house.

Since the founding of the People's Republic in 1949, Zhongnanhai has been the site of the residence and offices of the highest-ranking members of the Communist Party.

Summer Palace 颐和园

One of Beijing's most visited sights, the Summer Palace (yíhéyuán) is an immense park containing some newish Qing architecture. The site had long been a royal garden and was considerably enlarged and embellished by Emperor Qianlong in the 18th century. He deepened and expanded Kunming Lake with the help of 100,000 labourers, and reputedly surveyed imperial navy drills from a hilltop perch.

Empress Dowager Cixi began rebuilding in 1888 using money that was supposedly reserved for the construction of a modern navy – but she did restore a marble boat that sits immobile at the edge of the lake.

In 1900 foreign troops, annoyed by the Boxer Rebellion, had another go at roasting the Summer Palace. Restorations took place a few years later and a major renovation occurred after 1949, by which time the palace had once more fallen into disrepair.

The original palace was used as a summer residence, as its name implies. The residents of the Forbidden City packed up and decamped here for their holidays, so the emphasis was on cool features – water, gardens, hills. It was divided into four sections: court reception, residences, temples and strolling or sightseeing areas.

Three-quarters of the park is occupied by Kunming Lake, and most items of structural interest are towards the east or north gates. The main building is the **Hall of**

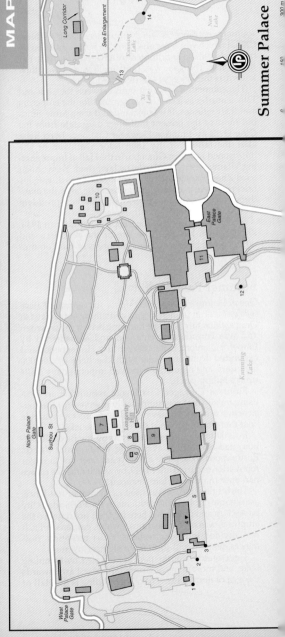

MAP 4

Summer Palace

Long Corridor

See Enlargement

Kunming Lake

Nan Lake

Xi Lake

To Central Beijing

13

14

15

0   150   300 m

North Palace Gate

Suzhou St

West Palace Gate

Longevity Hill

7

8

6

9

5

4

3

2

1

10

11

12

East Palace Gate

Kunming Lake

MAP 4 Summer Palace 颐和园

1	Rowing Boat Dock 划船码头	9	Buddhist Virtue Temple 佛香阁
2	Marble Boat 清晏船	10	Harmonious Interest Garden 谐趣园
3	Ferry Dock 码头	11	Benevolence & Longevity Hall 仁寿殿
4	Listening to the Orioles Restaurant (Tingliguan) 听鹂馆	12	Rowing Boat Dock 划船码头
5	Long Corridor 长廊	13	Jade Belt Bridge 玉带桥
6	Precious Clouds Pavilion 排云殿	14	Knowing in the Spring Pavilion 知春亭
7	Buddhist Tenants Hall 香崇宗印之阁	15	Bronze Ox 铜牛
8	Wisdom Sea Temple 智慧海		

GLENN BEANLAND

GLENN BEANLAND

The Summer Palace park was designed by the emperor Qianlong in the style of the landscape of southern China.

Benevolence & Longevity, just off the lake toward the east gate. It houses a hardwood throne and has a court-yard with bronze animals. In it the emperor-in-residence handled state affairs and received envoys.

Along the north shore of the lake is the **Long Corridor** *(cháng láng)*, over 700 metres long, which is decorated with mythical scenes. If the paint looks new it's because a lot of pictures were whitewashed during the Cultural Revolution.

On artificial Longevity Hill are a number of temples. The **Precious Clouds Pavilion** on the western slopes is one of the few structures to escape destruction by the Anglo-French forces. It contains some elaborate bronzes. At the top of the hill sits the **Buddhist Temple of the Sea of Wisdom**, made of glazed tiles; good views of the lake can be had from this spot.

Other sights are largely associated with Empress Cixi, like the place where she celebrated her birthdays, and exhibitions of her furniture and memorabilia.

The Tingliguan Restaurant serves imperial banquet food – fish from Kunming Lake, velvet chicken, dumplings – on regal tableware lookalikes. It has a splendid alfresco location and exorbitant prices, and is housed in what was once an imperial theatre; nowadays there are attached souvenir shops.

Another noteworthy feature is the **17-arch bridge** spanning 150 metres to South Lake Island; on the mainland side is a beautiful bronze ox. Also note the Jade Belt Bridge on the mid-west side of the lake; and the Harmonious Interest Garden at the north-east end which is a copy of a garden in Wuxi.

You can get around the lake by rowing boat, or on a pair of ice skates in winter. As with the Forbidden City moat, it used to be a common practice to cut slabs of ice from the lake in winter and store them for summer use.

The park is about 12 km north-west of the centre of Beijing (Map 1). The easiest way to get there is to take the subway to Xizhimen (close to the zoo), then a minibus. Bus No 332 from the zoo is slower but will get you there eventually. There are lots of minibuses returning to the city centre from the Summer Palace, but get the price and destination settled before departure. You can also get there by bicycle; it takes about 1½ to two hours from the city centre. Rather than taking the main roads, it's far more pleasant to bike along the road following the Beijing-Miyun Diversion Canal.

Foreigners are charged an outrageous Y45 for admission. This ticket does *not* get you into everything – there are some additional fees inside. Admission for Chinese costs Y20 – foreigners need to be a Beijing resident with a valid ID to get this price – and opening times are 7 am to 6 pm. Be sure you don't visit on a weekend or the only things you'll see will be camera flashes, cotton candy and 'I Love Beijing' T-shirts.

Old Summer Palace 圆明园

The original Summer Palace *(yuánmíngyuán)* was laid out in the 12th century. By the reign of Emperor Qianlong, it had developed into a set of interlocking gardens. Qianlong set the Jesuits to work as architects of European palaces for the gardens, adding elaborate fountains and baroque statuary.

In the second Opium War (1860), British and French troops torched the place and sent the booty abroad. Since the Chinese pavilions and temples were made of wood they did not survive fires, but a marble facade, some broken columns and traces of the fountains stick out of the rice-paddies. The effect is charming, and many people enjoy this sedate setting more than the touristy Summer Palace.

The ruins have long been a favourite picnic spot for foreign residents and Chinese twosomes seeking a bit of privacy. More recently, the government has decided to slowly restore the gardens, moats and buildings. It's uncertain yet just how far the restoration will go. Will it be allowed to remain as ruins or will it become another Chinese tourist circus like the Great Wall?

The site is enormous – 2½ km from east to west – so be prepared to do some walking. There are three entrance gates to the compound, all on the south side. The western section is the main area, Yuanmingyuan. The south-east corner of the site is the Beautiful Spring Garden. The eastern section is the Eternal Spring Garden *(chāngchūnyuán)*. It's here that you'll find the Great Fountain Ruins, considered the best preserved relic in the palace and featured prominently in the tourist brochures. In this area is also the fully restored 10,000 Flowers Maze.

Minibuses connect the new Summer Palace with the old one, for about Y5, but a taxi on the same route only costs Y10. There are some slower but pleasant trips you can do around the area by public transport. Take bus No 332 from the zoo to the Old Summer Palace and to the Summer Palace; change to bus No 333 for the Fragrant Hills; change to bus No 360 to go directly back to the zoo.

Another round-trip route is to take the subway to Pingguoyuan (the last stop in the west) and then take bus No 318 to the Fragrant Hills; change to No 333 for the Summer Palace, and then to No 332 for the zoo.

MAP 5

ROBERT STOREY

Old Summer Palace

Yuanmingyuan Donglu

Eternal Spring Garden

Entrance Gate

Entrance Gate

Beautiful Spring Garden

Blessing Sea

Black Lake

Yuanmingyuan Xilu

MAP 5 Old Summer Palace 圆明园

1	Purple Blue Lodge 紫碧山房	21	Open Sea Hill 海岳开襟
2	Library Pavilion 文源阁	22	Fuhai Restaurant 福海酒家
3	Wuling Spring Beauty 武陵春色	23	Rowboat Dock 船台
4	Universal Peace 万方安和	24	Clear Reflection of the Void 涵虚朗鉴
5	Apricot Blossoms in Spring Lodge 杏花春馆	25	Grace & Beauty Lodge 接秀山房
6	Guards' Citadel 舍卫城	26	Blessing Sea Fairy Hill Hall 瀛海仙山亭
7	Open World to the Public 鸿慈大公	27	Jade Terraces on Penglai Isles 蓬岛瑶台
8	Autumn Moon Over the Calm Lake 平湖秋月	28	Body Bathed in Virtue 澡身浴德
9	Far North Mountain Village 北远山村	29	Lakes & Hills View 湖山在望
10	Collecting Mysteries Tower 藏密楼	30	Broad Nutrient Palace 广育宫
11	Square Pots Wonderland 方壶胜境	31	New Fairyland 别有洞天
12	10,000 Flowers Maze 万花阵	32	Great Palace Entrance Gate 大宫门
13	Oceanic Banquet Hall 海宴堂	33	Xiyuan Restaurant 西苑饭店
14	Exhibition Hall 展览馆	34	Pine Moon Pavilion 松月亭
15	Great Fountain Ruins (European Gardens) 西洋楼	35	Contain Autumn Hall 涵秋馆
16	Racecourse 线法山	36	Phoenix & Unicorn Isles 凤麟洲
17	Lion's Forest 狮子林	37	Boat Dock 船台
18	Exquisite Jade Hall 玉玲珑馆	38	Enjoying Jasper Pavilion 槛碧亭
19	Containing Scriptures Hall 含经堂	39	Awareness Temple 正觉寺
20	Everlasting Thoughts Studio 思永斋		

ROBERT STOREY

MUSEUMS

As far as foreigners are concerned, Beijing's museums are worthwhile but poorly presented. There are almost no English explanations, not even in pamphlet form.

Chinese Revolution History Museum
中国革命历史博物馆

Housed in a sombre building on the east side of Tiananmen Square, access to the Chinese Revolution History Museum *(zhōngguó gémìng lìshǐ bówùguǎn;* Map 20) was long thwarted by special permission requirements. From 1966 to 1978 the museum was closed so that history could be reassessed in the light of recent events.

The presentation of history poses quite a problem for the Chinese Communist Party. It has failed to publish anything of note on its own history since it gained power, before, during or since the Cultural Revolution. This would have required reams of carefully worded revision according to what tack politics (here synonymous with history) might take, so it was better left unwritten.

There are actually two museums here combined into one – the Museum of History and the Museum of the Revolution. Explanations throughout most of the museums are entirely in Chinese, so you won't get much out of this labyrinth unless you're particularly fluent or pick up an English-speaking student. An English text relating to the museum is available inside.

The Museum of History contains artefacts and cultural relics (many of them copies) from year zero to 1919, subdivided into primitive communal groups, slavery, feudalism and capitalism/imperialism, laced with Marxist commentary. Without a guide you can discern ancient weapons, inventions and musical instruments.

The Museum of the Revolution is split into five sections: the founding of the Chinese Communist Party (1919-21), the first civil war (1924-27), the second civil war (1927-37), resistance against Japan (1937-45) and the third civil war (1945-49).

Military Museum 军事博物馆

Perhaps more to the point than the Museum of the Revolution, the Military Museum *(jūnshì bówùguǎn)* traces the genesis of the PLA from 1927 to the present and has some interesting exhibits: pictures of Mao in the early days, astonishing socialist-realist artwork, captured American tanks from the Korean War and other tools of destruction. Explanations are in Chinese only. You must have your bags checked at the door, presumably to prevent you from liberating a Sherman tank or MiG aircraft.

The museum is on Fuxing Lu on the western side of the city; to get there take the subway to Junshibowuguan (Map 23).

Natural History Museum 自然博物馆

This is the largest such museum in China and gets good reviews from travellers. The four main exhibition halls of the Natural History Museum (*zìrán bówùguǎn*) are devoted to flora and fauna, ancient fauna and human evolution. Some of the more memorable exhibits include a human cadaver cut in half to show the insides and a complete dinosaur skeleton. There is also plenty of pickled wildlife, though nothing worse than what you see for sale in some of the street markets. Some of the exhibits were donated by the British Museum, the American Museum of Natural History and other foreign sources.

The Natural History Museum is in the Tianqiao area, just west of Tiantan Park, just north of the park's west gate entrance (Map 20). Admission costs Y10. The museum is open daily except Monday, from 8.30 am until 4 pm.

Lu Xun Museum 鲁讯博物馆

Dedicated to China's No 1 Thinking Person's Revolutionary, the Lu Xun Museum (*lǔ xùn bówùguǎn*) contains manuscripts, diaries, letters and inscriptions by the famous writer. To the west of the museum is a small Chinese walled compound where Lu Xun lived from 1924 to 1926. The museum is off Fuchengmennei Dajie, west of the Xisi intersection on the north-western side of the city (Map 23).

China Art Gallery 中国美术馆

Back in Cultural Revolution days one of the safest hobbies for an artist was to retouch classical-style landscapes with red flags, belching factory chimneys or bright red tractors. You can get some idea of the state of the arts in China at the China Art Gallery (*zhōngguó měishù guǎn*). At times very good exhibitions of current work including photo displays are held in an adjacent gallery. Check the *China Daily* for listings. The arts and crafts shop inside has an excellent range of woodblock prints and papercuts. The gallery is west of the Dongsi intersection (Map 22).

Xu Beihong Museum 徐悲鸿纪念馆

Here you'll find traditional Chinese paintings, oils, gouaches, sketches and memorabilia of the famous artist Xu Beihong, noted for his galloping horse paintings. Painting albums are on sale, as well as reproductions and Chinese stationery. The Xu Beihong Museum (*xú bēihóng jìnìan guǎn*) is at 53 Xinjiekou Bei Dajie, Xicheng District (Map 23).

Song Qingling Museum 宋庆龄故居

Madam Song was the wife of Sun Yatsen, founder of the Republic of China. After 1981 her large residence was transformed into a museum dedicated to her memory and to that of Sun Yatsen. On display are personal items and pictures of historical interest. The Song Qingling Museum (*sòng qìnglíng gùjū*) is on the north side of Shisha Houhai Lake at 46 Beiheyan Lu (Map 23).

TEMPLES

Lama Temple 雍和宫

This is by far the most colourful temple in Beijing, with its beautiful gardens, stunning frescoes and tapestries and incredible carpentry.

The Lama Temple (*yōnghégōng*) was once modified to become the official residence of Count Yin Zhen. Nothing unusual in that, perhaps, but in 1723 he was promoted to emperor, and moved to the Forbidden City. His name was changed to Yong Zheng, and his former residence became Yonghe Palace. The green tiles were changed to yellow, the imperial colour, and – as was the custom – the place could not be used except as a temple. In 1744 it was converted into a lamasery, and became a residence for large numbers of monks from Mongolia and Tibet.

In 1792, Qianlong, having quelled an uprising in Tibet, instituted a new administrative system involving two gold vases. One was kept at the Jokhang Temple in Lhasa, where it was intended to be used for determining the reincarnation of the Dalai Lama (under the supervision of the Minister for Tibetan Affairs). The other was kept at the Lama Temple for the lottery for the Mongolian Grand Living Buddha. The Lama Temple

ROBERT STOREY

ROBERT STOREY

GLENN BEANLAND

The Lama Temple, home to members of the Yellow Hat sect, escaped damage during the Cultural Revolution.

thus assumed a new importance in ethnic minority control.

The lamasery has three richly-worked archways and five main halls strung in a line down the middle, each taller than the preceding one. Styles are mixed – Mongolian, Tibetan and Han – with courtyard enclosures and galleries.

The first hall, **Lokapala**, houses a statue of the Maitreya (future) Buddha, flanked by celestial guardians. The statue facing the back door is Weituo, guardian of Buddhism, made of white sandalwood. Beyond, in the courtyard, is a pond with a bronze mandala depicting Xumishan, the Buddhist paradise.

The second hall, **Yonghedian**, has three figures of Buddha – past, present and future.

The third hall, **Yongyoudian**, has statues of the Buddha of Longevity and the Buddha of Medicine (to the left). The courtyard following it has galleries with some nandikesvaras, or joyful buddhas, tangled up in multi-armed close encounters. These are coyly draped lest you be corrupted by the sight, and are to be found in other esoteric locations.

The **Hall of the Wheel of Law**, further north, contains a large bronze statue of Tsong Khapa (1357-1419), founder of the Gelukpa or Yellow Hat sect, and frescoes depicting his life. This Tibetan-style building is used for study and prayer.

The last hall, **Wanfu Pavilion**, has an 18-metre-high statue of the Maitreya Buddha in his Tibetan form, sculptured from a single piece of sandalwood and clothed in yellow satin. The smoke curling up from the yak-butter lamps transports you momentarily to Tibet, which is where the log for this statue came from.

In 1949 the Lama Temple was declared protected as a major historical relic. Miraculously it survived the Cultural Revolution without scars. In 1979 large amounts of money were spent on repairs and it was restocked with several dozen novices from Inner Mongolia, a token move on the part of the government to back up its claim that the Lama Temple is a 'symbol of religious freedom, national unity and stability in China'. The novices study Tibetan language and the secret practices of the Gelukpa (Yellow Hat) sect.

The temple is active again, though some question whether or not the monks in tennis shoes are really monks or PSB. Prayers take place early in the morning, not for public viewing, but if you inquire discreetly of the head lama you might be allowed to return the following morning. No photography is permitted inside the temple buildings, but the postcard industry thrives.

The temple is open daily, except Monday, from 9 am to 4 pm. You can get there by subway to the Yonghegong station (see Map 23). Entry costs Y10; the acoustiguide is Y20 and not worth it.

Confucius Temple & Imperial College
孔庙

Just down the hutong opposite the gates of the Lama Temple is the former Confucius Temple (*kǒng miào*) and the Imperial College (*guózijiān*). The Confucius Temple is the largest in the land after the one at Qufu. The temple was re-opened in 1981 after some mysterious use as a high-official residence and is now used as a museum, in sharp contrast to the Lama Temple.

The steles in the temple courtyard record the names of those successful in the civil service examinations (possibly the world's first) of the imperial court. To see his name engraved here was the ambition of every scholar, but it wasn't made easy. Candidates were locked in cubicles (about 8000 of them) measuring roughly 1½ by 1½ metres for a period of three days. Many died or went insane during their incarceration. Imagine that.

The Imperial College was the place where the emperor expounded the Confucian classics to an audience of thousands of kneeling students, professors and court officials; this was an annual rite. Built by the grandson of Kublai Khan in 1306, the former college was the only institution of its kind in China. It's now the Capital Library. Part of the 'collection' are the stone tablets commissioned by Emperor Qianlong. These are engraved with 13 Confucian classics – 800,000 characters or 12 years' work for the scholar who did it. There is an ancient 'Scholar-Tree' in the courtyard.

The easiest way to get there is by subway to the Yonghegong station (Map 23).

Great Bell Temple   大钟寺

The biggest bell in China, this one at the Great Bell Temple (*dàzhōng sì*) weighs a hefty 46½ tonnes and is 6¾ metres tall. The bell is inscribed with Buddhist sutras, a total of over 227,000 Chinese characters.

The bell was cast during the reign of Ming Emperor Yong Le in 1406 and the tower was built in 1733. Getting the bell from the foundry to the temple proved problematic, since back in those days it wasn't possible to contract the job out to a Hong Kong company. A shallow canal had to be built which froze over in winter, and the bell was moved across the ice by sled.

GLENN BEANLAND

GLENN BEANLAND

The Great Bell Temple houses the largest bell in China.

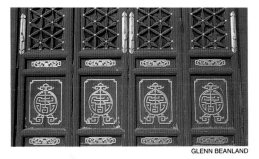

GLENN BEANLAND

Ornate carved doors are a feature of temple architecture.

Within the grounds of the monastery at this site are several other buildings (besides the Bell Tower itself). They include the Guanyin Hall, Sutra-keeping Tower, Main Buddha Hall and Four Devas Hall. This monastery is one of the most popular in Beijing and was re-opened in 1980.

The Great Bell Temple is almost two km due east of the Friendship Hotel on Beisanhuan Xilu (Map 23).

White Dagoba Temple 白塔寺

The White Dagoba Temple *(báitǎ sì)* can be spotted from the top of Jingshan, and is similar (and close) to the one in Beihai Park. It was used as a factory during the Cultural Revolution but re-opened after restoration in 1980. The dagoba dates back to Kublai Khan's days and was completed with the help of a Nepalese architect, though the halls date only from the Qing Dynasty. It lies off Fuchengmennei Dajie (Map 23).

Guangji Temple 广济寺

The Guangji (Universal Rescue) Temple *(guǎngjì sì)* is on the north-west side of Xisi intersection, and east of the White Dagoba Temple. It's the headquarters of the Chinese Buddhist Association (Map 23).

Fayuan Temple 法源寺

In a lane just east of the Niujie Mosque (see below) is the Fayuan (Source of Law) Temple *(fǎyuán sì)*. The temple was originally constructed in the 7th century and is still going strong. It's now the China Buddhism College and is open to visitors (Map 23).

White Cloud Temple 白云观

The White Cloud Temple (báiyúnguān) is in a district directly south of Yanjing Hotel and west of the moat. Once the Taoist centre of North China and the site of temple fairs, inside you'll find several courtyards containing a pool, bridge, several halls of worship and Taoist motifs. Check Map 23 for directions. Walk south on Baiyun Lu and cross the moat; continue south along Baiyun Lu, turn into a curving street on the left and follow it for 250 metres to the temple entrance.

MOSQUES & CATHEDRALS

Dongsi Mosque 东四清真寺

The Dongsi Mosque (dōngsì qīngzhēn sì) is one of two functioning mosques in Beijing, the other being Niujie Mosque. It's at 13 Dongsi Nan Dajie, just south of the intersection with Chaoyangmennei Dajie (Map 22).

Niujie Mosque 牛街礼拜寺

In the south-west sector of Beijing, south of Guang-'anmennei Dajie, is a Muslim residential area, with the handsome Niujie Mosque (niújiē lǐbài sì) facing Mecca. Niu Jie (Ox St) is an area worth checking out with a feel all its own (Map 23).

South Cathedral 南堂

This is the main functioning cathedral of Beijing – the others are in a comparatively sorry state. The South Cathedral (nántáng) is built on the site of Matteo Ricci's house – first built in 1703 and destroyed three times since then. The cathedral is on Qianmen Dajie at the Xuanwumen intersection (north-east side) above the subway station (Map 23).

Mass is held every morning at 6.30 am. On Sunday morning mass runs until noon.

North Cathedral 北堂

Also called the Cathedral of Our Saviour, the North Cathedral (běitáng) was built in 1887, but was badly damaged during the Cultural Revolution and converted to a factory warehouse. It was re-opened at the end of 1985 after restoration work was completed. The cathedral is at Xishiku, Xicheng, West District (Map 23).

PARKS

In imperial days the parks were laid out at the compass points: to the west of the Forbidden City lies Yuetan Park; to the north lies Ditan Park; to the south lies Taoranting Park and to the east is Ritan Park. To the south-east of the Forbidden City is the showpiece of them all, Tiantan Park.

All of these parks were venues for ritual sacrifices offered by the emperors. Not much remains of the shaman structures, bar those of the Temple of Heaven in Tiantan Park, but if you arrive early in the morning you can witness *taiji*, fencing exercises, or perhaps opera-singers and musicians practising. It's well worth experiencing the very different rhythms of the city at this time.

Temporary exhibitions take place in the parks, including horticultural and cultural ones, and there is even the odd bit of open-air theatre as well as some worthy eating establishments. If you take up residence in Beijing, the parks become very important for preserving sanity. They are open late too, typically until 8 pm.

Tiantan Park 天坛公园

The perfection of Ming architecture, Tiantan (*tiāntán*; Temple of Heaven) has come to symbolise Beijing. Its lines appear on countless pieces of tourist literature and its name serves as a brand name for a wide range of products from tiger balm to plumbing fixtures. In the 1970s the complex got a face-lift and was freshly painted after pigment research. It is set in a 267-hectare park, with four gates at the compass points, and bounded by walls to the north and east. It originally functioned as a vast stage for solemn rites performed by the Son of Heaven who came here to pray for good harvests, seek divine clearance and atone for the sins of the people.

With this complicated mix in mind, the unique architectural features will delight numerologists, necromancers and the superstitious – not to mention acoustic engineers and carpenters. Shape, colour and sound take on symbolic significance. The temples, seen in aerial perspective, are round, and the bases are square, deriving from the ancient Chinese belief that heaven is round, and the earth is square. Thus the north end of the park is semicircular and the south end is square (the Temple of Earth, also called Ditan, is on the northern compass point and the Temple of Heaven on the southern compass point).

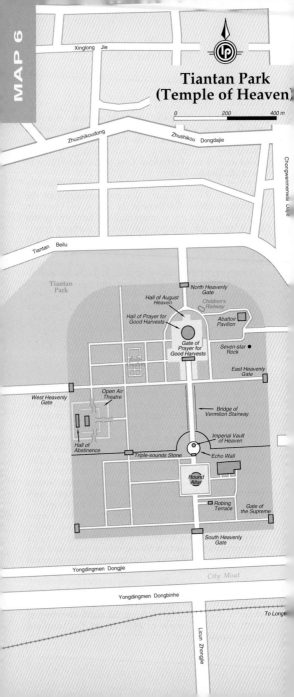

MAP 6

Tiantan Park
(Temple of Heaven)

0   200   400 m

Xinglong   Jie

Zhuzshikoudong   Zhushikou   Dongdajie

Chongwenmenwai Dajie

Tiantan   Beilu

Tiantan Park

North Heavenly Gate

Hall of August Heaven

Children's Railway

Hall of Prayer for Good Harvests

Abattoir Pavilion

Gate of Prayer for Good Harvests

Seven-star Rock

East Heavenly Gate

West Heavenly Gate

Open Air Theatre

Bridge of Vermilion Stairway

Imperial Vault of Heaven

Hall of Abstinence

Triple-sounds Stone

Echo Wall

Round Altar

Robing Terrace

Gate of the Supreme

South Heavenly Gate

Yongdingmen Dongjie

City Moat

Yongdingmen Dongbinhe

To Long

Licun Zhongjie

GLENN BEANLAND

Tiantan Temple, the symbol of Beijing. The common people were not allowed to see the imperial sacrifices made here.

Tiantan was considered highly sacred ground and it was here that the emperor performed the major ceremonial rites of the year. Just before the winter solstice, the emperor and his enormous entourage passed down Qianmen Dajie to the Imperial Vault of Heaven in total silence. Commoners were not permitted to view the ceremony and remained cloistered indoors. The procession included elephant chariots, horse chariots and long lines of lancers, nobles, officials and musicians, dressed in their finest, flags fluttering. The next day the emperor waited in a yellow silk tent at the south gate while officials moved the sacred tablets to the Round Altar, where the prayers and sacrificial rituals took place. The least hitch in any part of the proceedings was regarded as an ill omen, and it was thought that the nation's future was thus decided. This was the most important ceremony although other excursions to the Temple of Earth also took place.

Round Altar The five-metre-high Round Altar was constructed in 1530 and rebuilt in 1740. It is composed of white marble arrayed in three tiers, and its geometry revolves around the imperial number nine. Odd numbers were considered heavenly, and nine is the largest single-digit odd number. The top tier, thought to symbolise heaven, has nine rings of stones, each ring composed of multiples of nine stones, so that the ninth ring has 81 stones. The middle tier – earth – has the 10th to 18th rings. The bottom tier – man – has the 19th to 27th rings, ending with a total of 243 stones in the largest ring, or 27 times nine. The number of stairs and balustrades are also multiples of nine. If you stand in the centre of the upper terrace and say something, the sound waves are bounced off the marble balustrades, making your voice appear louder (nine times?).

Echo Wall Just north of the altar, surrounding the Imperial Vault of Heaven, is the Echo Wall, 65 metres in diameter. This enables a whisper to travel clearly from one end to your friend's ear at the other – that is, if there's not a group tour in the middle.

In the courtyard are the Triple Echo Stones. If you stand on the first one and clap or shout, the sound is echoed once, on the second stone twice, and on the third, three times. Should it return four times, you will almost certainly not find a hotel room for under Y900 that day, or any other day that is a multiple of three.

Imperial Vault of Heaven This octagonal vault was built at the same time as the Round Altar, and is structured along the lines of the older Hall of Prayer for Good Harvests, though it is smaller. It used to contain tablets of the emperor's ancestors, which were used in the winter solstice ceremony. Proceeding up from the Imperial Vault is a walkway: to the left is a molehill composed of excess dirt dumped from digging air-raid shelters and to the right is a rash of souvenir shops.

Hall of Prayer for Good Harvests The granddaddy of the whole complex is the Hall of Prayer for Good Harvests, which is a magnificent piece mounted on a three-tiered marble terrace. Built in 1420, it was burnt to cinders in 1889 and heads rolled in apportioning blame. The cause seems to have been lightning. A faithful reproduction based on Ming architectural methods was erected the following year, using Oregon fir for the support pillars.

The four pillars at the centre represent the seasons, the 12 in the next ring denote the months of the year, and the 12 outer ones are symbolic of the day, broken into 12 'watches'. Embedded in the ceiling is a carved dragon, a symbol of royalty. The patterning, carving and gilt decoration of this ceiling and its swirl of colour is a dizzy sight, enough to carry you into the Seventh Heaven.

In fact it looks peculiarly modern, like a graphic from a sci-fi movie of a UFO about to blast into space. All this is made more amazing by the fact that the wooden pillars ingeniously support the ceiling without nails or cement – for a building 38 metres high and 30 metres in diameter, that's an accomplishment not matched until Lego was invented. Capping the structure is a deep blue umbrella of tiles with a golden knob and two complementary eaves.

Other Tiantan, it should not be forgotten, is also a park and a meeting place. Get there at 6.30 am (before the ticket booth opens) to see taiji, dancing to Western music and some other games that people play. This is how Beijing awakes. It becomes just another Chinese parkland by 9 am as the tourists start to break the magic.

If you get a Chinese-priced ticket for Tiantan Park (Y0.50), you need to pay an extra Y5 to see the Hall of Prayer for Good Harvests. If you buy the overpriced tourist ticket (Y30), admission to everything is included. The park is open from 6 am to 8 pm (see Map 6).

Jingshan Park 景山公园

North of the Forbidden City is Jingsham Park(*jǐngshān; Coal Hill*), which contains an artificial mound made of earth excavated to create the palace moat. If you clamber to the top pavilions of this regal pleasure garden you get a magnificent panorama of the capital and a great overview of the russet roofing of the Forbidden City. On the east side of the park is a locust tree (not the original) where the last of the Mings, Emperor Chongzhen, hanged himself (after slaying his family) rather than see the palace razed by the Manchus. The hill supposedly protects the palace from the evil spirits – or dust storms – from the north, but which didn't quite work for Chongzhen.

Entrance to Jingshan Park is a modest Y0.50, or you can pay over 30 times as much for a souvenir 'tourist passport ticket'; the latter is optional (Map 23).

Beihai Park 北海公园

Just north-west of the Forbidden City, Beihai Park (*běihǎi gōngyuán*) is the former playground of the emperors. It's rumoured to have been the private pleasure domain of the great dragon-lady/witch Jiang Qing, widow of Mao who, until her death in May 1991, was serving a life sentence as No 1 of the Gang of Four. Half of the park is a lake. The island in the lower middle is composed of the heaped earth dug to create the lake – some attribute this to the handiwork of Kublai Khan.

The site is associated with the Great Khan's palace, the navel of Beijing before the creation of the Forbidden City. All that remains of the Khan's court is a large jar made of green jade, in the Round City near the south entrance.

MAP 7 Beihai Park 北海公园

1	Beihai Playground 北海体育场	15	Beihai Restaurant 北海餐厅
2	Glazed Pavilion 琉璃阁	16	Rowboat Dock 游船码头
3	Hall 大慈真如殿	17	Boat House 船坞
4	Tianwang Hall 天王殿	18	Painted Boat Studio 画舫斋
5	Nine Dragon Screen 九龙壁	19	Rowboat Dock 游船码头
6	Jingxin House 静心斋	20	Fangshan Restaurant 仿膳饭庄
7	Rowboat Dock 游船码头	21	Pavilion of Calligraphy 阅古楼
8	North Gate 北门	22	White Dagoba 白塔
9	Qincan Hall 亲蚕殿	23	East Gate 东门
10	Kindergarten 北海幼儿园	24	Falun Hall 法轮殿
11	Wanfulou 万福楼	25	West Gate 西门
12	Gardens 植物园	26	Light Receiving Hall 承光殿
13	Miniature Western Paradise 小西天	27	South Gate 南门
14	Five Dragon Pavilion 五龙亭		

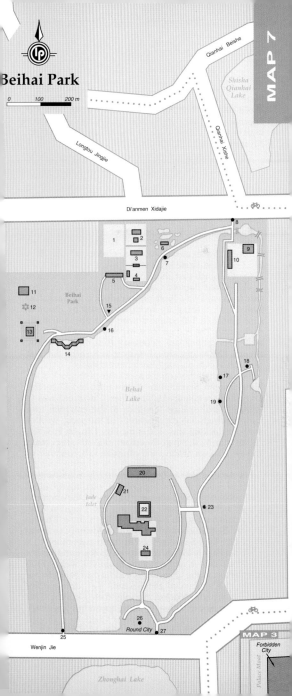

MAP 7

Beihai Park

0   100   200 m

Qianhai Beishe

Shisha
Qianhai Lake

Qianhai Xishe

Longtou Jingjie

Di'anmen Xidajie

1
2
3
6
4
5
7

8

9
10

11

Beihai
Park

12

13

15

14

16

18

17

19

Beihai
Lake

20

21

Jade
Islet

22

23

24

25

26

Round City   27

Wenjin Jie

MAP 3

Forbidden
City

Palace Moat

Zhonghai Lake

A present given in 1265, and said to have contained the Khan's wine, it was later discovered in the hands of Taoist priests who used it to store pickles. In the Light Receiving Hall, the main structure nearby, is a 1½-metre-high white jade Buddha inlaid with jewels, a gift from Myanmar (Burma) to Empress Dowager Cixi.

From the 12th century on, Beihai Park was landscaped with artificial hills, pavilions, halls, temples and covered walkways. In the present era the structures have been massively restored and Beihai Park is now one of the best examples of a classical garden found in China. Dominating Jade Islet on the lake, the **White Dagoba** is a 36-metre-high pop-art 'peppermint bottle' originally dating from 1651. It was put up for a visit by the Dalai Lama and was rebuilt in 1741. It's believed that Lamaist scriptures, robes and other sacred objects are encased in this brick-and-stone landmark.

On the north-east shore of the islet is the handsome double-tiered **Painted Gallery**, with unusual architecture for a walkway. Near the boat-dock is the Fangshan Restaurant, dishing up recipes favoured by Empress Cixi. She liked 120-course dinners with about 30 kinds of desserts. The restaurant is expensive and high class, and reservations are necessary (but check out the decor!). Off to one side, however, is a snack bar that dispenses royal pastries much more cheaply.

The big attraction on the north side of the park is the **Nine Dragon Screen**, five metres high and 27 metres long, made of coloured glazed tiles. The screen was to scare off evil spirits; it stands at the entrance to a temple which has disappeared. To the south-west of the boat-dock on this side is the Five Dragon Pavilion dating from 1651, where the emperors liked to fish, camp and sing songs around the campfire (a forerunner of karaoke).

On the east side of the park are the 'gardens within gardens'. These waterside pavilions, winding corridors and rockeries were summer haunts of the imperial family, notably Emperor Qianlong and Empress Cixi. They date back some 200 years, with structures like the Painted Boat Studio and the Studio of Mental Calmness. Until 1980 the villas were used as government offices.

Beihai Park is a relaxing place to stroll around, grab a snack, sip a beer, rent a rowing boat (Y10, with a Y100 deposit) or, as the Chinese do, cuddle on a bench in the evening. It's crowded at weekends. Swimming in the lake is not permitted, but in winter there's skating. This is nothing new in China – skating apparently goes back to the 18th century when Emperor Qianlong reviewed the imperial skating parties here. (See Map 7.)

Ditan Park 地坛公园

Although 'ditan' sounds just like the Chinese word for 'carpet', in this case it means 'Temple of Earth'. Ditan Park (*dìtán gōngyuán*) was built around 1530 as a place for the emperors to sacrifice lesser beings to keep on good terms with the Earth God. The park experienced many years of neglect, but re opened in 1984 as a sort of activity centre for the elderly. The park is just north of the magnificent Lama Temple (Map 23).

Ritan Park 日坛公园

Ritan means 'Temple of the Sun' and it's one of Beijing's older parks, having been built in 1530. Ritan Park (*rìtán gōngyuán*) was built as an altar for ritual sacrifice to the Sun God. Situated practically right in the middle of Jianguomenwai embassyland, it is a big hit with diplomats, their families and other notables who like to rub elbows with important foreigners (Map 21). The Ritan Restaurant is in the park and serves *jiaozi* in an older-style pavilion – this place is very popular with Westerners for snacks.

Yuetan Park 月坛公园

A small park west of the centre, this one's name means 'Temple of the Moon'. It is another one of Beijing's sacrificial parks, where the emperors reduced the surplus population to appease the Moon God. These days the Yuetan Park (*yuètán gōngyuán*; Map 23) is notable for the Emei Restaurant on the north side of the park, which serves hot Sichuan food with no compromise for foreign palates.

Yuyuantan Park 玉渊潭公园

Off to the west of Yuetan Park is the Jade Hole Pool (*yùyuāntán*). The park is notable for the palatial Diaoyutai State Guesthouse, the stomping ground of visiting diplomats and high-ranking cadres. Tourists wandering around the main gate will be politely told to get lost. Just to the south side of the park is the immense TV Tower, one of Beijing's most prominent landmarks. The park is just north of the Military Museum (Map 23).

Taoranting Park 陶然亭公园

Taoranting (*táoránting gōngyuán*), or Happy Pavilion Park, is in the southern part of Beijing. The park dates back to at least the Qing Dynasty, when it gained fame

ROBERT STOREY

Small viewing pavilion in Taoranting Park

chiefly because it was one of the very few accessible to
the masses (most of the others were the private play-
grounds of the emperors). It's one of the less inspiring
parks in Beijing, but has a good public swimming pool
with water slides (Map 23).

Zizhuyuan Park 紫竹园

The park's name means 'Purple Bamboo', a reference to
some of what has been planted here. This place doesn't
have much history to distinguish it, being mainly former
paddy fields, but during the Ming Dynasty there was a
Temple of Longevity *(wànshòu sì)* at this site. Zizhuyuan
Park *(zǐzhúyuàn gōngyuán)* is pleasant enough and there
is a reasonably large lake which makes a good venue for
ice skating in winter. Zizhuyuan is in a prestigious
neighbourhood just west of the zoo (Map 23).

Longtan Park 龙潭公园

Longtan (Dragon Pool) Park *(lóngtán gōngyuán)*, east of
the Temple of Heaven, is of chief interest to budget
travellers staying at the nearby Longtan Hotel in south-

east Beijing; visit the park at dawn to see taiji performances (Map 23).

The west side of Longtan Park has been converted into the Beijing Amusement Park, a world of balloons, cotton candy and nauseating rides (don't eat Sichuan food before getting on the 'Spider').

Grand View Garden 大观园

Off the south-west corner of town is Grand View Garden, also known as Daguanyuan Park (*dàguānyuán gōngyuán*). Unlike most of Beijing's parks which date back to imperial days, this one is new. Construction started in 1984 and was completed four years later. The park was built as a replica of the family gardens described in the classic Chinese novel *The Dream of the Red Chamber* (also translated as *The Dream of Red Mansions* and *The Story of the Stone*), written by Cao Xueqin in the late 18th century. While the park is not steeped in history, it could be of interest if you've read the novel. Otherwise, just relax and enjoy the birds, trees and colourful pavilions.

OTHER SIGHTS

Prince Gong's Residence 恭王府

To find this, you have to get off the main roads into the small alleys running around the Shisha Hai Lakes (Map 23). Prince Gong's Residence (*gōng wáng fǔ*) is more or less at the centre of the arc created by the lakes running from north to south. It's reputed to be the model for the mansion in Cao Xueqin's classic epic, *The Dream of the Red Chamber*. It's one of the largest private residential compounds in Beijing, with a nine-courtyard layout, high walls and elaborate gardens. Prince Gong was the son of a Qing emperor.

Ancient Observatory 古观象台

One interesting perspective on Beijing is the Ancient Observatory (*gǔguān xiàngtái*) mounted on the battlements of a watchtower, once part of the city walls. Dwarfed by embassy housing blocks, it's surrounded by traffic loops and highways just west of the Friendship Store, on the south-west corner of Jianguomennei Dajie and the second ring road. The views themselves are worth the visit. There are some English explanations. The observatory dates back to Kublai Khan's days when it was north of the present site. The Great Khan, as well

Things to See & Do

Underground City
In the late 1960s, with a Soviet invasion apparently hanging over them, the Chinese built huge civil defence systems, especially in northern China. (This hobby started before 1949 when the PLA used the tunnelling technique to surprise the enemy.) Civil defence officials proudly proclaimed that 10,000 shoppers in the Dazhalan area could seek shelter in five minutes (what about the other 70,000?) in the event of an attack.

Pressed for space, and trying to maximise the peacetime possibilities of the air-raid shelters (aside from the fact that the shelters are useless in the event of nuclear attack), Beijing has put them to use as warehouses, factories, shops, restaurants, hotels, roller-skating rinks, theatres and clinics.

The underground city *(dìxià chéng)* was constructed by volunteers and shop assistants living in the Qianmen area – about 2000 people and 10 years of spare-time work with simple tools. The people reap a few benefits now such as use of the warehouse space, and preferential treatment for relatives and friends who can stay in a 100-bed hotel – the views aren't great, but at least they can escape the traffic noise.

It's not one of the most inspiring sights in Beijing, but an estimated 600 people per day pay to catch a glimpse of the 32-km underground system. There are roughly 90 entrances to this particular complex and entrances are hidden in shops. One such shop happy to welcome tourists is at 62 Xidamochang Jie, a narrow hutong (see Map 20). To find it, start from the Qianmen subway station and walk east along this hutong for 15 minutes. Admission for foreigners costs Y5. A fluorescent wall map reveals the routing of the entire tunnel system. ∎

as later Ming and Qing emperors, relied heavily on astrologers before making a move.

The present Beijing Observatory was built from 1437 to 1446, not only to facilitate astrological predictions but to aid seafaring navigators. Downstairs are displays of navigational equipment used by Chinese ships. On the 1st floor are replicas of five 5000-year-old pottery jars, unearthed from Henan Province in 1972 and showing painted patterns of the sun. There are also four replicas of Han Dynasty eave tiles representing east, west, north and south. There is a map drawn on a wooden octagonal board with 1420 stars marked in gold foil or powder; it's a reproduction of the original, which is said to be Ming Dynasty but is based on an older Tang map. Busts of six prominent astronomers are also displayed.

On the roof is a variety of astronomical instruments designed by the Jesuits. The Jesuits, scholars as well as proselytisers, found their way into the capital in 1601 when Matteo Ricci and company were permitted to work with Chinese scientists. The emperor was keen to find out about European firearms and cannons from them.

The Jesuits outdid the resident Muslim calendar-setters and were given control of the observatory, becoming the Chinese court's advisors. Of the eight bronze instruments on display (including an equatorial armilla, celestial globe and altazimuth), six were designed and constructed under the supervision of the Belgian priest Ferdinand Verbiest, who came to China in 1659 to work at the Qing court. The instruments were built between 1669 and 1673, and are embellished with sculptured bronze dragons and other Chinese craftwork, a unique mix of east and west. The azimuth theodolite was supervised by Kilian Stumpf, also a missionary. The eighth instrument, the new armilla, was completed in 1744 by Ignaz Kögler. It's not clear which instruments on display are the originals.

During the Boxer Rebellion, the instruments disappeared into the hands of the French and the Germans. Some were returned in 1902, while others came back under the provisions of the Treaty of Versailles (1919).

More recently, government officials were caught off guard when local and foreign rock bands got together and staged a dance party in the ancient tower.

The observatory is open Wednesday through Sunday from 9 to 11 am and from 1 to 4 pm (Map 21).

Central TV Tower 中央电视塔

Though Westerners tend to be less than thrilled by TV towers, these appear to be a major drawcard for Chinese tourists. At 238 metres, Beijing's TV tower (zhōngyāng diànshìtái) is the tallest structure in the city. For a fee, tourists can go to the top and have a meal at a pricey restaurant. The purpose, of course, is to admire the view. Unfortunately, Beijing's smoggy skyline is not all that inspiring, but the trip is more rewarding at night.

The Central TV Tower is on the western side of Yuyuantan Park (Map 23). Bus Nos 323 and 374 stop there.

Beijing Financial St 金融街

Just inside the west section of the second ring road between Fuxingmennei and Fuchengmennei Dajie, developers are busily constructing the much ballyhooed 'Wall St of China' (Map 23). It's been officially dubbed the 'Beijing Financial St'. Despite the hoopla, skeptics point out that Shanghai will almost certainly blow away Beijing's attempt to become the country's financial centre. Currently, Beijing does not even have a stock exchange, though that is sure to change.

WALKING TOURS

Walking tours are close to impossible in sprawling Beijing. You can walk a bit in certain neighbourhoods like Wangfujing, Dazhalan and Jianguomenwai, but the city is so spread out that the obvious way to go is by bicycle.

BLOCKBUSTER BICYCLE TOUR

Tiantan Park (west side) – Natural History Museum – Dazhalan – Qianmen – Tiananmen Square – Chinese Revolution History Museum – Great Hall of the People – Tiananmen Gate – Forbidden City – Beihai Park – Jingshan Park – Prince Gong's Residence – Song Qingling Museum – Drum Tower – Bell Tower – Confucius Temple – Lama Temple – China Art Gallery – Kentucky Fried Chicken or McDonald's – Wangfujing – Tiantan Park (east side) – Home?

Obviously this tour only gives you a cursory glance at Beijing's many fine sights; indeed, you could spend a full day in just the Forbidden City itself. But if you start out early (such as at dawn) you can see a good chunk of town and take in some of Beijing's many moods, and you can always continue the tour the next day if your schedule permits.

For the following tour, nonstop cycling time is about two hours – Chinese bike, Western legs, average pace. The starting point is the west side of Tiantan Park, and the finishing point is the east side of the same park. Refer to Map 23 at the end of this book, in which the route is traced out.

The southern end of Qianmen Dajie is called Yongdingmen Dajie; it's here that you'll find the west entrance of **Tiantan Park**. The park is certainly worth exploring, but you can do that on the way back. Right now, our goal is just a little to the north, the **Natural History Museum** on the east side of Yongdingmen Dajie.

After you've had your dose of natural history, continue north to where Yongdingmen Dajie becomes Qianmen Dajie. Coming up on your left is **Dazhalan**, one

Hutong Hopping

A completely different side of Beijing emerges in the hutongs or back lanes. The original plan of the city allowed for enclosed courtyards buried down alleys, and though the politics have changed many of the courtyards remain. Given the choice between a high-rise block and a traditional compound, most residents of Beijing would opt for the latter. The compounds have loads more character – and offer courtyards to grow vegetables in.

There are over 3000 hutongs in Beijing, so there's a lot out there to discover. The word derives from Mongolian and means a passageway between tents or yurts. Many of the hutongs are named after the markets (fish, pig, rice, sheep) or trades (hats, bowstrings, trousers) once conducted along them. Others took their names after the seats of government offices or specialised suppliers to the palace (granaries, red lacquer, armour). Yet others were named after dukes and officers.

Around the Forbidden City of yore there were some very odd industries. Wet-Nurse Lane was full of young mothers who breastfed the imperial offspring. They were selected from around China on scouting trips four times a year. Clothes-Washing Lane was where the women who did the imperial laundry lived. The maids, grown old in the service of the court, were packed off to far-away places for a few years so that their intimate knowledge of the royal undergarments would be out of date by the time they got round to gossiping.

Walking along the hutongs kind of destroys the advantage of a lightning visit, and may well lead to you acquiring a Chinese entourage. Charging off on a bicycle is the best way to go. If you see an interesting compound you can stop and peer in, maybe even be invited in; the duller bits you can cruise by. ■

GLENN BEANLAND

of Beijing's most intriguing hutongs. Bikes cannot be ridden into this particular hutong, though you can explore most others on two wheels.

Slightly more than a stone's throw to the north is **Qianmen**, the front gate to the vast expanse of Tiananmen Square. Traffic is one way for north-south avenues on either side of the square. If you want to go to Tiananmen, dismount after the archway and wheel the bike to the parking areas along the sidewalk. Bicycles cannot be ridden across Tiananmen Square (apparently tanks are OK), but you can walk the bike. Nearby are the Chinese Revolution History Museum, Great Hall of the People, Mao's Mausoleum, Tiananmen Gate and the Forbidden City itself.

Over to the west side of the Forbidden City you're heading into the most sensitive part of the capital, the **Zhongnanhai** compound. On the right, going up Beichang Jie, you pass some older housing that lines the moat. On the left is a high wall which shields from view the area where top Party members live and work (it was decided not to rip down this section of the old walls). In 1973, when the new wing of the Beijing Hotel shot up, the PSB suddenly realised that guests with binoculars could observe activity in Zhongnanhai, so a fake building was erected along the western wall of the Forbidden City to short-circuit that possibility. Mysterious buildings, indeed, abound in this locale (including secret underground tunnels connecting them).

Then it's **Beihai Park**, which by this time of day should be bustling with activity. You can exercise your arms as well as your legs by hiring a rowing boat. There's a cafe near the south gate overlooking Beihai Lake, where you can get beer, coffee, tea or cold drinks.

Back on the bike and you'll soon bump into **Jingshan Park**. There's bicycle parking by the entrance. Jingshan Park is a splendid place to survey the smog of Beijing, get your bearings with 360° views and enjoy a good overview of the russet roofing of the Forbidden City opposite.

North of Jingshan Park it gets a bit tricky. You want to get off the main road into the small alleys running around the Shisha Hai Lakes. In this area, and worth checking out for a taste of literary history, is **Prince Gong's Residence**, thought to be the house which Cao Xueqin used as a model in his classic *The Dream of the Red Chamber*.

The lake district is steeped in history; if you consult a Beijing map you will see that the set of lakes connects from north to south. In the Yuan Dynasty, barges would come through various canals to the top lake (*jīshuǐtán*), a sort of harbour for Beijing. Later the lakes were used for pleasure-boating, and were bordered by the residences of high officials.

The larger lake to the north-west is the Shisha Houhai (Lake of the Ten Back Monasteries). Below that is the Shisha Qianhai (Lake of the Ten Front Monasteries).

Also around the lakes you'll find the **Song Qingling Museum**, the retirement residence of Sun Yatsen's respected wife.

Make a small detour here. If you go north-east through the hutongs you will arrive at the **Bamboo Garden Hotel**, which is a wonderful illustration of the surprises that hutongs hold. This was originally the personal garden of Sheng Xuanhuai, an important Qing official. There are exquisite gardens and courtyards, renovated compound architecture and an expensive restaurant (English menu, alfresco in summer). It's a quiet place to sip a drink.

Another small detour brings you to the Kaorouji Restaurant – not necessarily the cheapest place to get your roast chicken, but the balcony dining in summer is pleasant enough.

Back on the main drag and you come to the **Drum Tower** (gǔlóu). It was built in 1420 and has several drums which were beaten to mark the hours of the day, in effect the Big Ben of Beijing. Time was kept with a water clock. It's in pretty sad shape, but an impressive structure nonetheless with a solid brick base. Occasional exhibitions take place here since the tower is connected with local artisans.

Behind the Drum Tower, down an alley directly north, is the **Bell Tower**, which was originally built at the same time as the Drum Tower, but burnt down. The present structure is 18th-century, and the gigantic bell which used to hang there has been moved to the Drum Tower. Legend has it that the bellmaker's daughter plunged into the molten iron before the bell was cast. Her father only managed to grab her shoe as she did so, and the bell's soft sound resembled that of the Chinese for 'shoe' (xié). The same story is told about a couple of other bells in China – seems like committing suicide in molten iron was a serious social problem.

Back on the road you'll reach the former **Confucius Temple** and Imperial College, now a museum/library complex. Unless you can read stele-calligraphy, you probably won't spend much time here. A stele standing in the hutong ordered officials to dismount at this point but you can ignore that.

By contrast, just down the road is the **Lama Temple**, one of Beijing's finest. Along the way to the Lama

Temple you might pass through several decorated lintels; these graceful archways (páilóu), which commemorate mandarin officials or chaste widows, were ripped out of the thoroughfares of Beijing in the 1950s. The reason given was the facilitation of traffic movement. Some have been relocated in parks. The ones you see in this hutong are rarities.

This is the northernmost point of today's journey (you're still with us, aren't you?). Head south, and if you're ready for yet another museum there's the **China Art Gallery**, a slight detour to the west at the northern end of Wangfujing. Unfortunately, Wangfujing itself is closed to cyclists, so head back to the east on Dongsi Xi Dajie and you'll find Kentucky Fried Chicken. If the Colonel's fried chicken delights aren't what you had in mind, you could try McDonald's, at the southern end of Wangfujing. No matter what you think of the food, these restaurants are at least as popular as the Forbidden City – and just remember that none of China's emperors ever had the chance to taste a Big Mac, Chicken Nuggets or Egg McMuffin.

Launch yourself into the sea of cyclists, throw your legs into cruising speed and cycle the length of Dongdan south to the east entrance of **Tiantan Park**. If this is still day one of your bike tour, you're probably too exhausted to walk inside to see the Temple of Heaven – well, there's always tomorrow. From this point, you're well positioned to head home (wherever that is).

ACTIVITIES

Health Clubs

Sporting, recreational and club facilities are to be found in tourist hotels, and the National Olympic Sports Centre on Beisihuan Zhonglu (north-central section of the fourth ring road; Map 1). The International Club on Jianguomenwai – a place with signs telling you what not to do – can be dull during the daytime but livens up in the evening (Map 21). You might also want to try the Beijing International Health Land (☎ 466-1302) at 11 Xinyuan Xijie (Map 21).

Guests at major hotels can generally use all facilities for free, while non-guests must pay additional requisite fees. These fees can be high if calculated by the hour, but many hotels offer substantial discounts if you pay on a monthly basis (Y500 and up), quarterly or annually. Hotels offering this service include the Beijing-Toronto, China World, Capital, Great Wall Sheraton, Holiday Inn Lido, Landmark Towers, Kunlun and Shangri-la. If you don't mind commuting out to the airport, the Mövenpick Hotel has an excellent health club (The Splash) but you are obliged to become a member.

Basketball

This sport has not exactly captured the imagination of Beijingers. Mostly it's Americans who play this, and for this reason the only regular games are played at the US embassy every Sunday at 2 pm. There is now an attempt to get a basketball league started – ask at the US embassy for details.

Bowling

Hotels with bowling alleys include the Capital, Continental Grand, Grand View Garden, Holiday Inn Lido, International, Mandarin, New Century, Poly Plaza, Swissôtel, Tianlun Dynasty, Traders, Xinqiao, Yanxiang and the Zhongyuan. You can also find a bowling alley at the Beijing Recreation Centre, north of the National Olympic Sports Centre, on Anli Lu.

Golf

The art of poking a white ball around a lawn enjoys considerable prestige in face-conscious China. If your face needs a lift, check out the Beijing International Golf Course (☎ 974-6388) *(běijīng guójì gāo'ěrfū qiú chǎng)*. This Chinese-Japanese joint venture opened in mid-1986. The 18-hole golf course is 35 km north of Beijing close to the Ming Tombs in Changping County, and the course was used during the 1990 Asian Games (see Map 13). Pushing that little ball around is not cheap, but the course is in good condition and the scenery is spectacular. Visitor fees are Y350 on weekdays and Y400 on weekends and public holidays. You can rent a set of golf clubs and spiked golf shoes for an additional fee.

There is another 18-hole golf course which goes by a variety of names. It's officially named the Beijing Golf Course (☎ 513-7766) but is most commonly called the Airport Golf Course *(jīchǎng gāo'ěrfū qiú chǎng)*. It's just north of Capital Airport.

Closest to the city centre is the Chaoyang Golf Club (☎ 491-0385) *(cháoyáng gāo'ěrfū qiú chǎng)*– see Map 8.

Miniature Golf Mark Twain used to say that playing golf is a waste of a good walk. If you agree, you might find miniature golf more suitable.

Beijing's first outdoor miniature golf course opened in June 1995, in Ditan Park (Map 23). Playing one 18-hole round costs Y20. The Beijing-Toronto Hotel also has a miniature golf course in the basement, but this one costs a mind-boggling Y300 per hour.

Shooting

If being ripped off by street vendors and pedicab drivers is getting you down, you can work out your aggressions at the Beijing Shooting Range *(běijīng shèjí chǎng)* on the west side of town (near Badachu). Run for profit by the PLA, all the war toys are made in China including 'Red Star' pistols and AK-47s. If this doesn't suffice, west of the Ming Tombs is the International Shooting Range where you can play with bazookas and anti-aircraft guns! Cost is calculated per bullet – it's quite a bit more for artillery shells.

Swimming

Swimming is supposedly illegal at Longtan Lake (southeast Beijing) or the Miyun Canal, but that's where many locals take a dip on a hot summer day. An amazingly large number of them also drown.

Most tourist hotels have indoor pools, but large Olympic-sized pools are harder to find. Large ones can be found at the China World Hotel, Holiday Inn Lido (members only), Hotel New Otani, China Resources Hotel and Fragrant Hills Hotel. Perhaps cheapest and best for the serious swimmer are the pools at the National Olympic Sports Centre (☎ 491-0468, 491-0483) – see Map 1.

Some other hotels with pools open to the public include the Great Wall Sheraton, Holiday Inn Downtown, International, Jingguang Centre, Landmark, Palace, Peace, Shangri-La, Tianlun Dynasty, Xiyuan, Yanxiang and Zhaolong. There is a decent pool inside the Sino-Japanese Youth Exchange Centre (Map 21).

There are less expensive but less nice pools inside Shijingshan Amusement Park and Taoranting Park (Map 23).

Squash

There are four courts in the Holiday Inn Lido (☎ 437-6688 ext 1623). Lufthansa Centre (☎ 465-3388 ext 5721) chips in with three courts. The China World Hotel (☎ 505-2266 ext 33) and Hilton (☎ 466-2288 ext 7478) each have two courts. Out by the airport, the Mövenpick Hotel (☎ 456-5588 ext 1428) has one court.

Tennis

Known to the Chinese as 'net ball' *(wǎng qiú)*, the sport has an enthusiastic following and all public facilities are very crowded. It's much easier to find a vacant court at an upmarket hotel or club, but such places charge Y30 to Y100 per hour. Even then, reservations are usually mandatory. You can try any of the following venues:

Beijing Recreation Centre, near National Olympic Sports Centre, Beisihuan Zhonglu (north fourth ring road) (☎ 499-3401)
Friendship Hotel, Baishiqiao Lu (third ring road) (☎ 849-8888 ext 0740)
Great Wall Sheraton Hotel, Dongsanhuan Beilu (north-east third ring road) (☎ 500-5566)
International Club, Jianguomenwai (☎ 532-2046)
International Tennis Centre (☎ 701-3872)
New Classical Tennis Club, National Olympic Sports Centre, Beisihuan Zhonglu (north fourth ring road) (☎ 491-2233 ext 218)
Ritan Park, Jianguomenwai (☎ 502-5555)
Shangri-La Hotel, 29 Zhizhuyuan Lu, Haidian District (☎ 841-2211 ext 2881)
Sino-Japanese Centre, Dongsanhuan Lu (east third ring road) (☎ 466-3311 ext 3186)

Horseback Riding

Several horse-riding parks *(qímǎ chǎng)* have opened to the north-west of Beijing in the Western Hills. The nearest is at the Fragrant Hills, but the best of the lot is Kangxi Grasslands (see the Excursions chapter; Map 8). Prices are reasonable, especially the further out you get from the city.

Hash House Harriers

This is mainly for foreign residents of Beijing, so if you're just passing through you might not be enthusiastically welcomed. Hash House Harriers is a loosely-strung international club with branches all over the world. It appeals mainly to young people, or the young at heart. Activities typically include a weekend afternoon's easy jogging session followed by a dinner and beer party which can extend until the wee hours of the morning.

Beijing's Hash is very informal. There is no club headquarters and no stable contact telephone or address. Nonetheless, finding the Hash is easy. Some embassy employees know about it, otherwise check the notice-board at Mexican Wave, a bar and restaurant on Dongdaqiao Lu (east of the Friendship Store; Map 21). Various bars and beer houses are also likely places to find Hash members; simply ask any likely-looking foreign resident of Beijing. The usual meeting time and place for the Hash is on Sunday afternoons at 3 to 4 pm in front of Mexican Wave, but this is certainly not engraved in stone. In summer there are runs on Monday evenings.

Parks

If you arrive early in the morning you can watch (or participate in) taiji and fencing exercises, or perhaps see opera singers and musicians practising. The best parks for pursuing these activities (more or less in order) are Tiantan, Beihai, Ritan, Ditan and Zhongshan parks.

COURSES

Language

Beijing is a good place to study Chinese, but prices and the quality of instruction vary widely. A bottom-end price quote for four hours of instruction per day, five days a week is US$400 per month for the first month, US$100 per week thereafter if you stay a long time. Dormitory housing starts at around US$10 a day for private room, or half that amount to share the room. There have been complaints from students that universities try to hit foreigners with all sorts of various hidden surcharges – 'study licences' and so on. It's probably to your advantage to sign up for a one-month course, and if you like it you can extend later.

Most universities welcome fee-paying foreign students. One place popular with foreigners is Beijing Language Institute (BLI) *(yǔyán xúeyuán)*, east of Qinghua University. Another place worth trying is the Central Nationalities Institute *(zhōngyāng mínzú xuéyuàn)*.

Or rather than study, perhaps you'd like to be the teacher. You can set yourself up as an unwaged professor at the Beijing 'English corner' in Zhizhuyuan Park in the western Haidian District. Students come here to practise their English and foreigners come to meet the locals – a fair exchange.

If you belong that 1% (or less) of the world's population that can speak Esperanto, check out the China Esperanto League (☎ 832-6682; fax 832-1808), 24 Bai-wanzhuang.

Places to Stay

In China, you can't simply stay in any hotel which has a vacancy – the hotel must be designated a 'tourist hotel'. It's no use trying to force your way into a Chinese-only hotel; even if the staff would love you to stay, they dare not break the rules, which are enforced by the PSB.

During the summer peak season, hotels (especially cheap ones) tend to fill up quickly and you may have to scramble to find something affordable. It's advisable to ring ahead before embarking on a long taxi journey in search of an elusive vacant room, though many hotel operators cannot speak English. When the operator answers, ask to speak to the reception desk *(zǒng fúwù tái).*

For more information on the taxes and discounts applicable to hotels in Beijing, see under Costs in the Facts for the Visitor chapter.

The following hotel lists are arranged according to the maps at the front and back of the book.

PLACES TO STAY – BOTTOM END

Beijing offers little in the way of cheap accommodation but there are a few budget places mostly in the outlying areas of town. In China's pricey capital city, any hotel charging under Y400 in the high season would have to be considered 'bottom end'.

At the present time, the two favourite bottom-end haunts for backpackers are the Jinghua Hotel and Lihua Hotel, about the only two places in town with dormitories. Other hotels which get good reviews include the Far East, Longtan and Lüsongyuan. A lot of foreigners stay in the Tiantan Sports Hotel because of its convenient location, but the rooms aren't so good.

The following list of hotels with rooms priced below Y400 is in alphabetical order. Make allowances for the fact that future renovations (and greed) may drive prices to even more astronomical levels.

Beijing (Map 1)

Complant Hotel (☎ 762-6688) *(zhōngchéng bīnguǎn),* 1 Dingan Dongli, Puhuangyu, 100075. Standard doubles are Y380.

Fengtai Hotel (☎ 381-4448) *(fēngtái bīnguǎn),* 67 Zhengyang Dajie, Fengtai District, 100071 (near Fengtai railway station). Rates are low – Y60 without air-conditioner or Y80 with it. Bus No 335 from the Wukesong subway station (East-West Line) can get you there.

Furong Hotel (☎ 502-2921) *(fúróng bīnguǎn),* Bailizhuang, Chaoyang Lu, Chaoyang District, 100025. Doubles cost Y180.

Hainan Hotel (☎ 256-5550; fax 256-8395) *(hǎinán fàndiàn),* Zhongguancun, Haidian District. Doubles cost Y200.

Jiali Hotel (☎ 437-3631) *(jiālì fàndiàn),* 21B Jiuxianqiao Lu, Chaoyang District, 100016. Standard doubles cost Y300.

Jinghua Hotel (☎ 722-2211) *(jīnghuá fàndiàn),* Nansanhuan Xilu (southern part of the third ring road). A favourite with backpackers, dorm beds cost Y26 to Y28. Doubles with private bath are Y140 to Y162. Bus Nos 2 and 17 (or minibus No 14) from Qianmen drop you off nearby.

Jingtai Hotel (☎ 721-2476, 722-4675) *(jīngtài bīnguǎn),* 65 Yongwai Jingtaixi (a small alley running off Anlelin Lu). Rooms without/with attached bath cost Y120/200 but this place is scheduled for renovation – prices may rise to over Y300.

Lihua Hotel (☎ 721-1144) *(lìhuá fàndiàn),* 71 Yangqiao, Yongdingmenwai. A well-established backpackers' hotel, dorms cost Y25 to Y30 and doubles are Y140 to Y162. Bus No 343 is the best way to get there but No 14 will also do.

Yongdingmen Hotel (☎ 721-3344) *(yǒngdìngmén fàndiàn),* 77 Anlelin Lu. It's currently closed for renovation and prices will probably rise to about Y300. Take bus No 39 from the main Beijing railway station.

Zhongguancun Hotel (☎ 256-5577) *(zhōngguāncūn jiǔdiàn),* 16A Zhongguancun, Haidian District. Doubles cost Y256.

Tiananmen Square & Dazhalan Area (Map 20)

Far East Hotel (☎ 301-8811; fax 301-8233) *(yuǎndōng fàndiàn),* 90 Tieshuxie Jie, Qianmenwai, Xuanwu District – actually on the west end of Dazhalan (south-west of Qianmen). Double rooms cost Y292.

Jianguomenwai & Sanlitun Area (Map 21)

Guanghua Hotel (☎ 501-8866; fax 501-6516) *(guānghuá fàndiàn),* 38 Dongsanhuan Beilu, Chaoyang District, 100020 (near China World Trade Centre). Rooms cost Y280 to Y332.

Guoan Hotel (☎ 500-7700) *(guóān bīnguǎn),* Guandongdian Beijie, Dongdaqiao, Chaoyang District, 100020. Doubles begin at Y400.

Huayuan Hotel (☎ 467-8661) *(huáyuán fàndiàn),* 28 Beixiaoyun Lu, Dongsanhuan, 100027. Standard doubles are Y350.

Wangfujing Area (Map 22)

Fangyuan Hotel (☎ 525-6331) *(fāngyuán bīnguǎn)*, 36 Deng-shikou Xijie, Dongcheng District, 100006. Doubles begin at Y198.

Lüsongyuan Hotel (☎ 401-1116, 403-0416) *(lǚsōngyuán bīnguǎn)*, 22 Banchang Hutong, Dongcheng District, 100007. Doubles cost Y298. It can be difficult to find this place – when you approach the hutong from either end, it doesn't seem that there could be a building of such high standard halfway down. The hutong is one way and many taxi drivers are reluctant to drive down it in the wrong direction, but others are willing to do so. The hotel is directly north of the China Art Gallery, second hutong north of Di'anmen, turn left – bus No 104 from the main Beijing railway station comes close.

Central Beijing (Map 23)

Beihai Hotel (☎ 601-2229; fax 601-7848) *(běihǎi bīnguǎn)*, 141 Di'anmen Xi Dajie, 100009. Doubles cost Y210 to Y230.

Beijing Commercial Business Complex (☎ 329-2244) *(běijīng shāngwù huìguǎn)*, Building No 1, Yulin Li, Youanmenwai, 100054. Official rates for doubles are Y350 to Y450, but prices as low as Y280 are possible by polite negotiation.

Big Bell Hotel (☎ 225-3388; fax 225-2605) *(dàzhōngsì fàndiàn)*, 18 Beisanhuan Xilu, Haidian District, 100086. Standard doubles are Y280.

Desheng Hotel (☎ 202-4477) *(déshèng fàndiàn)*, 4 Beisanhuan Zhonglu. All rooms cost Y252.

Evergreen Hotel (☎ 842-1144) *(wànniánqīng bīnguǎn)*, 25 Xisanhuan Beilu, Haidian District, 100081. Standard doubles cost Y260.

Feixia Hotel (☎ 301-2228; fax 302-1764) *(fēixiá fàndiàn)*, Building 5, Xibianmen Xili, Xuanwu District, 100053. Rooms cost Y130. One star.

Hademen Hotel (☎ 701-2244) *(hādémén fàndiàn)*, 2A Chongwen-menwai Dajie, 100062. Rates are Y320 to Y450.

Hebei Hotel (☎ 401-5522) *(héběi fàndiàn)*, 11A Cheniandian Hutong, Andingmennei, 100009. Rooms begin at Y332.

Jimen Hotel (☎ 201-2211) *(jìmén fàndiàn)*, Huangtingzi, Xueyuan Lu, Haidian District, 100088. Doubles begin at Y200.

Leyou Hotel (☎ 771-2266; fax 771-1636) *(lèyóu fàndiàn)*, 13 Dongsanhuan Nanlu, 100021 – east of Longtan Park (south-east Beijing). Doubles go for Y276 to Y380. Take bus Nos 28 or 52 to the terminus.

Longtan Hotel (☎ 771-1602; fax 771-4028) *(lóngtán fàndiàn)*, 15 Panjiayuan Nanli, Chaoyang District, 100021. Doubles cost Y300 while suites are Y510 and Y780. The hotel is opposite Longtan Park in the south of the city.

Overseas Chinese Hotel (☎ 401-6688) *(huáqiáo fàndiàn)*, 5 Beixinqiao Santiao, 100007. Room rates are Y383 to Y680. Two stars.

Qiaoyuan Hotel (☎ 303-8861, 301-2244) *(qiáoyuán fàndiàn)*, Dongbinhe Lu, Youanmenwai. At one time Beijing's largest budget hotel, it is currently under renovation and prices are expected to rise to at least Y300.

Shangyuan Hotel (☎ 225-1166) *(shàngyuán fàndiàn)*, Xie Jie, Xizhemenwai, Haidian District, 100044 – near the Xizhimen (north) railway station. Doubles are Y278. Two stars.

Tiantan Sports Hotel (☎ 701-3388; fax 701-5388) *(tiāntán tǐyù bīnguǎn)*, a huge place at 10 Tiyuguan Lu, Chongwen District, 100061. Doubles cost Y288. Take the subway one stop from the main railway station to Chongwenmen, then bus Nos 39, 41 or 43.

Traffic Hotel (☎ 701-1114, 711-2288) *(jiāotōng fàndiàn)*, 35 Dongsi Kuaiyu Nanjie. Has 82 comfortable rooms priced from Y238 to Y268. The hotel is in a narrow alley running south from Tiyuguan Lu – signs in English point the way. Bus No 41 runs on Tiyuguan Lu and drops you off at the alley's entrance. One star.

Yuanwanglou Hotel (☎ 201-3366) *(yuǎnwànglóu bīnguǎn)*, 13 Beisanhuan Xilu (north third ring road). Standard doubles cost Y300. Two stars.

Outside Central Beijing

The Shijingshan District (about 7 km to the west of the city centre along Fuxingmen Dajie) has a number of hotels:

Jingyan Hotel (☎ 887-6261) *(jīngyàn fàndiàn)*, 29 Shijingshan Lu, 100043. Doubles cost Y200.

Yuquan Hotel (☎ 821-0033) *(yùquán fàndiàn)*, Yuquan Lukou Xi, 100039. Rooms are cheap at Y132.

Ziwei Hotel (☎ 887-8031) *(zǐwēi bīnguǎn)*, 40 Shijingshan Lu, 100043. Doubles cost Y400.

North-west of central Beijing at the Botanical Gardens is the *Wofosi Hotel* (☎ 259-1561) *(wòfósì fàndiàn)*, which has doubles costing Y207.

PLACES TO STAY – MIDDLE

By Beijing's pricey standards, a hotel under US$100 should be considered 'mid-range'. The following fall into this category:

Beijing (Map 1)

Park Hotel (☎ 761-2233) *(bǎilè jiǔdiàn)*, 36 Puhuangyu Lu, 100078. Doubles cost Y550. Three stars but not worth it.

Yanxiang Hotel (☎ 437-6666; fax 437-6231) *(yānxiáng fàndiàn)*, 2A Jiangtai Lu, Dongzhimenwai (along the way to the airport in north-east Beijing). Rates are Y480 to Y960. Three stars.

Tiananmen Square & Dazhalan Area (Map 20)

Beiwei Hotel (☎ 301-2266; fax 301-1366) *(běiwěi fàndiàn)*, 13 Xijing Lu, Xuanwu District (on the western side of Tiantan Park). Standard rooms are Y420, superior Y630 and suites Y766. Two stars.

Dongfang Hotel (☎ 301-4466; fax 304-4801) *(dōngfāng fàndiàn)*, 11 Wanming Lu, 100050 (south of Qianmen). Standard doubles are Y450, superior rooms cost Y650. Three stars.

Qianmen Hotel (☎ 301-6688; fax 301-3883) *(qiánmén fàndiàn)*, 175 Yong'an Lu (south-west of Qianmen). Doubles/suites are Y617/935. Three stars.

Rainbow Hotel (☎ 301-2266; fax 301-1366) *(tiānqiáo bīnguǎn)*, 11 Xijing Lu, Xuanwu District, 100050 (south-west of Qianmen). Rooms are priced from Y630 to Y766. Three stars.

Jianguomenwai & Sanlitun Area (Map 21)

Guangming Hotel (☎ 467-8822) *(guāngmíng fàndiàn)*, Liangmaqiao Lu, Chaoyang District, 100016. Doubles cost Y570. Three stars.

Guotai Hotel (☎ 501-3366) *(guótài fàndiàn)*, 12 Yongan Xili, Jianguomenwai Dajie, 100022. Doubles are Y460.

Huadu Hotel (☎ 500-1166; fax 500-1615) *(huádū fàndiàn)*, 8 Xinyuan Nanlu, Chaoyang District, 100027. Rates are Y638 to Y978. Three stars.

Landmark Hotel (☎ 501-6688) *(liàngmǎhé dàshà)*, 8 Dongsanhuan Beilu, 100004. Rates are Y700 to Y1250. Four stars.

Ritan Hotel (☎ 512-5588) *(rìtán bīnguǎn)*, 1 Ritanlu (near Ritan Park). The hotel was under renovation at the time of writing so rates were unavailable.

Twenty-First Century Hotel (☎ 466-3311) *(èrshíyī shìjì fàndiàn)*, 40 Liangmaqiao Lu. Rooms range from Y560 to Y1250. Three stars.

Wangfujing Area (Map 22)

Grand Hotel (☎ 201-0033; fax 202-9893) *(yuánshān dà jiǔdiàn)*, 20 Yumin Dongli, Deshengmenwai, Xicheng District. Doubles are Y555 to Y639. Three stars. Avoid confusing this with the Grand Hotel Beijing.

Peace Hotel (☎ 512-8833; fax 512-6863) *(hépíng bīnguǎn)*, 3 Jinyu Hutong, Wangfujing. Standard/deluxe rooms are Y696/1044. Four stars.

Central Beijing (Map 23)

Bamboo Garden Hotel (☎ 403-2229; fax 401-2633) *(zhúyuán bīnguǎn)*, 24 Xiaoshiqiao Hutong, Jiugulou Dajie, 100009. Singles/doubles cost Y579/766.

Chongqing Hotel (☎ 422-8888) *(chóngqìng fàndiàn)*, 15 Guangxi-men Beili, Chaoyang District, 100028 (west side of Exhibition Centre). Rooms cost from Y498. Three stars.

Chongwenmen Hotel (☎ 512-2211; fax 512-2122) *(chóngwénmén fàndiàn)*, 2 Chongwenmen Xi Dajie, 100062. Standard rooms are Y490, suites Y610.

Holiday Inn Downtown (☎ 832-2288; fax 832-0696) *(jīndū jiàrì fàndiàn)*, 98 Beilishi Lu, Xicheng District, 100037. Rates are Y650 to Y1740. Three stars.

Huabei Hotel (☎ 202-2266, 202-8888) *(huáběi dà jiǔdiàn)*, Anhuaqiao, 19 Gulouwai Dajie, 100011. Rooms go for Y480 to Y580. Three stars.

Hua Thai Apartment Hotel (☎ 771-6688; fax 771-5266) *(huátài fàndiàn)*, Jinsong Dongkou (south-east Beijing). Rooms are actually apartments with kitchen facilities. Twin rooms are Y412; rooms with four beds costs Y720.

International Hotel (☎ 512-6688; fax 512-9972) *(guójì fàndiàn)*, 9 Jianguomennei Dajie, 100005. Doubles are Y705 to Y830, suites cost Y1000 to Y4980. Four stars.

Longdu Hotel (☎ 254-2277) *(lóngdū bīnguǎn)*, 400 Xiaonan-zhuang, Wanquanhe Lu, Haidian District, 100080. Standard doubles are Y450.

Media Centre Hotel (☎ 851-4422) *(méidiyà zhōngxīn)*, 11B Fuxing Lu. Room rates are Y650 to Y1300. Three stars.

The 1.5 Millionth Guest

Passing the Beijing Hotel we noticed that there was a huge sign (in English and Chinese) over the entrance saying 'The Beijing Hotel Welcomes its 1.5 Millionth Visitor!' The staff, dressed in neat uniforms, were all waiting in the freezing cold. The steps were covered in red carpet and there were plants and flowers everywhere. About 20 photographers were waiting to record this event. We speculated as to who would be the lucky guest and concluded that whoever it was, he or she was unlikely to be the 1.5 millionth visitor who casually entered the swinging doors and asked to register.

Our theory was confirmed when a large black limousine came up, stopped and had the door opened by a porter. The cameras started clicking and out stepped the most ragged peasant we saw in all of Beijing. He was warmly welcomed into the hotel and brought through the swinging doors. Without further delay – after the disappearance of the camera crews – the lucky 'guest' reappeared through the swinging doors and disappeared back into the black limo, presumably never to see the Beijing Hotel again. Within minutes the carpet and flowers disappeared into the back of a van. I'd love to have known how this obviously staged event was reported in the press.

Brian Malone

Minzu Hotel (☎ 601-4466; fax 601-4849) *(mínzú fàndiàn),* 51
Fuxingmennei Dajie, 100046 (west of CAAC and Xidan).
Standard Y700, superior Y1230. Three stars.

Olympic Hotel (☎ 831-6688; fax 831-8390) *(aòlínpīkè fàndiàn),* 52
Baishiqiao Lu, Haidian District, 100081. Doubles cost
Y680, suites are Y1360. Three stars.

Tiantan Hotel (☎ 701-2277; fax 701-6833) *(tiāntán fàndiàn),* 1
Tiyuguan Lu, Chongwen District (east of Tiantan Park).
Standard/deluxe rooms cost Y655/697. Three stars.

Xinqiao Hotel (☎ 513-3366) *(xīnqiáo fàndiàn),* 2 Dong Jiaomin
Xiang. Rates are Y640 to Y950. Three stars.

Xinxing Hotel (☎ 851-6688) *(xīnxīng bīnguǎn),* 17 Xisanhuan
Zhonglu, 100036. Standard double rooms are Y482.

Yanjing Hotel (☎ 853-6688) *(yānjīng fàndiàn),* 19 Fuxingmenwai
Dajie (west Beijing). Standard/deluxe rooms cost
Y560/947. Three stars.

Yongan Hotel (☎ 501-1188) *(yǒngān bīnguǎn),* 5A Non-
gzhanguan Beilu, 100026. Doubles begin at Y747.

Yuexiu Hotel (☎ 301-4499; fax 301-4609) *(yuèxiù dà fàndiàn),* 24
Dong Dajie, Xuanwumen, 100051. Rates are Y420 and
Y550. Three stars.

Zhumulangma Hotel (☎ 401-8822) *(zhūmùlǎngmǎ bīnguǎn),* 149
Gulou Xi Dajie, 100009. Rates begin at Y540.

PLACES TO STAY – TOP END

The vast majority of hotels in Beijing which accept foreigners are top-end hotels. It's worth noting that while
many government-run tourist hotels rate themselves as
four-star and five-star (with prices to match), service is
often not up to international standards. A good example
of this is the State-owned Beijing Hotel, which continues
to 'win awards'.

A personal favourite of ours is the Holiday Inn Lido.
It's only rated four stars, but in many ways comes out
ahead of its five-star competitors.

The line-up of Beijing's top-end accommodation
includes the following:

Beijing (Map 1)

China Resources Hotel (☎ 501-2233) *(huárùn fàndiàn),* 35 Jianguo
Lu, Chaoyang District, 100025. Rooms cost from Y910 to
Y6640. Four stars.

Continental Grand Hotel (☎ 491-5588; fax 491-0106) *(wǔzhōu dà
jiǔdiàn),* 8 Beichen Donglu, Beisihuan Zhonglu,
Andingmenwai, 100101 (in the National Olympic Sports
Centre). Standard rooms are Y830, superior Y1660 and
suites Y2490. Four stars.

Grace Hotel (☎ 436-2288; fax 436-1818) *(xīn wànshòu bīnguǎn),*
8 Jiangtai Xilu, Chaoyang District, 100016. Twins cost
Y1080. Four stars.

Holiday Inn Lido (☎ 437-6688) (*lìdū jiàrì fàndiàn*), Jichang Lu, Jiangtai Lu, 100037 (on the road to the airport). Rooms cost Y1000 to Y1660. Officially only four stars, but perhaps the best hotel in Beijing!

Jianguomenwai & Sanlitun Area (Map 21)

Beijing Asia Hotel (☎ 500-7788; fax 500-8091) (*běijīng yàzhōu dà jiǔdiàn*), 8 Xinzhong Xijie, Gongren Tiyuchang Beilu, 100027. Double rooms cost Y860, suites Y1380. Three stars.

Beijing Toronto Hotel (☎ 500-2266; fax 500-2022) (*jīnglún fàndiàn*), 3 Jianguomenwai Dajie, 100020. Room rates are Y1245 to Y1910. Four stars.

Chains City Hotel (☎ 500-7799; fax 500-7668) (*chéngshì bīnguǎn*), 4 Gongren Tiyuchang Donglu, Chaoyang District, 100027. Standard Y860, superior Y1035. Three stars.

China World Hotel (☎ 505-2266; fax 505-3167) (*zhōngguó dà fàndiàn*), 1 Jianguomenwai Dajie, 100004 (inside China World Trade Centre). Prices are Y2240 to Y3530. Five stars.

CVIK Hotel (☎ 512-3388; fax 512-3542) (*sàitè fàndiàn*), 22 Jianguomenwai Dajie (across from Friendship Store). With 341 rooms, prices range from Y1037 to Y1825. Four stars.

Gloria Plaza Hotel (☎ 515-8855; fax 515-8533) (*kǎilái dà jiǔdiàn*), 2 Jianguomennan Dajie, 100022. Rooms cost from Y1160 up to Y9960. Four stars.

Great Wall Sheraton (☎ 500-5566; fax 500-3398) (*chángchéng fàndiàn*), Dongsanhuan Beilu, 100026. Rooms cost Y1870 to Y2280. Five stars.

Hilton Hotel (☎ 466-2288; fax 465-3052) (*xīěrdùn fàndiàn*), 1 Dongfang Lu, Dongsanhuan Beilu, 100027. Room prices are Y1900 to Y2740. Five stars.

Jianguo Hotel (☎ 500-2233; fax 500-2871) (*jiànguó fàndiàn*), 5 Jianguomenwai Dajie, 100020. Superior rooms are Y1160 and deluxe twins cost Y2325. Four stars.

Jingguang New World Hotel (☎ 501-8888; fax 501-3333) (*jīngguǎng xīn shìjiè fàndiàn*), Hujialou, Chaoyang District, 100020. Rates are Y1410 to Y3490. Five stars.

Kempinski Hotel (☎ 465-3388) (*kǎibīnsījī fàndiàn*), Lufthansa Centre, 50 Liangmaqiao Lu, 100016. Room rates are Y1820 to Y2400. Five stars.

Kunlun Hotel (☎ 500-3388; fax 500-3228) (*kūnlún fàndiàn*), 2 Xinyuan Nanlu, Chaoyang District, 100004. Doubles cost Y1245 to Y1495. Five stars.

New Otani (☎ 512-5555; fax 512-5346) (*chángfù gōng*), 26 Jianguomenwai Dajie, 100022. Doubles are Y1660 to Y1825, suites are Y2490 to Y5400. Five stars.

Poly Plaza (☎ 500-1188) (*bǎolì dàshà*), 14 Dongzhimen Nan Dajie. Rooms cost Y1044 to Y1500. Three stars.

SAS Royal Hotel (☎ 466-3388) (*huángjiā dà fàndiàn*), 6A Beisanhuan Donglu, 100028. Standard/suite rooms cost Y1330/2075. Four stars.

Swissôtel (☎ 501-2288; fax 501-2501) – see the map key for the Hong Kong-Macau Centre *(běijīng gǎng'aò zhōngxīn)* which it's also called, on the corner of Gongren Tiyuchang Beilu & Chaoyangmen Bei Dajie. Doubles are priced from Y1494 to Y1992. Five stars.

Traders Hotel (☎ 505-2277) *(guómào fàndiàn)*, China World Trade Centre, 1 Jianguomenwai Dajie. Rooms cost Y1495 to Y2075, but business discounts negotiable. Four stars.

Yuyang Hotel (☎ 466-9988; fax 466-6638) *(yúyáng fàndiàn)*, 18 Zhong Jie, Xinyuan Xili, Chaoyang District, 100027. Rooms are priced from Y996 to Y1826.

Zhaolong Hotel (☎ 500-2299; fax 500-3319) *(zhàolóng bīnguǎn)*, Dongsanhuan Beilu & Gongren Tiyuchang Beilu (east Beijing on the third ring road). Doubles cost Y1180. Four stars.

Wangfujing Area (Map 22)

Beijing Hotel (☎ 513-7766; fax 513-7307) *(běijīng fàndiàn)*, 33 Dongchang'an Jie, 100004. Rooms go for Y1330 to Y2650.

Guangdong Regency Hotel (☎ 513-6666; fax 513-4248) *(yuèhǎi huángdū jiǔdiàn)*, 2 Wangfujing Dajie, 100006. Standard/ suite rooms cost Y1162/2490. Four stars.

Holiday Inn Crowne Plaza (☎ 513-3388; fax 513-2513) *(guójì yìyuàn huángguān jiàrì fàndiàn)*, 48 Wangfujing Dajie, Dengshixikou, 100006. Rooms cost Y1245, Y1910 and Y2075. Five stars.

Jinlang Hotel (☎ 513-2288; fax 512-5839) *(jīnláng dà jiǔdiàn)*, 75 Chongwenmennei Dajie, Dongcheng District. Doubles cost Y870, suites are Y1500. Three stars.

Novotel Hotel (☎ 513-8822; fax 513-9088) *(sōnghè dà jiǔdiàn)*, 88 Dengshikou Jie, Dongcheng District, 100006 (north part of Wangfujing). Rooms are priced from Y913 to Y1411. Three stars.

Palace Hotel (☎ 512-8899; fax 512-9050) *(wángfǔ fàndiàn)*, 8 Jinyu Hutong, Dongdanbei Dajie, 100006. Doubles cost Y2158 to Y3154, suites up to Y18,260. Five stars.

Taiwan Hotel (☎ 861-2682; fax 866-3850) *(táiwān fàndiàn)*, 5 Jinyu Hutong, Wangfujing. Rates are Y978 to Y1564. Three stars.

Tianlun Dynasty Hotel (☎ 513-8888; fax 513-7866) *(tiānlún wángcháo fàndiàn)*, 50 Wangfujing Dajie. Standard/suite rooms are Y1180/1800. Four stars.

Central Beijing (Map 23)

Capital Hotel (☎ 512-9988; fax 512-0323) *(shǒudū bīnguǎn)*, 3 Qianmendong Dajie, 100006. Doubles are Y1350 to Y2494. Four stars.

Debao Hotel (☎ 831-8866; fax 833-4205) *(débǎo fàndiàn)*, Building 22, Debao Xinyuan, Xicheng District, 100044 (east side of the zoo). Standard/suite rates are Y1080/1950.

Exhibition Centre Hotel (☎ 831-6633) *(zhǎnlǎn guǎn bīnguǎn)*, 135 Xizhimenwai Dajie, 100044. Standard doubles cost Y650. Three stars.

Friendship Hotel (☎ 849-8888; fax 849-8866) *(yǒuyí bīnguǎn)*, 3 Baishiqiao Lu, 100873 (at third ring road). Standard rooms cost Y921 to Y1322. Two to four stars.

Grand Hotel Beijing (☎ 513-7788) *(běijīng guìbīnlóu fàndiàn)*, 35 Dongchang'an Jie, 100006. Standard/suite rooms cost Y2160/3320. Five stars. Don't confuse this with the other Grand Hotel.

Grand View Garden Hotel (☎ 326-8899) *(dàguānyuán jiǔdiàn)*, 88 Nanciyuan, Xuanwu District, 100054. All rooms cost Y1000. Four stars.

Mandarin Hotel (☎ 831-9988; fax 831-2136) *(xīndàdū fàndiàn)*, 21 Chegongzhuang Lu, 100044 (south of the Beijing Zoo). Standard rooms cost Y830, suites are Y1395. Four stars.

New Century Hotel (☎ 849-2001; fax 831-9183) *(xīn shìjì fàndiàn)*, 6 Shoudu Tiyuguan Nanlu, 100046 (south-west of Beijing Zoo). Room rates are Y1411 to Y2158. Five stars.

Shangri-La Hotel (☎ 841-2211; fax 841-8002) *(xiānggé lǐlā fàndiàn)*, 29 Zhizhuyuan Lu, Haidian District. Rates are Y1660 to Y3320. Five stars.

Xiyuan Hotel (☎ 831-3388; fax 831-4577) *(xīyuàn fàndiàn)*, 1 Sanlihe Lu (immediately south of the Beijing Zoo). Rates are from Y900 to Y1200. Four stars.

Yanshan Hotel (☎ 256-3388; fax 256-8640) *(yānshān dà jiǔdiàn)*, 138A Haidian Lu, Haidian District, 100086. Standard/ suite rooms are Y850/1245. Three stars.

Zhongyuan Hotel (☎ 831-8888; fax 831-9887) *(zhōngyuàn bīnguǎn)*, 18 Xie Jie, Gaoliangqiao, Xizhimenwai (north-west of the Xizhimen railway station). Rates are Y747 to Y871. Four stars.

Airport

Last but not least, out at the airport is the *Mövenpick Hotel* (☎ 456-5588; fax 456-5678) *(guódū dà fàndiàn)*. Doubles start at Y954, and the hotel has a four-star rating.

LONG TERM

For those planning to live, work or study long-term in Beijing, the good news is that the standard of accommodation has been steadily improving. Years ago, foreigners had little choice but to live in luxury hotels. The bad news is that China's housing market is anything but free. Lots of regulations govern just where, when and how a foreigner can live.

The two basic rules are this: government policy is to keep Chinese and foreigners separated, and foreigners are expected to pay the earth for apartments. If you harbour dreams of living with a Chinese family as a paying guest in their dirt-cheap flat, you can stop dreaming, because it's impossible. The PSB will eventually find out, you'll be kicked out and your host family will face the consequences. Ditto for finding a quaint Chinese farmhouse in the suburbs.

If you are coming to study, your school will almost certainly have some sort of dormitory. If you teach or work for the government, your housing will probably be provided for free or at the Chinese price (next to nothing).

Housing costs really begin to escalate when you go to work for a foreign company or embassy, or if you want to set up your own office. In fact, it's not unusual for foreigners to live in their offices because maintaining two addresses is prohibitively expensive. Beijing's apartment blocks are almost entirely government-owned, and the lack of a free market means you don't just browse through the Chinese newspapers looking at the classified ads because there aren't any.

Most foreigners are exiled to special high-priced compounds. You will find some occasional ads in the *China Daily* or *Business Beijing* for luxury flats and villas. Foreigners' apartments tend to be in big residential and office towers along Jianguomenwai and the Sanlitun area in north-east Beijing – examples would include the Capital Mansion, the Landmark Towers or the China World Trade Centre. The villas are also found in north or north-east Beijing, around such places as the National Olympic Sports Centre and the airport. Flats rent for about US$70 to US$85 per sq metre, which typically works out to be US$5000 per month for an average-sized apartment. Villas cost about double this rate.

If you're ready to make Beijing your permanent home, you can purchase a flat or villa. Bottom-end flats begin at around US$1700 per sq metre, but double this price is not unusual. At least in theory, purchasing a flat or villa gains you a permanent residence visa, though given China's ever-changing regulations and disregard for the law, you shouldn't bet your life on it.

Places to Eat

CHINESE FOOD

Eating out in the capital is a true adventure, one that should be seized with both chopsticks.

The northern capital has always been supplied with an abundance of produce from the rest of China, and this is reflected in the spectrum of restaurants on offer. From quick snacks at a street stall to a 12-course (or larger) imperial banquet, you're not going to be stuck for variety. You could also spend months working through all Beijing's different variants of Chinese regional cooking.

However prices are escalating rapidly. The days are gone when a budget traveller could afford to visit an upmarket restaurant and rub elbows with Beijing's bloated cadres. On the other hand, even upmarket hotels often charge very reasonable prices for breakfast and sometimes for lunch too, though dinner can be pricey. There is a surprisingly wide range of restaurants in the major hotels too.

Northern Cuisine

Despite the relatively small variety of produce which can be grown in the north, Beijing has still developed its own distinctive cuisine, centred on the cold northlands of China. Since this is the country's wheat belt, steamed breads, dumplings and noodles figure more prominently than rice. The other local grain, millet, supplies Beijingers with a hearty winter gruel, usually eaten with beef and pickles, and is very filling.

Beef, chicken and of course duck are the most common meats. There are relatively few local vegetables, cabbages being the main exception. Others are tomatoes, shallots and leeks.

In general, Beijingers like their food relatively bland and less spicy than elsewhere in China. However, you'll find a wide variety of pickled side-dishes to go with your noodles.

One of the most common ways of preparing food in the north is by the *bào* ('explode-frying') method. Food is deep-fried (with a loud noise) in smoking-hot peanut oil for only about 60 seconds, to seal in the nutrients and flavours.

GLENN BEANLAND

GLENN BEANLAND

GLENN BEANLAND

Top & Middle: Two of the main north China specialities –
Beijing Duck and Mongolian Hotpot.
Bottom: Sharkfin soup is becoming an expensive rarity.

Representative dishes in a Beijing-style restaurant might include cold spiced pork as an appetiser, then a choice of at least a dozen chicken recipes. Among these look for beggar's chicken (*qǐgàijī*), supposedly created by a beggar who stole the emperor's chicken and had to bury it in the ground to cook it. The dish is wrapped in lotus leaves and baked all day in hot ashes. Other typical dishes to keep an eye out for are:

Jiaozi The standard budget fare, dumplings (or *jiǎozi*), can be steamed, boiled or fried. They're normally prepared in small bamboo steamers, stacked on top of each other, and sold on street stalls. Buy them by the *jin* – half a jin is plenty for one person. Smaller alternatives are *bǎozi* and *shāomai*. Spring rolls (*chūn juǎn*) are common and come with a variety of fresh fillings.

Beijing Duck This is the one thing you're most likely to want to try in Beijing. It is made on the same principle as that other great delicacy, paté de foie gras, namely by force-feeding ducks. By the time they get to your table, the birds have been plucked, blown up like a balloon (to separate the skin from the flesh), basted in honey and vinegar, wind-dried and grilled. In the restaurants, the duck is served in stages. First come boneless meat and crispy skin with a side dish of shallots, plum sauce or sweet flour paste, and crepes. This is then followed by duck soup made of bones and all the other parts except the quack.

Mongolian Hotpot Mongolian hotpot, which is nothing like a slow-cooked casserole hotpot in the Western sense, was originally prepared in the helmets and shields of Mongol warriors. It's basically a winter dish – a brass pot with charcoal inside, placed at the centre of the table. You cook thick strips of mutton and vegetables yourself, fondue fashion, in the chafing-dish on top, spicing as you like.

Muslim Barbecue Uighurs from China's Xinjiang Province add Muslim cuisine to Beijing's multi-ethnic menu. A standard Uighur meal consists of flatbread (*náng*) consumed with sweet Uighur tea (*sānpào tái* or *bābǎo chá*), some vegetable dishes, noodles (*miàn*) and kebabs (*ròuchuàn*).

Imperial Food Imperial food (*gōngtíng cài* or *mǎnhàn dàcān*) is cuisine fit for an emperor and will clean your wallet out very fast. In 1982 a group of Beijing chefs set about reviving the imperial pastry recipes, and even went so far as to find the last emperor's brother to try their products out on.

Cantonese Cuisine

This is southern Chinese cooking, the pride of Hong Kong and Guangzhou. A favourite is *dim sum*, a snack-like variation served for breakfast and lunch (but never dinner). It consists of all sorts of little delicacies served from pushcarts wheeled around the restaurant. It's justifiably famous and highly addictive stuff.

Cantonese dinners are somewhat less attractive to Western palates. The Cantonese are said to eat anything with four legs but the table – specialities are abalone, dried squid, 1000-year eggs (traditionally made by soaking eggs in horses' urine), shark's fin soup, snake soup and dog stew. Other culinary exotica include ant-eaters, pangolins (a sort of armadillo), cats, rats, owls, monkeys, turtles and frogs.

Chaozhou Cuisine

This is similar to Cantonese food, though the emphasis is less on dim sum and more on seafood. Specialities are abalone, shark's fin soup, roast pig and a snake dish known as 'Dragon's Duel Tiger' which is a combination of wild cat and snake meat. The Chinese do interesting things with edible fungi (more politely called 'truffles') of which there are numerous species with different tastes.

Hunan Cuisine

This style of cooking is similar to Sichuan cuisine, but also borrows the Cantonese concept of making anything palatable. If the French can do it with frogs, why not the Chinese with dogs? Anyone for hot dog? Hunan menus typically include onion dog, dog soup (reputed to be an aphrodisiac) and dog stew. For those with canine sensi-bilities, perhaps a switch to Hunan-style duck spiced with hot pepper, or some seafood, and several styles of noodles would be preferable.

Sichuan Cuisine

Sichuan food is China's spiciest cuisine – we are talking about chillies that can do damage. Some tourists liken it to tear gas, but most foreigners conclude that it's great stuff. One speciality is smoked duck which is cooked in peppercorns, marinated in wine for 24 hours, covered in tea leaves and cooked again over a charcoal fire. Other dishes to try are frogs' legs, shrimps with salt and garlic, dried chilli beef, bean curd with chilli, fish in spicy bean sauce and eggplants in garlic.

Useful Terms

restaurant
cāntīng 餐厅
menu
cài dān 菜单
bill (cheque)
zhàng dān 帐单
set meal (no menu)
tàocān 套餐
to eat/let's eat
chī fàn 吃饭
chopsticks
kuàizi 筷子
knife and fork
dāochā 刀叉
spoon
tiáogēng 调羹
I'm vegetarian.
Wǒ chī sù. 我吃素
vegetarian dishes
shūcài lèi 蔬菜类
Have you got any...?
Nǐ yǒu méiyǒu...? 你有没有...?
Please bring me one order of...
Qǐng nǐ chǎo yīpán...gěi wǒ. 请你炒一盘...给我
How much does this dish cost?
Zhèzhǒng cài duōshǎo qián? 这种菜多少钱?
What's the total cost for everything?
Yígòng duōshǎo qián? 一共多少钱?
Do you have any of the dishes on this list?
Càidān lǐmiàn yǒu méiyǒu zhèzhǒng cài?
菜单里面有没有这种菜?
That was very tasty.
Hěn hǎo chī. 很好吃

Rice & Bread

steamed rice
mǐfàn 米饭
rice noodles
mǐfěn 米粉
fried rice (assorted)
shíjǐn chǎofàn 什锦炒饭
fried rice Cantonese-style
guǎngzhōu chǎofàn 广州炒饭
Western-style bread
miànbāo 面包

fried roll
   yínsī juǎn 银丝卷
steamed buns
   mántóu 馒头
steamed meat buns
   bāozi 包子
fried bread stick
   yóutiáo 油条
dumplings
   jiǎozi 饺子
prawn cracker
   lóngxiā piàn 龙虾片

Vegetable Dishes
fried rice with vegetables
   shūcài chǎofàn 蔬菜炒饭
fried noodles with vegetables
   shūcài chǎomiàn 蔬菜炒面
spicy peanuts
   wǔxiāng huāshēng mǐ 五香花生米
fried peanuts
   yóuzhà huāshēng mǐ 油炸花生米
spiced cold vegetables
   liángbàn shíjǐn 凉拌什锦
Chinese salad
   jiācháng liángcài 家常凉菜
bean curd
   dòufǔ 豆腐
beansprouts
   dòuyá 豆芽
fried rape with mushrooms
   dōnggū pácài dǎn 冬菇扒菜胆
fried bean curd in oyster sauce
   háoyóu dòufǔ 蚝油豆腐
spicy hot bean curd
   mápó dòufǔ 麻婆豆腐
bean curd casserole
   shāguō dòufǔ 沙锅豆腐
bean curd & mushrooms
   mógū dòufǔ 磨菇豆腐
fried garlic
   sù chǎo dàsuàn 素炒大蒜
fried eggplant
   sùshāo qiézi 素烧茄子
fried beansprouts
   sù chǎo dòuyá 素炒豆芽
fried green vegetables
   sù chǎo qīngcài 素炒青菜
fried green beans
   sù chǎo biǎndòu 素炒扁豆
fried cauliflower & tomato
   chǎo fānqié càihuā 炒蕃茄菜花

broiled mushroom
 sù chǎo xiānme 素炒鲜蘑
black fungus & mushroom
 mù'ěr huákǒu mó 木耳滑口磨
assorted hors d'oeuvre
 shíjǐn pīnpán 什锦拼盘
assorted vegetarian food
 sù shíjǐn 素什锦

Egg Dishes
preserved egg
 sōnghuā dàn 松花蛋
fried rice with egg
 jīdàn chǎofàn 鸡蛋炒饭
fried tomatoes & eggs
 xīhóngshì chǎo jīdàn 西红柿炒鸡蛋
egg & flour omelette
 jiān bǐng 煎饼

Beef Dishes
fried rice with beef
 niúròusī chǎofàn 牛肉丝炒饭
noodles with beef (soupy)
 niúròu tāng miàn 牛肉汤面
spiced noodles with beef
 niúròu gān miàn 牛肉干面
fried noodles with beef
 niúròu chǎomiàn 牛肉炒面
beef with white rice
 niúròu fàn 牛肉饭
beef platter
 niúròu tiěbǎn 牛肉铁板
beef with oyster sauce
 háoyóu niúròu 蚝油牛肉
beef braised in soy sauce
 hóngshāo niúròu 红烧牛肉
beef with tomatoes
 fānqié niúròu piàn 蕃茄牛肉片
beef with green peppers
 qīngjiāo niúròu piàn 青椒牛肉片
beef curry & rice
 gālí niúròu fàn 咖哩牛肉饭
beef curry & noodles
 gālí niúròu miàn 咖哩牛肉面

Chicken Dishes
fried rice with chicken
 jīsī chǎofàn 鸡丝炒饭
noodles with chicken (soupy)
 jīsī tāng miàn 鸡丝汤面

fried noodles with chicken
  jīsī chǎomiàn 鸡丝炒面
chicken leg with white rice
  jītuǐ fàn 鸡腿饭
spicy hot chicken & peanuts
  gōngbào jīdīng 宫爆鸡丁
fruit kernel with chicken
  guǒwèi jīdīng 果味鸡丁
sweet & sour chicken
  tángcù jīdīng 糖醋鸡丁
sauteed spicy chicken pieces
  làzi jīdīng 辣子鸡丁
sauteed chicken with green peppers
  jiàngbào jīdīng 酱爆鸡丁
chicken slices & tomato sauce
  fānqié jīdīng 蕃茄鸡丁
mushrooms & chicken
  cǎomó jīdīng 草磨鸡丁
chicken pieces in oyster sauce
  háoyóu jīdīng 蚝油鸡丁
chicken braised in soy sauce
  hóngshāo jīkuài 红烧鸡块
sauteed chicken with water chestnuts
  nánjiè jīpiàn 南芥鸡片
sliced chicken with crispy rice
  jīpiàn guōbā 鸡片锅巴
chicken curry
  gālī jīròu 咖哩鸡肉
chicken curry & rice
  gālī jīròu fàn 咖哩鸡肉饭
chicken curry & noodles
  gālī jīròu miàn 咖哩鸡肉面

Duck Dishes
Beijing Duck
  běijīng kǎoyā 北京烤鸭
duck with white rice
  yāròu fàn 鸭肉饭
duck with noodles
  yāròu miàn 鸭肉面
duck with fried noodles
  yāròu chǎomiàn 鸭肉炒面

Pork Dishes
pork chop with white rice
  páigǔ fàn 排骨饭
fried rice with pork
  ròusī chǎofàn 肉丝炒饭
fried noodles with pork
  ròusī chǎomiàn 肉丝炒面
noodles, pork & mustard greens
  zhàcài ròusī miàn 榨菜肉丝面

pork with crispy rice
    ròupiàn guōbā 肉片锅巴
sweet & sour pork fillet
    tángcù lǐjī 糖醋里肌
pork fillet with white sauce
    huáliū lǐjī 滑溜里肌
shredded pork fillet
    chǎo lǐjī sī 炒里肌丝
spicy hot pork pieces
    gōngbào ròudīng 宫爆肉丁
sauteed diced pork & soy sauce
    jiàngbào ròudīng 酱爆肉丁
pork cubelets & cucumber
    huángguā ròudīng 黄瓜肉丁
sauteed shredded pork
    qīngchǎo ròusī 青炒肉丝
shredded pork & hot sauce
    yúxiāng ròusī 鱼香肉丝
shredded pork & green peppers
    qīngjiāo ròusī 青椒肉丝
shredded pork & bamboo shoots
    dōngsǔn ròusī 冬笋肉丝
pork with oyster sauce
    háoyóu ròusī 蚝油肉丝
boiled pork slices
    shuǐzhǔ ròupiàn 水煮肉片
pork, eggs & black fungus
    mùxū ròu 木须肉
pork & fried onions
    yángcōng chǎo ròupiàn 洋葱炒肉片

Seafood Dishes
fried rice with shrimp
    xiārén chǎofàn 虾仁炒饭
fried noodles with shrimp
    xiārén chǎomiàn 虾仁炒面
diced shrimp with peanuts
    gōngbào xiārén 宫爆虾仁
sauteed shrimp
    qīngchǎo xiārén 清炒虾仁
deep-fried shrimp
    zhà xiārén 炸虾仁
fried shrimp with mushroom
    xiānmó xiārén 鲜蘑虾仁
squid with crispy rice
    yóuyú guōbā 鱿鱼锅巴
sweet & sour squid roll
    suānlà yóuyú juàn 酸辣鱿鱼卷
fish braised in soy sauce
    hóngshāo yú 红烧鱼
braised sea cucumber
    hóngshāo hǎishēn 红烧海参

clams
  gé 蛤
crab
  pángxiè 螃蟹
lobster
  lóngxiā 龙虾

Soup
three kinds seafood soup
  sān xiān tāng 三鲜汤
squid soup
  yóuyú tāng 鱿鱼汤
hot & sour soup
  suānlà tāng 酸辣汤
tomato & egg soup
  xīhóngshì dàn tāng 西红柿蛋汤
corn & egg thick soup
  fènghuáng lìmǐ gēng 凤凰栗米羹
egg & vegetable soup
  dànhuā tāng 蛋花汤
mushroom & egg soup
  mógu dànhuā tāng 蘑菇蛋花汤
fresh fish soup
  shēng yú tāng 生鱼汤
vegetable soup
  shūcài tāng 蔬菜汤
cream of tomato soup
  nǎiyóu fānqié tāng 奶油蕃茄汤
cream of mushroom soup
  nǎiyóu xiānmó tāng 奶油鲜蘑汤
pickled mustard green soup
  zhàcài tāng 榨菜汤
bean curd & vegetable soup
  dòufu cài tāng 豆腐菜汤
wonton soup
  húndùn tāng 馄饨汤
clear soup
  qīng tāng 清汤

Weird Stuff
goat, mutton
  yáng ròu 羊肉
dog meat
  gǒu ròu 狗肉
deer meat (venison)
  lùròu 鹿肉
snake
  shé ròu 蛇肉
frog
  qīngwā 青蛙
eel
  shàn yú 鳝鱼

turtle
   hǎiguī   海龟

Condiments
garlic
   dàsuàn   大蒜
black pepper
   hújiāo   胡椒
hot pepper
   làjiāo   辣椒
hot sauce
   làjiāo jiàng   辣椒酱
ketchup
   fānqié jiàng   蕃茄酱
salt
   yán   盐
MSG
   wèijīng   味精
soy sauce
   jiàng yóu   酱油
vinegar
   cù   醋
sesame seed oil
   zhīmá yóu   芝麻油
butter
   huáng yóu   黄油
sugar
   táng   糖
jam
   guǒ jiàng   果酱
honey
   fēngmì   蜂蜜

DRINKS

Non-alcoholic Drinks

Tea is the most commonly served brew in Beijing; it didn't originate in China but in South-East Asia. Indian tea is not generally available in restaurants, but if you need the stuff, large supermarkets stock Lipton and Twinings. Coffee addicts will find a plentiful supply of Maxwell House and Nescafé in all the shops, but seldom in restaurants.

Coca-Cola, first introduced into China by American soldiers in 1927, is now produced in Beijing. Fanta and Sprite are widely available, both genuine and copycat versions. Sugary Chinese soft drinks are cheap and sold everywhere – some are so sweet they'll turn your teeth inside out. Jianlibao is a Chinese soft drink made with honey rather than sugar, and is one of the better brands. Lychee-flavoured carbonated drinks are unique to China and get rave reviews from foreigners. Fresh milk is rare but you can buy imported UHT milk at high prices from Western-style supermarkets.

A surprising treat is fresh sweet yoghurt, available from street stalls and shops everywhere. It's usually sold in what look like small milk bottles and is consumed by drinking with a straw rather than eating with a spoon. This excellent stuff would make a great breakfast if you could find some decent bread to go with it.

Alcoholic Drinks

If tea is the most popular drink in Beijing then beer must be number two. By any standards the top brands are great stuff. The best known is Tsingtao, made with a mineral water which gives it its sparkling quality. It's really a German beer since the town of Qingdao (formerly spelled 'Tsingtao') where it's made was once a German Concession and the Chinese inherited the brewery. Experts in these matters claim that draft Tsingtao tastes much better than the bottled stuff.

Beijing has a number of local brews – the best is reputed to be Yanjing. Another brand, simply called Beijing Beer, tastes much like coloured water. San Miguel is brewed in Canton and is available from some shops in Beijing. Real Western imports are sold in the Friendship Store and five-star hotels at five-star prices.

China has probably cultivated vines and produced wine for over 4000 years, but Westerners give them mixed reviews. The word 'wine' gets rather loosely translated; many Chinese 'wines' are in fact spirits. Rice wine – a favourite with Chinese alcoholics due to its low price – is intended mainly for cooking rather than drinking. *Hejie jiu* (lizard wine) is produced in the southern province of Guangxi; each bottle contains one dead lizard suspended perpendicularly in the clear liquid. Wine with dead bees or pickled snakes is also desirable for its alleged tonic (or aphrodisiac) properties. In general, the more poisonous the creature, the more potent are the alleged tonic effects.

Maotai, a favourite of the Chinese, is a spirit made from sorghum (a type of millet) and is used for toasts at banquets. It tastes rather like rubbing alcohol and makes a good substitute for petrol or paint thinner.

Chinese women don't drink (except beer) in public; women who hit the booze are regarded as prostitutes. However, Western women can easily violate this social

Drinks Vocabulary

fizzy drink (soda)
  qìshuǐ 汽水
Coca-Cola
  kěkǒu kělè 可口可乐
tea
  chá 茶
coffee
  kāfēi 咖啡
coffee creamer
  nǎijīng 奶精
water
  kāi shuǐ 开水
mineral water
  kuàng quán shuǐ 矿泉水
beer
  píjiǔ 啤酒
vodka
  fútèjiā jiǔ 伏特加酒
whisky
  wēishìjì jiǔ 威士忌酒
Maotai spirit
  Máotái jiǔ 矛台酒
red grape wine
  hóng pútáo jiǔ 红葡萄酒
white grape wine
  bái pútáo jiǔ 白葡萄酒
rice wine
  mǐ jiǔ 米酒
milk
  niúnǎi 牛奶
soybean milk
  dòujiāng 豆浆
yoghurt
  suānnǎi 酸奶
fruit juice
  guǒzhī 果汁
orange juice
  liǔchéng zhī 柳橙汁
coconut juice
  yézi zhī 椰子汁
pineapple juice
  bōluó zhī 波萝汁
mango juice
  mángguǒ zhī 芒果汁
hot
  rède 热的
ice cold
  bīngde 冰的
ice cube
  bīng kuài 冰块

taboo without unpleasant consequences, since the Chinese expect weirdness from Westerners anyway. As a rule Chinese men are not big drinkers, but toasts are obligatory at banquets. If you really can't drink, fill your wine glass with tea and say you have a bad stomach. In spite of all the toasting and beer drinking, public drunkenness is strongly frowned upon.

Imported alcohol – like XO, Johnny Walker, Kahlua, Napoleon Augier Cognac, etc – is highly prized by the Chinese for its prestige value rather than exquisite taste. The snob appeal plus steep import taxes translates into absurdly high prices, so don't walk into a hotel bar and order this stuff unless you've brought a wheelbarrow full of cash. If you can't live without Western spirits, take advantage of your two-litre duty-free allowance on entry to China.

RESTAURANTS

Although in 1949 Beijing had an incredible 10,000 snack bars and restaurants, by 1976 that number had dwindled to less than 700. Restaurants, a nasty bourgeois concept, were all to have been phased out and replaced with revolutionary dispensaries dishing out rice. The free-enterprise reforms of the past 15 years have changed all that. An explosion of privately owned eateries has taken place. Gone are the famines and ration cards, and the connections needed to buy a loaf of bread or a bottle of cooking oil. No one is pretending they're all five-star restaurants, but the number of places to eat in Beijing must have exceeded that 10,000 mark by now.

Northern Style
Beijing Duck There are plenty of places which specialise in this.

Otherwise known as the 'Old Duck', the *Qianmen Quanjude Roast Duck Restaurant* (☎ 511-2418) *(qiánmén quànjùdé kǎoyādiàn)* is at 32 Qianmen Dajie, on the east side, near the Qianmen subway station (Map 20). As the nickname implies, this is one of the oldest restaurants in the capital, dating back to 1864. However, it has come right up to date with a fast food section offering duckburgers. Price depends on which section of the restaurant you sit in – salubrious surroundings cost more and the cheap section is very crowded.

The *Bianyifang Duck Restaurant* (☎ 702-0505) *(biàn-yifǎng kǎoyādiàn)* is another famous house at 2 Chongwenmenwai Dajie, by the Hademen Hotel (Map

23). Language is not really a problem; you just have to negotiate half or whole ducks. In the cheap section the locals will show you the correct etiquette, like when to spit on the floor.

Mongolian Hotpot Mongolian hotpot is so good in Beijing that it's hard to believe it can be so bad in Mongolia. Look for the symbol shaped like the hotpot on little foodstalls and restaurants in the hutongs.

Nengren Ju (☎ 601-2560) is appropriately right next to Kublai Khan's creation, the White Dagoba Temple (Map 23). There are also plenty of hotpot places along Dazhalan from Qianmen to the Far East Hotel (Map 20).

In the top-end price category, the New Century Hotel (Map 23) incorporates the *Gold Hot Pot Restaurant* (☎ 849-1303).

Muslim Barbecue Muslim barbecue is dirt cheap if you know the right place to look for it. The right place is the west end of Baiwanzhuangxi Lu, a street in a neighbourhood known as Ganjiakou not far south of the zoo (Map 23). This is where Beijing's Uighur minority congregates. It's often best to eat with a small group (two to four persons) so you can get several dishes and sample everything. Alternatively, you can just drift from stall to stall sampling as you go.

Out in tourist hotel-land this type of cuisine costs considerably more. One place you might try is *Hongbinlou* (☎ 601-4832) *(hóngbīnlóu fànzhuāng)* at 82 Xi Chang'an Jie, just east of Xidan intersection (Map 23).

The *Moslem Restaurant* (☎ 831-3388 ext 5150) in the Xiyuan Hotel (Map 23) can accommodate you and your credit card.

Imperial Food Imperial cuisine is served up in the *Fangshan Restaurant* (☎ 401-1889) in Beihai Park (Map 7). The Summer Palace is home to the *Tingliguan Imperial Restaurant* (☎ 258-2504). There is also an imperial restaurant at Fragrant Hills Park. *Gloria Showcase Restaurant* (☎ 515-8855 ext 333) in the Gloria Plaza Hotel (Map 21) also does imperial cuisine at imperial prices.

Li Family Restaurant (☎ 601-1915) *(lì jiā cài)* is at 11 Yangfang Hutong which runs off Deshengmennei Dajie (Map 23). The setting on the south side of Shisha Houhai Lake is almost as impressive as the food. This place does dinners only and reservations are essential.

Cantonese Style

No self-respecting tourist hotel in Beijing is without a
Cantonese restaurant dishing up dim sum to its Hong
Kong clientele. Remember that dim sum is for breakfast
and lunch only – at night they offer mostly seafood.

For something that's not inside a tourist hotel, you
might try the *Renren Restaurant* (☎ 511-2978) *(rénrén dà
jiǔlóu)* at 18 Qianmen Dong Dajie (Map 20).

The *Hibiscus Restaurant* in the Media Centre Hotel
(Map 23) does a superb and affordable (Y48) Cantonese
buffet, but only on weekends. Operating hours are 11.30
am to 2 pm, and 6 to 10.30 pm. The hotel is at 11B Fuxing
Lu, on the west side of the Military Museum.

Windows on the World (☎ 500-3335) actually dishes up
both Western and Cantonese food. The Western 'execu-
tive lunch' is actually quite a deal at Y55 per person.
You'll find this place on the 28th floor of the CITIC
building on Jianguomenwai (Map 21).

Chaozhou Style

Zuihong Chaozhou Food City (☎ 303-6530) *(zuìhóng
cháozhōu chéng)*, Building 3, Zhengyang Market,
Qianmen Xi Dajie, looks like it was lifted lock, stock and
lobsters straight out of Hong Kong. It's just a little hard
to find, stuck in an alley near Dazhalan (Map 20).

Certainly easier to find but pricier is the *Chaozhou
Seafood Restaurant* (☎ 512-9988 ext 3583) in the Capital
Hotel (Map 23). Ditto for the *Chao Ming Yuan* (☎ 521-8833
ext 6702) in the Peace Hotel (Map 22) and the *Chiu Chow
Garden* (☎ 512-8899 ext 7576) in the Palace Hotel (Map
22).

Out in the western area of town, check out the *Crystal
Palace Chaozhou Restaurant* (☎ 853-1014) *(shuǐjīnggōng
cháozhōu jiǔlóu)*, 15A Nanlishi Lu, Xicheng District (Map
23). The emphasis here is heavily on seafood.

Hunan Style

The *Quyuan* (☎ 606-2316) *(qǔyuán jiǔjiā)* is at 133 Xidan
Beidajie (west side), north of Chang'an, in a red-fronted
building by an overhead bridge (Map 23).

The *Shaoshan Mao's Restaurant* (☎ 421-9340) *(sháoshān
máojiā càiguǎn)*, 4 Hepingli Zhongjie (Map 23), dishes up
revolutionary cooking prepared by the late chairman's
townsfolk. The Hunan food served here is hot and
spicy.

Sichuan Style

The classic place to go is the *Sichuan Restaurant* (☎ 603-3291) *(sìchuān fàndiàn)* at 51 Xi Rongxian Hutong (Map 23). To get there go south from Xidan intersection (where Xidan meets Chang'an), turn left into a hutong marked by traffic lights and a police-box, and continue along the hutong until you find the grey wall entrance. This restaurant is housed in the sumptuous former residence of Yuan Shikai, a general who tried to set himself up as an emperor in 1914.

Emei Restaurant (☎ 852-3069) *(éméi fàndiàn)* is another time-honoured Sichuan eatery. It's at 4 Yuetan Beijie by the entrance to Yuetan Park (Map 23).

GLENN BEANLAND

Sichuan food is famous for its very hot spices.

At the south-west gate of Ritan Park (Map 21) is *Shenxian Douhua Village* (☎ 500-5939) *(shénxiān dòuhuā cūn)*. Another reasonably priced Sichuan restaurant is located on the west side of the Qianmen semi-circle.

Just next to the main building of the Holiday Inn Lido (Map 1) is a charming wooden house where you'll find the *Sichuan Yandianzi Restaurant* (☎ 437-3561 ext 6028). Less charming but still excellent is *Dragon Court* (☎ 701-2277 ext 2102) in the Tiantan Hotel (Map 23). The Great Wall Sheraton Hotel (Map 21) is where you'll find *Yuen Tai Restaurant* (☎ 500-5566 ext 2162). The Beijing Hotel's (Map 22) contribution is *Yiyuan Garden Restaurant* (☎ 513-7766 ext 1383).

Vegetarian

Strict Buddhists eat only vegetarian food on the first and 15th day of each lunar month, though you can find vegetarian food at any time if you know where to look. Oddly, the Buddhist definition of vegetarian food excludes garlic, onions and leeks.

The Yangzhou-style *Gongdelin Vegetarian Restaurant* (☎ 511-2542) *(gōngdélín sùcàiguǎn)*, at 158 Qianmen Nan Dajie (Map 20), is probably the best in the city. It serves up wonderful veggie food with names to match. How about the 'peacock in pride' or 'the fire is singeing the snow-capped mountains'?

The other notable place is *Vegetarians* (☎ 512-6688), located inside the International Hotel (Map 23).

Cheap Eats

If you're looking for cheap eats, the hutongs are so packed with small eateries and foodstalls that it would take a book larger than this one to list them all. Good areas to explore include the Qianmen region at the south end of Tiananmen Square, Wangfujing to the east and all around parklands such as Tiantan, Ritan and Beihai.

Special mention should go to the *Dong'anmen Night Market* which gets going from around 6 to 9 pm daily. All sorts of exotic eats from pushcarts are available, including tiny four-legged beasties roasted on a skewer. The night market is at the northern end of Wangfujing near the Bank of China (Map 22).

Dongdan Fastfood (dōngdān kuài cāntīng) is in fact a traditional but cheap Chinese restaurant strategically situated in the Wangfujing area. It's on the north-west corner at Dongchang'an Jie and Dongdan Bei Dajie (Map 22). The fried chicken is perhaps the most Western thing on the menu.

Along similar lines is the *Dumpling King (jiǎozi dàwáng)* at Wangfujing and Dong'anmen Dajie (northwest corner; Map 22). There is no English sign on the place.

Zoo Food

Even we couldn't make this up. A restaurant inside the Beijing Zoo (Map 23) dishes up deer, pheasants, turtles, monkeys, etc, but thankfully no panda bears. See for yourself at the *Binfengtan Restaurant* (☎ 831-4411 ext 515) *(bīnfēngtáng fànzhuāng)*.

OTHER ASIAN FOOD

Let it not be forgotten that Beijing is the most cosmopolitan city in China. Foreign embassy staff, business people and tourists have carved their own culinary niche.

Indian

The *Shamiana Indian Restaurant* (☎ 832-2288 ext 7107) in the Holiday Inn Downtown (Map 23) is where you can get your chappatis and tandoori chicken. The tariff will run upwards of Y100 per person.

Omar Khayyam (☎ 513-9988 ext 20188) is in the Asia Pacific Building (Map 21) at 8 Yabao Lu, next to the International Post & Telecommunications Office in the Jianguomenwai area. This restaurant also does vegetarian food.

Indonesian

Rasa Sayang (☎ 437-6688 ext 1847) is buried within the cavernous corridors of the Holiday Inn Lido (Map 1).

Japanese

Japanese restaurants seem to be expensive no matter where you go in the world. In keeping with this tradition, you'll find Beijing's Japanese restaurants located in upmarket hotels. Hotels with trendy Japanese restaurants include the Beijing Hotel (Map 22) , Capital Hotel (23), China World Hotel (21), Grace Hotel (1), the Hilton (21), Hong Kong-Macau Centre (21), Kunlun Hotel (21), Media Centre Hotel (23), New Century Hotel (23), the New Otani (21), Palace Hotel (22) and Rainbow Hotel (20).

Korean

On the 2nd floor of the Gloria Plaza Hotel (Map 21) is *The Golden Turtle* (☎ 515-8855 ext 3255). The International Hotel (Map 23) chips in with the *Bobea Won Restaurant* (☎ 512-9844) on the 1st and 3rd floors. The Jingguang New World Hotel (Map 21) has the *Meigetsukan Restaurant* (☎ 501-2032) on the 2nd floor.

Malaysian

The *Asian Star Restaurant* (☎ 591-6716) *(yàzhōu zhīxīng xīnmǎyìn cāntīng)* is a combination eatery. Cuisine on offer includes dishes from Malaysia, Singapore and India, a delight for curry enthusiasts. The restaurant is at 26 Dongsanhuan Beilu (the third ring road).

Thai

Sawasdee (☎ 513-8822 ext 2430) is in the Novotel Hotel (Map 22). The Holiday Inn Lido (Map 1) is the place to go for the *Borom Piman Thai Restaurant* (☎ 437-6688 ext 2899).

Vietnamese

The *Saigon Inn* (☎ 515-8855) is in the Gloria Plaza Hotel (Map 21). *Ma Cherie* (☎ 500-3388 ext 5247) is in the Kunlun Hotel (Map 21).

WESTERN FOOD

All the large tourist hotels serve Western food of varying quality and price. Travellers pining for a croissant or strong coffee will be pleased to know that Beijing is the best place in China to find such delicacies.

Brazilian

With its emphasis on barbecues and salads, Brazilian cuisine has been an instant hit with expats. *Parati Restaurant* (☎ 506-2054), 120 Sanlitun Nanlu, is out in the Sanlitun embassyland (Map 21). It has great ambience and draws a steady stream of expats.

Another favourite is *Churrascaria Beijing-Brasil Restaurant* (☎ 605-6957) *(běijīng bāxī kǎoròu dian)* at 46 Fuxingmennei Dajie.

GLENN BEANLAND

GLENN BEANLAND

Sweet potatoes, nuts and strips of dried fruit paste are common healthy snacks.

GLENN BEANLAND

GLENN BEANLAND

Top: Small restaurant: Chinese eateries pride
themselves on using the freshest ingredients.
Bottom: Food stall, including imported fruit.

French

Maxim's de Paris (☎ 505-4853) *(bālí mǎkèxīmǔ cāntīng)* is not just in Paris – a branch can be found within the precincts of the China World Trade Centre (West Wing; Map 21). Dinner for two – *sacré bleu* – is a cool Y300 or so, excluding that Bordeaux red or the Alsatian Gewürztraminer.

Le Bistrot (☎ 505-2288 ext 6198) is in the same building as Maxim's – perhaps this is Beijing's French Quarter?

German

On the 1st floor of the cavernous Lufthansa Centre (just north of the Great Wall Sheraton; Map 21) is *Paulaner Brauhaus* (☎ 465-3388 ext 5732), an excellent German restaurant. This place brews its own genuine German beer!

It's easy to confuse the foregoing with the *Hof Brauhaus* (☎ 508-1605), 15 Dongsanhuan Beilu, 100 metres south of the Zhaolong Hotel (Map 21). The décor and beer are German, but the food is an unusual German-Cantonese mix. There is also a *Brauhaus* (☎ 505-2266 ext 6565) in the China World Hotel (Map 21).

Italian

The *Metro Cafe* (☎ 501-3377 ext 7706), 6 Gongren Tiyuchang Xilu, is a charming spot across the street on the west side of the Worker's Stadium (Map 21).

The *Royal Inn* (☎ 461-8580), 55 Dongzhimenwai Xiejie (Map 21), does a mean bruchetta and spaghetti napolitana.

If you want to go upmarket, the *Revolving Italian Bar Restaurant* (☎ 500-3388 ext 5507) is on the 29th floor of the Kunlun Hotel (Map 21). You can't beat the food but it's not a place for acrophobiacs.

Mexican

Mexican Wave (☎ 506-3961) is on Dongdaqiao Lu near the intersection with Guanghua Lu (Map 21). Dongdaqiao Lu is the major north-south road on Jianguomenwai between the Friendship Store and the Jianguo Hotel. Mexican Wave serves set lunches (Western not Mexican food) from noon until 2.30 pm; dinners (Mexican style) are from around 6 pm onwards. Most dishes range from Y35 to Y70.

Russian

The *Moscow Restaurant* (☎ 894454) *(mòsīkē cāntīng)* is on the west side of the Soviet-designed Exhibition Centre in the zoo district (Map 23). The vast interior has chandeliers, a high ceiling and fluted columns. You can get a table overlooking the zoo (which has, by the way, no connection with the menu). Unlike Moscow, there are no queues here, but the food is genuinely Russian – borsch, cream prawns au gratin, pork à la Kiev, beef stroganoff, black bread, soups and black caviar. It's moderately priced.

Coffee Shops

All major hotels have coffee shops, but *Johnny's Coffee* (☎ 466-4331), Xibahedongli Building 11, is worth a special mention. It's *the* place to get your Blue Mountain and croissants. You'll find it opposite the International Exhibition Centre (Map 21), and it's open daily from 8 am to 10 pm.

Fast Food

From the day of its grand opening in 1992, *McDonald's (màidāngláo)* has been all the rage with Beijingers. Though prices are low, this is one of Beijing's most prestigious restaurants, the venue for cadre birthday parties and a popular hang-out for the upper crust. McDonald's occupies a prime piece of real estate on the corner of Wangfujing just east of the Beijing Hotel (Map 22). In 1994, the city government tried to cancel the lease and kick McDonald's out to make way for a shopping mall. Ronald McDonald (whose plastic statue stands guard by the door) refused to budge, and the issue nearly escalated into a major commercial dispute with the US government before the Chinese side backed down. Business was so good that a second (but smaller) McDonald's opened in 1993 at the Chang'an Market on Fuxingmenwai Dajie near the Yanjing Hotel (Map 23). Other branches have since popped up everywhere, and all are open from 7 am until 11 pm.

By comparison, *Kentucky Fried Chicken (kěndéjī jiāxiāng jī)* enjoys a relatively longer history in Beijing, having spread its wings in 1987. At the time of its opening, it was the largest KFC in the world. The colonel's smiling face is just across the street from Mao's mausoleum in Tiananmen Square – if this doesn't make the late chairman turn over in his grave, nothing will. A smaller Kentucky Fried has hatched one block east of Wangfu-

jing on the south-western corner of Dongsi Xi Dajie and
Dongsi Nan Dajie (Map 22).

Pizza Hut (bìshèngkè) has arrived on the Beijing fast-food
scene with two branches. One is on Dongzhimenwai
Dajie in the Sanlitun area (next to the Australian
embassy; Map 21). The other hut is less conspicuous –
it's at 33 Zhushikou Xi Dajie, the second major road
south of Qianmen (first big road south of Dazhalan
Dajie; Map 20).

Uncle Sam's Fastfood (shānmǔ shūshū kuàicān) is on the
south side of Jianguomenwai opposite the Friendship
Store (Map 21). At least the pastries and drinks are not
bad.

Ice cream has caught on in a big way in Beijing. *Ciao
Ciao* is a classy chain with cones for Y10 to Y16.

SELF-CATERING

Bakeries

Chinese bread is about as tasty as a dried-out sponge,
but a few entrepreneurs in Beijing have started to intro-
duce edible baked goods to the masses. One fine effort
in this direction is *Vie de France (dà mòfáng miànbāo diàn)*,
which boasts genuine croissants and prices a fraction of
what you'd pay in Paris. This bakery currently has two
branches – one is at the Qianmen Zhengyang Market,
just south-west of Chairman Mao's mausoleum and
adjacent to the enormous Kentucky Fried Chicken (Map
20). The other branch is on the south-east corner of Xidan
and Xichang'an Dajie, across the street from the CAAC
office (Map 23).

Within the confines of the *Friendship Store*, there is a
bakery off to the right as you enter the store (Map 21).
Prices here are also very low but the selection is limited.

Another place to look are some of the big hotels – a
few have sent the staff off to Europe for a wintertime
crash course in making German black bread and Danish
pastries. Unfortunately, hotel prices tend to be high. The
deli in the *Holiday Inn Lido* (Map 1) stocks delectable
chocolate cake for around Y30 a slice.

Supermarkets

Beijing has several notable supermarkets, a good one
being *CVIK Plaza* on the south side of Jianguomenwai
(Map 21). It's a department store across the street from
the CITIC building and adjacent to SCITE Tower – the
supermarket is in the basement.

On the eastern fringe of Jianguomenwai is the China World Trade Centre – go down into the basement to find a fully fledged *Wellcome* supermarket, imported lock, stock and shopping carts from Hong Kong (Map 21). The Wellcome slogan 'low everyday prices' doesn't quite describe the situation in Beijing, but you'll find all the familiar goodies right down to the 'No Frills Dried Lemon Peel'.

Just next to the CITIC building is the *Friendship Store* – when you enter the building turn sharply right to find the food section (Map 21). The supermarket is decidedly mediocre, but new competition may force an improvement soon.

If you're out in Sanlitun embassyland, there's a small *Friendship Supermarket* serving the diplomatic (and not so diplomatic) crowd – the selection is limited but you can score chocolate chip cookies and other imported delicacies. The store is at 5 Sanlitun Lu (Map 21). In the same neighbourhood just north of the Great Wall Sheraton Hotel is the enormous *Lufthansa Centre* – yes, it is a ticket office for a German airline, but also a multi-storey shopping mall. There is a supermarket of sorts in here, but you may have a hard time finding the food amongst the Walkmans, computers and colour TVs.

Entertainment

Back in the days of Mao, 'nightlife' often meant revolutionary operas featuring evil foreign and Kuomintang devils who eventually were defeated by heroic workers and peasants inspired by the 'little red book'. Fortunately, performances have improved considerably. The *China Daily* carries a listing of cultural evenings recommended for foreigners; also worth checking is *Beijing Weekend*, which is published once a week. Offerings include concerts, theatre, ethnic minority dancing and some cinema. You can reserve ahead by phoning the box office via your hotel, or by picking up tickets at CITS (for a surcharge) – or take a risk and just roll up at the theatre.

CINEMA

Chinese movies *(diànyǐng)* are out of the boring stage and starting to delve into some contemporary issues, even verging on Cultural Revolution aftershock in a mild manner (see Cinema in the Facts about Beijing chapter). There are about 50 cinemas in the capital showing a mix of Chinese and foreign films. European and US films are not dubbed but appear with Chinese subtitles. On the other hand, films made in Hong Kong have English subtitles and Mandarin dialogue. Some good cinemas are:

Changhong. Cinema (chánghóng diànyǐng yuàn), 75 Longfusi Dongjie, Dongcheng District (☎ 404-1160)
Dizhi Auditorium Cinema (dìzhì diànyǐng yuàn), 30 Yangrou Hutong, Xicheng District (☎ 603-5385; Map 23)
French Embassy Cinema Hall (fǎguó dàshǐguǎn), Sanlitun Office Building 1-12, Sanlitun embassy compound (☎ 532-1422)
Huashi Cinema (huāshì diànyǐng yuàn), 135 Xihuashi Dajie, Chongwen District (☎ 511-2442; Map 23)
Original English Film Club (yīngwén diànyǐng jùlèbù), Holiday Inn Crowne Plaza, 48 Wangfujing Dajie (☎ 513-3388 ext 1209; Map 22)
Shoudu Cinema (shǒudū diànyǐng yuàn), Xichang'an Jie (Map 23)
Sino-Japanese Youth Exchange Centre (zhōngrì qīngnián jiāoliú zhōngxīn), 40 Liangmaqiao Lu, near the Sanlitun embassy compound (☎ 500-4466 ext 103; Map 21)
Tuxin Cinema (túxīn diànyǐng yuàn), National Library, 39 Baishiqiao Lu, Haidian District (☎ 841-5566 ext 5734; see Map 23 for the library)

Ziguang Cinema (zǐguāng diànyǐng yuàn), 168 Chaoyangmenwai Dajie, Chaoyang District (☎ 500-3868; find the
street on Map 21)

THEATRE

Entertainment is cheap compared to the West, but prices
are rising. Beijing is on the touring circuit for foreign
troupes, and these are also listed in the *China Daily.*
They're somewhat screened for content, but they've
been beefing up what's available. When Arthur Miller's
Death of a Salesman was acted out by Chinese at the
Capital Theatre, it was held over for two months by
popular demand.

The same theatre staged some avant-garde Chinese
theatre. It put on two plays by Gao Xingjian, incorporat-
ing theatre of the absurd and traditional Chinese
theatrical techniques. One of the plays, *Bus-stop*, is based
on eight characters who spend 10 years at a bus stop,
only to discover that the service was cancelled long ago.
That's either a vicious comment on the Beijing bus
service, or a sly reference to Gao's stint in a re-education
camp during the Cultural Revolution. Or maybe it's a
direct steal from Samuel Beckett or Luigi Pirandello.

The most likely venue for Western-style drama is the
Capital Theatre (☎ 524-9847) *(shǒudū jùcháng)* at 22
Wangfujing Dajie (Map 22). The other likely place is the
Experimental Theatre for Modern Drama (☎ 403-1009)
(zhōngyāng shíyàn jù huà jùyuàn), at 45 Mao'er Hutong,
which runs off Di'anmen Dajie east of Shisha Qianhai
Lake (Map 23).

CLASSICAL MUSIC

In the classic concert department they've presented
Beethoven's Ninth played on Chinese palace instruments, such as tuned bells copied from those found in
an ancient tomb. Other classical instruments are being
revived for dance-drama backings.

If it's Beethoven or Mozart you want to hear, the place
to go is the *Beijing Concert Hall* (☎ 601-8092) *(běijīng
yīnyuè tīng)* at 1 Bei Xinhua Jie, Liubukou, Xichang'an Jie
(Map 23). Go to Hepingmen subway station and walk
north; it's just before Xichang'an Jie. Another option is
the auditorium at the *Central Music Conservatory* (☎ 605-
3531) *(zhōngyāng yīnyuè xuéyuàn lǐtáng),* 43 Baojia Jie,
Xicheng District. There are also concerts in the atrium
lobby of the *Swissôtel* (☎ 501-2288 ext 2213; Map 21).

ROBERT STOREY

Cinema advertising: ghost stories and 'spaghetti easterns' are all the rage.

At the *Liuhexuan Teahouse* in Longtan Park, traditional bands sometimes perform by the shores of Longtan Lake.

JAZZ & ROCK

Real culture shock strikes when East meets West over the music score. China's leadership has had a hard time deciding how to react – in the beginning, Western music was vehemently denounced by the government as another form of dangerous 'spiritual pollution'. China's first concert featuring a foreign rock group was in April 1985, when the British group 'Wham!' was allowed to perform. The audience remained deadpan – music fans who dared to get up and dance in the aisles were hauled off by the PSB. Since then, things have become considerably more liberal and China has produced some notable bands (see Music in the Facts for the Visitor chapter).

Rock concerts, when they happen, will be announced well in advance in Beijing's various English-language publications which cater to foreigners.

Sanwei Bookstore (☎ 601-3204), 60 Fuxingmennei Dajie, is a trendy bookshop for intellectuals, but also has a charming Chinese teahouse on the 2nd floor. Jazz bands sometimes play here and it's open nightly until 10 pm. Live performances may cost up to Y30 for admission. The bookstore is opposite the Minzu Hotel (Map 23).

EXPAT BARS & NIGHTCLUBS

(All these places are on Map 21.)

The *Water Hole* (☎ 507-4761), 3 Guanghuaxili, is just around the corner from the famous Mexican Wave. This place does good beer and burgers to the accompaniment of fine music.

Local Joint (☎ 595-7687), Yong'anxili, shares its kitchen with an adjoining Sichuan restaurant and can boast the best Chinese food of any pub in Beijing. It's in an alley behind the Guotai Hotel.

Jazz Ya (☎ 415-1227), 18 Sanlitun Beilu, is just what the name implies – a jazz bar. Just next door at 58 Sanlitun Beilu is *City Pub House*, which puts on live Western bands on Friday and Saturday nights.

Carella Cafe (☎ 501-6655), otherwise known as the Car Wash, is at the south-east corner of the Worker's Stadium in the Sanlitun area.

The *Underground Club* (☎ 506-4466 ext 6196), 1A Jianguomenwai (adjacent to the China World Trade Centre), is worth visiting just for its stunning Australian aboriginal decor. The dance floor is in the basement, and there are live bands on Friday and Saturday nights. At lunchtime it's also a superb restaurant.

The legendary *Hard Rock Cafe* (☎ 501-6688) is in the west wing of the Landmark Towers, 8 Dongsanhuan Beilu (the third ring road). It's open from 11 am to 2 am.

The *Poachers Inn* (☎ 532-3063) is the most British thing in Beijing besides the UK embassy. Admission costs half-price for members – bring a photo on your first visit and become a member straight away. Opening hours are from 2 pm to 3 or 4 am, but it's closed on Sunday – things get hopping about 10 pm. It's on the 2nd floor of the International Store opposite the Belgium embassy in the Sanlitun area.

The *Redwood Bar* (☎ 501-9517) is a cosy place in the Sanlitun Diplomatic Apartments, across from the Zhaolong Hotel.

Cafe Cafe (☎ 507-1331 ext 5127), Dongdaqiaoxie Jie, is another beer garden-sort-of-place with good pub grub.

Sophia's Choice (☎ 500-4466), Sino-Japanese Youth Exchange Centre, 40 Liangmaqiao Lu, is in the Sanlitun area. Folk bands often perform here.

The *Pig & Whistle* (☎ 437-6688 ext 1976) is on the ground floor of the Holiday Inn Lido. Opening hours are 5 pm until 1 am on weekdays, and from noon until 1 am on weekends and holidays.

Frank's Place (☎ 507-2617) is a beer-garden setting popular with expats. You may have to compete for space at the crowded outdoor tables on summer weekends.

You'll find Frank's on Gongren Tiyuchang Donglu, just across the street (east side) from the Workers' Stadium. In the same vicinity as Frank's is *Berena's Bistro* (☎ 592-2628), at 6 Gongren Tiyuchang Donglu. It's open from 11 am to 2 am.

The *Rasput-Inn* (☎ 507-1331 ext 5050) is at 1 Sanlitun Lu, alongside the Liangma River just south of the towering Capital Mansion. It's an unusual Sino-Russian joint venture, featuring chess matches and satellite TV.

Opposite the Canadian embassy on Dongzhimenwai at Xindong Lu is *Xanadu Bar & Grill* (☎ 416-2272). The New Zealand steaks are unsurpassed.

Cafe Kranzler (☎ 465-3388 ext 5700) is buried deep within the bowels of the Kempinski Hotel. There's live music in the evenings and top-drawer food.

Check out *Schiller's Bar & Restaurant* (☎ 461-9276) on Liangmahe Nanlu, across from the Lufthansa Centre.

Expats give good reviews to the beer gardens in the *Jianguo Hotel* and *Great Wall Sheraton*.

DISCOS

NASA Disco (☎ 201-6622) advertises 'advanced designed style appealing to radicals'. It can accommodate 1500 dancers and is open from 8 pm until 2 am. It's at the corner of Xueyuan Lu and Xitucheng Lu, just north of the third ring road (Map 23). It's opposite the Jimen Hotel. Admission costs Y40, or Y60 on Friday and Saturday.

JJ's Disco (☎ 607-9691) is an enormous Chinese dance venue at 74 Xinjiekou Bei Dajie (Map 23). Your admission ticket buys you a chance in JJ's lottery – first prize is a bicycle. The disco operates from around 8 pm until 2 am – cover charge is Y50 but rises to Y80 on Friday and Saturday night.

Nightman Disco has a good location just around the corner from the SAS Royal Hotel (Map 21). It's at the corner of Xikanhezhong Jie and Qisheng Nanlu.

KARAOKE

Want to be a singing star? Karaoke bars give you an opportunity to stand in front of the microphone and croak along with a music tape. It's all the rage with Chinese, though to many Westerners it makes as much sense as underwater bungee jumping. As a foreigner, the Chinese audience will probably give you polite applause, though for the sake of international relations you should probably limit yourself to no more than two numbers.

There's no need to list the karaoke venues here, because there are so many that you'll have a hard enough time avoiding them. Remember that some of the karaoke places try to cheat customers in a big way, with outrageous service charges for 'talking to the hostesses'. Some of the hostesses hang out on the street near their place of employment and try to trick unsuspecting males (even domestic tourists) into going inside for 'a few drinks'. The bill for a couple of cokes could amount to six months in wages for the average Chinese worker.

SONG & DANCE SHOWS

These come in different varieties, from Western style to Chinese or occasionally in the style of China's ethnic minorities. They advertise in the *China Daily*, but may be cancelled despite being advertised in the newspapers.

The *International Theatre* (☎ 501-0290) in the Poly Plaza – a hotel at 14 Dongzhimen Nan Dajie – is probably your best bet (Map 21). A more expensive possibility is the 'Dynasty Show' at the *Gloria Plaza Hotel* (Map 21) from 6.30 to 9 pm nightly. Or you can dive in with the locals at the *Beijing Music Hall* in Zhongshan Park (the southwest corner of the Forbidden City; Map 3).

BEIJING OPERA

Special performances of Beijing opera (*jīngjù*) are put on for foreigners nightly at 7.30 pm in the *Liyuan Theatre* (☎ 301-6688 ext 8860 or 8986), which is inside the Qianmen Hotel at 175 Yong'an Lu (Map 20). Ticket prices depend on seat location, starting at Y8. For Y20 you can sit at a table and enjoy snacks and tea while watching the show. For Y40 you get better snacks and a table with a better location. Performances here last just 1½ hours with sporadic translations flashed on an electronic signboard. You can get dressed up in an opera costume (with full facial makeup) for a photo-taking session.

The *Laoshe Teahouse* (☎ 303-6830), at 3 Qianmen Xi Dajie, has nightly shows though basically it's all in Chinese. The performances vary from comedy acts to musical routines. Prices depend on the type of show and where you sit – the range is typically from Y40 to Y130. Showtime is from 7.30 to 9.30 pm.

Along similar lines is the *Tianqiao Happy Teahouse* (☎ 304-0617) at 113 Tianqiao Market, Xuanwu District

(Map 20). It's open daily except Monday from 7 to 9 pm and has an admission charge of Y80 to Y100.

ACROBATICS

Two thousand years old, and one of the few art forms condoned by Mao, acrobatics *(tèjì biǎoyǎn)* is the best deal in town.

The best place to catch an acrobatics show is the *Chaoyang Theatre (cháoyáng jùchǎng)* at 36 Dongsanhuan Beilu in the north-eastern part of Beijing (Map 21). Shows run from 7.15 to 8.40 pm and cost Y30.

The *Beijing Amusement Park* (☎ 511-3611), which is adjacent to Longtan Park and east of Tiantan Park (Map 23), often has performances.

The *International Club* (☎ 532-2188) *(guójì jùlèbù)*, at 21 Jianguomenwai Dajie (west of the Friendship Store; Map 21), occasionally has performances.

One other place to check is the *Rehearsal Hall of the Beijing Acrobatics Troupe* (☎ 303-1769) *(běijīng zájì tuán)* in Dazhalan (the Qianmen area).

THEME PARKS

If you want to avoid being smothered by cotton candy and blinded by popping camera flashes, it's important to avoid Beijing's theme parks on weekends and holidays. On more sedate weekdays, you can sometimes really enjoy these places.

Chinese Ethnic Culture Park
中华民族园

Beijing's answer to Disneyland, this theme park gives you a chance to see China's 56 nationalities in their native habitat. Or rather, to see Han Chinese dressed up in minority costumes. The area is also dressed up with small-scale imitations of famous Chinese scenic spots such as a fake Jiuzhaigou Dragon Waterfall. Perhaps the best thing about the place is the opportunity to sample some ethnic minority speciality foods.

The *Chinese Ethnic Culture Park* is to the west of the National Olympic Sports Centre (Map 1).

World Park 世界公园

A monument to kitsch, Beijing's *World Park* displays miniaturised reproductions of world-famous architectural wonders. Exhibits include France's Eiffel Tower,

America's Statue of Liberty and the great pyramids of Egypt. Since most Chinese are unable to travel abroad, this is as close as they can come to an overseas holiday. Perhaps this explains why the World Park is the largest theme park in China.

The park is south-west of the centre, about three km due south of Fengtai railway station. If you don't plan to travel by taxi, you'll have to take a bus to Fengtai railway station and a minibus from there to the park.

Beijing Amusement Park 北京游乐园

On the west side of Longtan Park in the south-east corner of the city is *Beijing Amusement Park* (Map 23). This one is a cut above other Chinese parklands, probably because it's a joint-venture with an American company. The rides are in good nick, and the 360° rollercoaster is not for coronary patients. Admission is a rather steep Y45, but all rides and shows are included free except for the go-carts and boats. If you're under 140 cm, you get in free. Bus Nos 60 and 116 from Chongwenmen Dajie will get you there.

Beijing Zoo 北京动物园

For humans, Beijing Zoo (*běijīng dòngwùyuán*) may be OK – an enormous park, pleasant lakes, good birds – but after you've been there you'll probably look as pissed-off as the animals. No attempt has been made to re-create their natural environments; they live in tiny cages with little shade or water. The Panda House, right by the gates, has four dirty specimens that would be better off dead, and you'll be happier looking at the stuffed toy pandas on sale in the zoo's souvenir shop. Parents can buy their children miniature plastic rifles with which they can practise shooting the animals. The children also enjoy throwing rocks at the monkeys and jabbing them with sticks. Some of the monkeys fight back by throwing their faeces.

Admission is a modest Y10, but there is an extra charge for the Panda House and other surcharges for special exhibits.

Getting to the zoo is easy enough; take the subway to the Xizhimen station. From there, it's a 15-minute walk to the west or a short ride on any of the trolley buses (Map 23).

Near the zoo are the *Beijing Planetarium* and the bizarre Soviet-style *Beijing Exhibition Hall* (irregular industrial displays, theatre, Russian restaurant) which looks like a cross between a missile and a wedding-cake decoration.

Shijingshan Amusement Park
石景山游乐园

It's one of Beijing's oldest amusement parks and looks the worse for wear. It's a land of rusting ferris wheels, roller coasters and other things liable to make you vomit.

The park is in the far west of Beijing where the fifth ring road intersects Shijingshan Lu. Take the East-West Line to Bajiaocun station.

HORSE RACING

Gambling is illegal in China, but the government has made an exception for horse racing. The fact that the revenue goes into the government's coffers of course had nothing to do with this decision.

The race track *(pǎo mǎ chǎng)* is about 10 km north of Capital Airport on the way to Huairou. It's on the east side of the road near the Beijing Golf Course and some new super expensive housing. Race times vary according to season, so you'll have to check with locals for the schedule.

Shopping

The Chinese produce some interesting items for export – tea, clothing and Silkworm missiles – the latter not generally for sale to tourists.

Within China the consumer boom has arrived, though the types of goods on offer are markedly different from what gets exported. A notable difference is that goods produced for the domestic market are often inferior quality. There is an awful lot of junk on sale, such as zips which break literally the first time you use them, imitation Walkmans which last a week, electrical appliances which go up in smoke the first time they're plugged in. Keep in mind the Latin expression *caveat emptor* ('let the buyer beware'). Always test zips, examine stitching and, in the case of electrical appliances, plug them in and make sure they won't electrocute you before handing over the cash. Chinese sales clerks expect you to do this; they'll consider you a fool if you don't.

A word about antiques – most are fakes. There is, of course, nothing wrong with buying fakes as long as you're paying the appropriate prices. Remember that you need special certificates to take genuine antiques out of China. For fakes, be sure you have receipts to prove that they are fakes, otherwise the goods may get confiscated.

There are several notable Chinese shopping districts offering abundant goods and low prices: Wangfujing, Qianmen (including Dazhalan hutong) and Xidan. Pricier but more luxurious shopping areas can be found in the embassy areas of Jianguomenwai and Sanlitun. There are also some specialised shopping districts such as Liulichang and Zhongguancun (see further on for details).

Tourist attractions like the Forbidden City and Tiantan, as well as major hotels, have garish souvenir shops stocking arts and crafts. Otherwise, speciality shops are scattered around the city core. Stores are generally open from 9 am to 7 pm seven days a week; some are open from 8 am to 8 pm. Bargaining is not a way of life in the government stores, but on the free market it certainly is.

Down jackets are one of the best bargains you can find in Beijing and are essential survival gear if you visit northern China during winter. Good buys are stationery (chops, brushes, inks), prints, handicrafts, clothing and antiques. Small or light items to buy are silk scarves and underwear, T-shirts, embroidered purses, papercuts, wooden and bronze buddhas, fold-up paper lanterns and kites.

A description of the shopping districts and bargains to be had is as follows:

WANGFUJING 王府井

This prestigious shopping street is just east of the Beijing Hotel – it's a solid block of stores and a favourite haunt of locals and tourists seeking bargains (Map 22). Westerners now call it 'McDonald's St' due to the restaurant which occupies the north-east corner of the main intersection. In pre-1949 days it was known as Morrison St, catering mostly to foreigners. The name Wangfujing derives from a 15th-century well.

At the time of writing, Wangfujing was in the middle of a major three-year renovation. When finished, there will be an 800-metre long underground street with three levels. It will be a solid mass of stores, restaurants, pubs and karaoke lounges.

Shopping Guide	
Antiques	Hongqiao Market, Liulichang
Arts & Crafts	Wangfujing
Books	Jianguomenwai, Wangfujing
Chinese Herbal Medicines	Dazhalan, Wangfujing
Clothing	Dazhalan, Jianguomenwai, Qianmen
Fabrics	Dazhalan, Jianguomenwai
Musical Instruments	Qianmen
Photography	Jianguomenwai, Wangfujing
Pottery	Qianmen
Technology	Zhongguancun

Wangfujing's biggest emporium is the Beijing Department Store (*běijīng bǎihuò dàlóu*). Of prime interest to foreign travellers is the Foreign Languages Bookstore (*wàiwén shūdiàn*) at shop No 235. This is not only *the* place in China to buy English-language books, but the music tape section upstairs is pretty impressive as well.

Soon to open is the Xindong'an Shopping Centre, which will be one of the biggest shopping malls in the land.

Wangfujing is the place to go to buy film, though the Friendship Store also offers very competitive prices. You can even find slide film here, but check the expiry dates. Wangfujing is also a good place to go for photo processing or to obtain passport photos in a hurry.

XIDAN 西单

Officially known as Xidan Bei Dajie, this street aspires to be a little Wangfujing (Map 23). It's certainly a popular place with the locals. As for foreign tourists, the Xidan area, west of the Zhongnanhai compound, is a bit disappointing. There is no shortage of things to buy, but it's mostly of the 'cheap junk that breaks easily' variety. However, it's a good street for budget travellers in search of practical everyday items.

All this may change soon with the opening of the Xidan International Mansion after nearly two years' construction.

To the west of Xidan, near Beijing Financial St, is the Vantone New World Shopping Mall (*wàntōng xīn shìjiè shāngchéng*), Beijing's newest.

DAZHALAN 大栅栏

If Wangfujing is too organised for you, the place to go and rub shoulders with the proletariat is Dazhalan, a hutong running west from the top end of Qianmen (Map 20). It's a heady jumble of silk shops, department stores, theatres, herbal medicine, food and clothing specialists and some unusual architecture.

Dazhalan has a definite medieval flavour to it, a hangover from the days when hutongs sold specialised products – one would sell lace, another lanterns, another jade. This one used to be called 'Silk Street'. The name Dazhalan refers to a wicket-gate that was closed at night to keep undesirable prowlers out.

In imperial Beijing, shops and theatres were not permitted near the city centre, and the Qianmen-Dazhalan

Name Chops

The traditional Chinese name chop or seal has been used for thousands of years. It is quite likely that people began using name chops because Chinese characters are so complex and few people in ancient times were able to read and write. In addition, chops date back to a time when there was no other form of identification such as fingerprinting, picture ID cards or computer files.

A chop served both as a form of identification and as a valid signature. All official documents in China needed a chop to be valid. Naturally, this made a chop quite valuable, for with another person's chop it was possible to sign contracts and other legal documents in their name.

Today, most Chinese are literate, but the tradition lives on. In fact, without a chop it is difficult or impossible to enter into legally-binding contracts in China. A chop is used for bank accounts, entrance to safe-deposit boxes and land sales. Only red ink is used for a name chop.

If you live in China for work or study, you will almost certainly need to have a chop made. If you're staying a short time, a chop makes a great souvenir. A chop can be made quickly, but first you will need to have your name translated into Chinese characters.

There are many different sizes and styles of chops. Inexpensive small chops can be carved from wood or plastic, while expensive ones can be carved from ivory, jade, marble or steel. Most Chinese people have many chops to confuse a possible thief, though they run the risk of confusing themselves as well. One chop might be used for their bank account, another for contracts and another for a safe-deposit box. Obviously, a chop is important and losing one can be a big hassle.

Since the people who carve chops don't check your ID, it might occur to you that obtaining a fake or forged chop would be very easy. Indeed, it is. It's also a very serious crime in China. ∎

District was outside the gates. Many of the city's oldest shops can be found along or near this crowded hutong.

Just off the beginning of Dazhalan at 3 Liangshidian Jie is Liubiju, a 400-year-old pickle and sauce emporium patronised by discriminating shoppers. Nearby is the Zhimielou Restaurant, which serves imperial snacks. On your right as you go down Dazhalan is a green concave archway with columns at No 5; this is the entrance to Liufuxiang, one of the better-known material and silk stores and a century old.

A famous shop is the Tongrentang at No 24, selling Chinese herbal medicines. It's been in business since 1669, though it doesn't appear that way from the renovations. It was a royal dispensary in the Qing Dynasty, and creates its pills and potions from secret prescriptions used by royalty. All kinds of weird ingredients – tiger bone, rhino horn, snake wine – will cure you of anything from fright to encephalitis, or so they claim. Traditional doctors are available on the spot for consultation; perhaps ask them about fear of Chinese railway ticket-offices (patience pills?).

Dazhalan runs about 300 metres deep off the western end of Qianmen. At the far end where the hubbub dies down is a bunch of Chinese hotels. Dazhalan was once the gateway to Beijing's red-light district; the brothels were shut down in 1949 and the women packed off to factories.

Qianmen Dajie, and Zhushikou Xi Dajie leading off to the west, are interesting places in which to meander. On Qianmen Dajie there are pottery stores at Nos 99 and 149, ethnic-minority musical instruments at Nos 18 and 104, and a nice second-hand shop at No 117. At 190 Qianmen Dajie is the Army Store, just the place to stock up on green PLA overcoats and Snoopy hats.

LIULICHANG 琉璃厂

Not far to the west of Dazhalan is Liulichang, Beijing's antique street (Map 20). Although it's been a shopping area for quite some time, only recently has it been dressed up for foreign tourists. The stores here are all designed to look as if they're straight out of an ancient Chinese village, and this makes for good photography even if you don't buy anything.

Most of the shops are State-run and seem to specialise in surly service and ridiculously high prices. Almost everything on sale looks antique, but most are fakes. Overall, you'll probably do better antique-hunting in Tianjin's antique market, which is particularly impressive at weekends (see the Excursions chapter).

JIANGUOMENWAI 建国门外

The Friendship Store (☎ 500-3311) (yǒuyí shāngdiàn), at 17 Jianguomenwai (Map 21), is the largest in the land – this place stocks both touristy souvenirs and practical everyday items. Not long ago, the Friendship Store was *the* place to shop in Beijing – so exclusive that only foreigners and cadres were permitted inside. But these days anyone can go in. The touristy junk is upstairs, but the ground floor is where the really useful items are found – tinned and dried foods, tobacco, wines, spirits, coffee, Chinese medicines and film. The book and magazine section is a gold mine for travellers long starved of anything intelligent to read. To the right are a supermarket and deli.

CVIK Plaza is a huge department store with an enormous selection – the best deal is the supermarket and restaurant in the basement. There are, of course, lots of pricey luxuries on offer: the latest fashion, make-up and perfumes. Kitchenwares are in basement No 2. CVIK Plaza is on the south side of Jianguomenwai, opposite the CITIC building.

GLENN BEANLAND

This calligraphy shop in Dazhalan sells hanging scrolls.

The Xiushui Silk Market (xiùshuǐ dōngjiē) is on the north side of Jianguomenwai between the Friendship Store and the Jianguo Hotel. Because of the prestigious location amidst the luxury hotels, this place is elbow to elbow with foreign tourists at times – go early to avoid crowds and forget it on Sundays. This market is one of the best places to pick up good deals in upmarket clothing – everything from silk underwear and negligees to leather moneybelts. Bargaining is expected here, though it's sometimes difficult because of all the foreign tourists willing to throw money around like water.

Ritan Park is north of the Friendship Store – on the west side of the park and intersecting with it at a 90° angle is Yabao Lu Clothing Market. This place is enormous – no Beijing department store could hope to match the variety and low prices on offer here. Bargaining is *de rigueur*.

SANLITUN 三里屯

The Sanlitun embassy compound is in north-east Beijing, close to the Great Wall Sheraton Hotel (Map 21). Like Jianguomenwai, the stores here are decidedly upmarket.

The Lufthansa Centre (yānshā shāngchéng), also known as the Kempinski Hotel (kǎibīnsījī fàndiàn), falls into a category by itself, being Beijing's first flashy multistorey shopping mall. You can buy everything here from computer floppy disks to bikinis (but who in China wears the latter?). A supermarket is in the basement.

HONGQIAO MARKET 红桥商场

Sadly, Hongqiao Market (hóngqiáo shìcháng) is not as interesting as it was in the recent past. In 1994, the market was moved across the street from its former location in Tiantan Park. The new building looks spiffy on the outside, but the market has lost its colour. Nevertheless, it's worth a peek if you're in the neighbourhood.

Most of the goods are under 100 years old, so they may not meet the textbook definition of 'antique'. This is no big deal as long as you're not paying antique prices. There are plenty of reasonably priced second-hand goods here.

Besides the old stuff, there are intriguing speciality items; for example, you can buy a 'little red book' for Y50 (be sure to bargain). One favourite among foreigners is a 'youth of China' alarm clock with a picture of a rosy-cheeked female Red Guard enthusiastically waving the little red book.

Hongqiao Market is on the east side of Tiantan Donglu, one block north of the Tiantan Sports Hotel (Map 23).

ZHONGGUANCUN 中关村

This is Beijing's hi-tech district, but unless you're stocking up on laser eye-surgery equipment, the real attraction here are the computer shops. However, it's not recommended that you buy a computer here unless you are going to live in Beijing for a while. You'll find lower prices, better quality and a wider selection in Hong Kong. On the other hand, foreigners living in Beijing report that most of the shops here are good about honouring their warranties, an important consideration because sending a machine to Hong Kong for service isn't practical.

All this having been said, Zhongguancun has a few specialised items to interest computer freaks. Much of the world's Chinese-language software originates in this neighbourhood, including that which was used to produce this book. Pirating software is a big local industry too but if you're interested, be aware that most Chinese software is copy-protected and many of the pirated programmes are infected with computer viruses.

Zhongguancun is in Haidian District in the northwest part of Beijing, not far from the Summer Palace (Map 1). Just off Zhongguancun is the shopping district for low-tech consumer goods (music tapes, clothing, food, etc), known as Haidian Tushucheng.

MISCELLANEOUS

If there's anything you think is impossible to buy in Beijing, check out Watson's (qūchénshì), in the Holiday Inn Lido (Map 1). This place sells every vitamin known to humanity, sunscreen (UV) lotion, beauty creams, tampons and the widest selection of condoms in China.

Excursions

All the places in this chapter can be visited as day trips from Beijing, although in several cases you might find it worth staying overnight. At the back of this book we've provided maps of many of the sites mentioned here.

GREAT WALL 长城

Construction on the Great Wall *(cháng chéng)* began 2000 years ago during the Qin Dynasty (221-207 BC) when China was unified under Emperor Qin Shihuang. Separate walls, built by independent kingdoms to keep out marauding nomads, were linked up. The effort required hundreds of thousands of workers, many of them political prisoners, and 10 years of hard labour under General Meng Tian. An estimated 180 million cubic metres of rammed earth was used to form the core of the original wall, and legend has it that among the building materials used were the bodies of dead workers.

The wall never really did perform its function as a defence line to keep invaders out. As Genghis Khan supposedly said, 'The strength of a wall depends on the courage of those who defend it'. Sentries could be bribed. However, it did work very well as a kind of elevated highway, transporting men and equipment across mountainous terrain. Its beacon tower system, using smoke signals generated by burning wolves' dung, transmitted news of enemy movements quickly back to the capital. To the west in Gansu Province was Jiayuguan Pass, an important link on the Silk Road, where there was a Customs post of sorts, and where unwanted Chinese were ejected through the gates to face the terrifying wild west.

Marco Polo makes no mention of China's greatest public works project. Both sides of the wall were under the same government at the time of his visit, but the Ming Great Wall had not been built. During the Ming Dynasty (1368-1644) a determined effort was made to rehash the whole project, this time facing it with bricks and stone slabs, some 60 million cubic metres of them. This created double-walling running in an elliptical shape to the west of Beijing, and did not necessarily follow the older earthen wall. This Ming project took over 100 years, and costs in human effort and resources were phenomenal.

The wall was largely forgotten after that, but now it's reached its greatest heights as a tourist attraction. Lengthy sections of it have been swallowed up by the sands, claimed by the mountains, intersected by road or rail, or simply returned to dust. Other bits were carted off by local peasants to construct their own four walls, a hobby that no one objected to during the Cultural Revolution. The depiction of the wall as an object of great beauty is a bizarre one, since until recent times it was a symbol of tyranny.

Badaling Great Wall 八达岭长城

Most foreigners see the wall at Badaling (bādálǐng; Map 11), 70 km north-west of Beijing at an elevation of 1000 metres. It was restored in 1957 with the addition of guard rails. The section is almost eight metres high with a base of 6½ metres and a width at the top of almost six metres. It runs for several hundred metres after which, if you keep going, are the unrestored sections where the crowds peter out. Originally the wall here could hold five horsemen riding abreast; nowadays it's about 15 tourists walking abreast.

The Great Wall Circle Vision Theatre was opened in 1990 and is a 360° amphitheatre showing 15-minute films about the wall. You hear about the wall's history and legends via a narration in English or Chinese; other languages may be added later.

To get up on top of the wall, there is an admission fee of Y25. The wall also has a cable car, which costs Y70 for foreigners. Badaling recently added a zoo and foreigners are charged Y28.

Getting There & Away CITS, CTS, big hotels and everyone else in the tourist business does a tour to Badaling. Prices border on the ridiculous, with some hotels asking over Y300 per person.

There are cheapie Chinese tours (around Y15) departing from a number of venues. Some depart from the south side of Tiananmen Square (near Kentucky Fried Chicken). Others depart from the car park in front of the main Beijing railway station (west side of station; Map 23), but don't get confused with the buses heading for Tianjin (which depart from the exact same spot). You can also catch buses from the car park of the Workers' Stadium (gōngrén tǐyùguǎn) – this is on Gongren Tiyuchang Beilu next to the Beijing Asia Hotel and the Dongsishitiao subway station (Map 23). Departures are only in the morning, around 7.30 to 8 am. But first ask about the itinerary – some tour operators don't just go

JO O'BRIEN

Badaling: most visitors see the 10,000 km Great Wall where it comes closest to Beijing.

straight to Badaling, but instead take you to numerous other sites, all of which carry hefty admission fees for foreigners:

Our Chinese tour went to a revolutionary monument, a theme park, movie studio, wax museum, history museum and *finally* the Great Wall. We departed from our hotel at 6.10 am and arrived at the Great Wall at 4.30 pm! All these different sights were not interesting!

Carol M Johnson

Local buses also ply the route to the wall but it's slow going; take bus Nos 5 or 44 to Deshengmen, north of Xihai Lake, then No 345 to the terminal at Changping, then a numberless bus to the wall. Alternatively, bus No 357 goes part way along the route and then you hitch. Another route is bus No 14 to Beijiao long-distance bus station, which is north of Deshengmen, then a numberless bus to the wall. Going on local buses saves some money but it's a headache even if you speak Chinese.

You can reach the wall by express train from the main Beijing railway station, getting off at Qinglongqiao. Buy the ticket from the foreigners' ticketing office the day before – the office opens at 8 am and there are long queues. The train to Qinglongqiao leaves Beijing at 8.50 am and the journey takes two hours. There are actually three stations within one km of the wall – Qinglongqiao, New Qinglongqiao and Badaling, but the first is by far the closest to your destination. Qinglongqiao station is notable for the statue of Zhan Tianyou, the engineer in charge of building the Beijing-Baotou line. No trains stop at all three stations and many only stop at Qinglongqiao. Trains from Qinglongqiao continue westwards to Datong, Hohhot and beyond. Qinglongqiao station has a left-luggage room.

At Qinglongqiao, get off the train and follow the tracks back the same way the train came. Pass through the tunnel (the left one since there are two side by side) and you will have a road to your right. Follow it to a parking lot and the entrance to the wall, a 10-minute walk in total. Returning to Beijing is easy; there are many minibuses in the afternoon. The price is Y10 (asking price is Y50). The minibuses drop you off at a subway station.

A microbus-style taxi to the wall and back will cost at least Y250 for an eight-hour hire with a maximum of five passengers – you are expected to buy lunch for the driver. Considering that this works out to less than Y60 per person, it's certainly not unreasonable.

Mutianyu Great Wall   慕田峪长城

To take some of the pressure off crowded Badaling, a second site for Great Wall viewing has been opened at Mutianyu (*mùtiányù*; Map 12), 90 km north-east of Beijing. This part of the wall is less of a carnival than Badaling, but the recent addition of souvenir shops and a cable car is starting to attract the armadas of Japanese tour buses. Nevertheless, Mutianyu is the place most preferred by individual travellers and is still much less crowded than Badaling.

Getting There & Away A small number of Chinese tour buses go to Mutianyu – look for them near Kentucky Fried Chicken near Tiananmen Square, the main

Beijing railway station or the Workers' Stadium.
Entrance to the wall at Mutianyu costs Y15. The cable-car
ride costs Y30 one way or Y40 for the return trip.

Everyday there is a direct bus to Mutianyu from
Dongzhimen bus station at 7.30 am. The fare is Y6 one
way. Coming back, there are two buses, one at 1 pm and
the other at 4 pm. You must change buses at Huairou on
the return journey. The fare is Y3 from Mutianyu to
Huairou and then another Y3 from Huairou to Beijing.
The total cost of the trip is Y12. It takes about two hours
to get there.

Simatai Great Wall 司马台长城

If you prefer your wall without the benefit of handrails,
cable cars and tacky souvenir shops, Simatai (*sīmǎtái*;
Map 8) is the place to go. Of all the parts of the wall near
Beijing which are open to tourism, the 19-km section at
Simatai is the least developed (for now). Many consider
this part of the wall to be the most beautiful.

This section of the wall dates from the Ming Dynasty
and has some unusual features like 'obstacle-walls',
which are walls-within-walls used for defending against
enemies who'd already scaled the Great Wall. There are
135 watchtowers at Simatai, the highest being
Wangjinglou. Small cannon have been discovered in this
area, as well as evidence of rocket-type weapons such as
flying knives and flying swords.

Simatai is not for the chicken-hearted because this
section of the wall is very steep. A few slopes have a 70°
incline and you need both hands free, so bring a daypack
to hold your camera and other essentials. One narrow
section of footpath has a 500-metre drop-off, so it's no
place for acrophobiacs.

An early Western visitor was Lord Macartney, who
crossed nearby Gubei Pass on his way to Chengde in
1793. His party made a wild guess that the wall contained almost as much material as all the houses in
England and Scotland.

In the early 1970s a nearby PLA unit destroyed about
three km of the wall to build barracks, setting an
example for the locals who likewise used parts of the
wall to build their houses. The story goes that in 1979 the
same PLA unit was ordered to rebuild the section which
had been torn down.

A small section of the wall at Simatai has already been
renovated, but most of it remains in its non-com-
mercialised, crumbling condition. Seeing the wall in its
undisturbed state is a sharp contrast to Badaling and
Mutianyu, which are so well restored that you may get

the impression the wall was built just yesterday to serve CITS tour groups. Perhaps it was.

There is a small restaurant at the car park near the base of the wall, and at the present time prices are still reasonable, although it's not a bad idea to come prepared with some snacks and water. There is a Y15 admission charge.

Getting There & Away Simatai is 110 km north-east of Beijing, and due to the far distance and lack of tourist facilities there is little public transport. Buses to Simatai cost Y20 for the round-trip and depart just once daily from the Dongzhimen bus station at 7 am (Map 21). The journey takes from two to three hours, and the bus departs Simatai at 3 pm (but ask to be sure).

For budget travellers, the best deal around is offered through the Jinghua Hotel – Y70 for the return journey by minibus. Ring up their booking office (☎ 761-2582 after 4 pm) for more details.

If you don't do a tour through the Jinghua Hotel, you can hire a microbus taxi for the day for about Y400. Tour operators also gather at Tiananmen Square and ask ridiculous prices for foreigners.

TOMBS

Dying is a big deal in China, especially if you're an emperor. Since they had to go, the royal families decided to go in style. Around Beijing are three major tomb sites, and each tomb holds (or held) the body of an emperor, his wives, girlfriends and funerary treasures. All of the tombs have been plundered at one time or other, but recent efforts at restoration have benefitted China's cultural pride, not to mention the tourist industry.

The three tomb sites around Beijing open to tourists are the Ming Tombs, Western Qing Tombs and Eastern Qing Tombs. Of the three, the Ming Tombs are by far the most frequently visited.

Ming Tombs 十三陵

The general travellers' consensus on the Ming Tombs (shísānlíng; Map 13) is that you'd be better off looking at a bank vault which is, roughly, what the tombs are. However, the scenery along the way is charming.

Aware of the fact that many visitors have found the tombs disappointing, the Beijing municipal government is busy dressing up the area. New facilities include a golf course, the Dingling Museum (with a wax Genghis Khan), the Nine Dragons Amusement Park, an archery and rifle range, shops, cafes, a 350-room hotel, swimming pool, aquarium, camp site, picnic area, fountain (with 200-metre waterjet), fishing pier (on the Ming Tombs Reservoir) and a bicycle racing velodrome. Another feature is the Old Beijing Miniature Landscape Park, a model of ancient Beijing which contains over 100 miniature 'buildings'. There are also helicopter rides over the tombs and the nearby Great Wall. Plans call for the construction of additional facilities, including a horse race track, cross-country skiing area and Mongolian yurts for use as a summer hotel.

The seven-km road known as the 'spirit way' starts with a triumphal arch then goes through the Great Palace Gate, where officials had to dismount, and passes a giant tortoise (made in 1425) bearing the largest stele in China. This is followed by a guard of 12 sets of stone animals. Every second one is in a reclining position, legend has it, to allow for a 'changing of the guard' at midnight. If your tour bus driver whips past them, insist on stopping to look – they're far more interesting than the tombs – because the drivers prefer to spend half an hour at the Ming Tombs Reservoir which is dead boring. Beyond the stone animals are 12 stone-faced human statues of generals, ministers and officials, each distinguishable by headgear. The stone figures terminate at the Lingxing Gate.

Dingling was the first of the tombs to be excavated and opened to the public. In total, 13 of the 16 Ming emperors are buried in this 40-sq-km area which is why another name for this site is the Thirteen Tombs. Besides

ROBERT STOREY

Stone guardian figure - more interesting than the tombs

Dingling two other tombs, Changling and Zhaoling, are open to the public.

Dingling, the tomb of Emperor Wan Li (1573-1620), is in fact the second largest tomb. Over six years the emperor used half a million workers and a heap of silver to build his necropolis and then held a wild party inside the completed chambers. It was excavated between 1956 and 1958 and you can now visit the underground passageways and caverns. Entry costs Y30. The underground construction covers 1195 sq metres, is built entirely of stone and is sealed with an unusual lock stone. The tomb yielded 26 lacquered trunks of funerary objects, some of which are displayed on site, while others have been removed to Beijing's museums and replaced with copies.

Wan Li and his royal spouses were buried in double coffins surrounded by chunks of uncut jade. The jade was thought to have the power to preserve the dead (or could have bought millions of bowls of rice for starving peasants), so the Chinese tour literature relates. Meanwhile experts on cultural relics as well as chefs are studying the ancient cookbooks unearthed from Dingling with a view to serving Wan Li's favourite dishes to visitors, using replicas of imperial banquet tableware.

Another tomb, Changling, was started in 1409 and took 18 years to complete. This is the final resting place of Emperor Yong Le. According to the story, 16 concubines were buried alive with his corpse. This was the second of the Ming Tombs to be excavated and opened to the public (Y25). It consists mainly of displays of funerary objects.

Zhaoling is the ninth of the Ming Tombs and was opened to visitors in 1989. This is the tomb of Emperor Longqing, who died in 1572, and three of his wives.

Getting There & Away The tombs lie 50 km north-west of Beijing and four km from the small town of Changping. The tour buses usually combine them with a visit to the Great Wall. You can also get there on the local buses. Take bus Nos 5 or 44 to Deshengmen terminal. West of the flyover is the terminal of bus No 345 which you take to Changping, a one-hour ride. Then take bus No 314 to the tombs (or hitch the last stretch).

Changping main railway station is on the main Beijing to Baotou train line. There is another station, Changping north, which is closer to the Ming Tombs, but relatively few trains stop there.

Western Qing Tombs 清西陵

The Western Qing Tombs (*qīng xīlíng*) are in Yixian County, 110 km south-west of Beijing. If you didn't see enough of Dingling, Yuling, Yongling and Deling at the Ming Tombs, well, there's always Tailing, Changling, Chongling and Muling at the Western Qing Tombs.

The tomb area is vast and houses the corpses of the emperors, empresses and other members and hangers-on of the royal family. The tomb of Emperor Guangxu (Chongling) has been excavated. His was the last imperial tomb and was constructed between 1905 and 1915.

Not many tours go to these tombs. Your best bet is to share a chartered taxi.

Eastern Qing Tombs 清东陵

The area of the Eastern Qing Tombs (*qīng dōng líng*; Map 14) could be Death Valley, housing as it does five emperors, 14 empresses and 136 imperial consorts. In the mountains ringing the valley are buried princes, dukes, imperial nurses, and so on.

The approach to the tomb area is a common 'spirit way', similar to that of the Ming Tombs but with the addition of marble-arch bridges. The materials for the tombs come from all over China, including 20-tonne logs which were pulled over iced roads, and giant stone slabs.

Emperor Qianlong (1711-99) started preparations when he was 30, and by the time he was 88 the old boy had used up 90 tonnes of his silver. His resting place covers half a sq km. Some of the beamless stone chambers are decorated with Tibetan and Sanskrit sutras; the doors bear bas-relief bodhisattvas.

Empress Dowager Cixi also got a head start. Her tomb, Dingdong, was completed some three decades before her death. The phoenix (symbol of the empress) appears above that of the dragon (the emperor's symbol) in the artwork at the front of the tomb – not side by side as on other tombs. Both tombs were plundered in the 1920s.

In Zunhua County, 125 km east of Beijing, the Eastern Qing Tombs have a lot more to see in them than the Ming Tombs, although you may be a little jaded after the Forbidden City.

Getting There & Away The only way to get there is by bus and it's a long haul. Tour buses are considerably more comfortable than the local rattletraps and take three or four hours to get there; you have about three hours on site.

WESTERN HILLS 西山

Within striking distance of the Summer Palace and often combined with it on a tour are the Western Hills (xī shān), a former villa-resort area.

Fragrant Hills Park 香山公园

The part of the Western Hills closest to Beijing is known as the Fragrant Hills (xiāngshān gōngyuán; Map 18).

You can scramble up the slopes to the top of Incense-Burner Peak, or take the crowded chairlift (Y15 one way). From the peak you get an all-embracing view of the countryside. The chairlift is a good way to get up the mountain, and from the summit you can hike further into the Western Hills and leave the crowds behind.

The Fragrant Hills area was razed by foreign troops in 1860 and 1900 but a few bits of original architecture still poke out. A glazed-tile pagoda and the renovated Temple of Brilliance (zhāo miào) – a mock Tibetan temple built in 1780 – are both in the same area. The surrounding heavily wooded park was a hunting ground for the emperors, and once contained a multitude of pavilions and shrines, many of which are now being restored. It's a favourite strolling spot for Beijingers and destined to become another Chinese Disneyland – the chairlift and hundreds of souvenir shops are foreboding signs of horrors to come. It's possible to stay here at the four-star Fragrant Hills Hotel (☎ 259-1166) (xiāngshān fàndiàn).

Admission to the park costs a mere Y0.50. There are a couple of ways of getting to the Fragrant Hills by public transport: bus No 333 from the Summer Palace, bus No 360 from the zoo, and bus No 318 from Pingguoyuan (the westernmost stop on the East-West Line).

Azure Clouds Temple 碧云寺

Within walking distance of the north gate of Fragrant Hills Park is the Azure Clouds Temple (bìyún sì; Map 8), whose landmark is the Diamond Throne Pagoda. Of Indian design, it consists of a raised platform with a central pagoda and stupas around it. The temple was first built in 1366, and was expanded in the 18th century with the addition of the Hall of Arhats, containing 500 statues representing disciples of Buddha. Dr Sun Yatsen's coffin was placed in the temple in 1925 before being moved to Nanjing. In 1954 the government renovated Sun's memorial hall, which has a picture display of his revolutionary activities.

ROBERT STOREY

Lift your spirits at Fragrant Hills

Sleeping Buddha Temple 卧佛寺

About halfway between the Fragrant Hills and the Summer Palace is the Sleeping Buddha Temple (*wòfósì*; Map 8). During the Cultural Revolution the buddhas in one of the halls were replaced by a statue of Mao (since removed). The drawcard is the huge reclining buddha, 5.2 metres long and cast in copper; its weight is unknown but could be up to 50 tonnes. The history books place it in the year 1331 but it's most likely a copy. Pilgrims used to make offerings of shoes to the barefoot statue.

Xiangshan Botanical Gardens
香山植物园

About two km east of Fragrant Hills Park and just to the south of the of the Sleeping Buddha Temple is the Xiangshan Botanical Gardens (*xiāngshān zhíwù yuán;*

Map 8). While not spectacular, the gardens are a botanist's delight and certainly a pleasant place for a stroll. Most of the time, the gardens are uncrowded.

BADACHU 八大处

Directly south of the Fragrant Hills is Badachu (*bādàchù*; Map 17), the Eight Great Sites, also known as Eight Great Temples (*bādà sì*). It has eight monasteries or temples scattered in wooded valleys. The Second Site has the Buddha's Tooth Relic Pagoda, built to house the sacred fang and accidentally discovered when the Allied army demolished the place in 1900.

Since 1994, the ancient culture has been dressed up with a new amusement park ride – a roller-toboggan course. A chairlift carries you up the hill to the top of the toboggan course. The rollerway has a length of 1700 metres and speeds up to 80 km/h can be achieved.

Admission to Badachu costs Y2. The easiest way to reach the area is to take the East-West Line to the last stop at Pingguoyuan and catch a taxi (Y10) from there. Alternatively, take bus No 347, which runs there from the zoo (it crosses the No 318 route).

TANZHE TEMPLE 潭柘寺

About 45 km directly west of Beijing is Tanzhe Temple (*tánzhè sì*; Map 8), the largest of all the Beijing temples, occupying an area 260 by 160 metres. The Buddhist complex has a long history dating as far back as the 3rd century (Jin Dynasty). Structural modifications date from the Tang, Liao, Ming and Qing dynasties. It therefore has a number of features – dragon decorations, mythical animal sculptures and grimacing gods – no longer found in temples in the capital.

Translated literally, Tanzhe means 'Pool Cudrania'. The temple takes its name from its proximity to the Dragon Pool (*lóng tán*) and some rare Cudrania (*zhè*) trees. Locals come to the Dragon Pool to pray for rain during droughts. The Cudrania trees nourish silkworms and provide a yellow dye and the bark of the tree is believed to cure women of sterility, which may explain why there are so few of these trees left at the temple entrance.

The temple complex is open to the public daily from 8.30 am until 6 pm. To get there, one option is to take bus No 336 from Zhanlanguan Lu, which runs off Fuchengmenwai Dajie (north-west of Yuetan Park; Map

23), to the terminal at Mentougou and then hitch or take a taxi. A direct route is bus No 307 from Qianmen to the Hetan terminal and then a numberless bus to the temple. Alternatively, take the subway to Pingguoyuan, bus No 336 to Hetan and the numberless bus to the temple.

JIETAI TEMPLE 戒台寺

About 10 km south-east of the Tanzhe Temple is a similar but smaller compound, Jietai Temple *(jiètái sì*; Map 8). The name roughly translates as 'Temple of Ordination Terrace'. The temple was built around 622 AD, during the Tang Dynasty, with major improvements made by later tenants during the Ming Dynasty. The main complex is dotted with ancient pines, all of which have quaint names. Nine Dragon Pine is claimed to be over 1300 years old.

It's roughly 35 km from Jietai Temple to Beijing, and a journey out here is usually combined with a visit to Tanzhe Temple.

STONE FLOWER CAVE 石花洞

Following the same highway westwards that takes you to Jietai Temple also brings you to Stone Flower Cave *(shí huā dòng*; Map 8). This is considered the most scenic set of caves in the Beijing area, and of course it's lit up with coloured lights and has souvenir stands outside.

The cave is 55 km south-west of central Beijing and will require a bus tour or chartered taxi to reach.

MARCO POLO BRIDGE 卢沟桥

Publicised by the great traveller himself, the Reed Moat Bridge *(lúgōuqiáo*; Map 8) is made of grey marble, is 260 metres long and has over 250 marble balustrades supporting 485 carved stone lions. First built in 1192, the original arches were washed away in the 17th century. The bridge is a composite of different eras and was widened in 1969. It spans the Yongding River near the little town of Wanping.

Long before CITS, Emperor Qianlong also did his bit to promote the bridge. In 1751 he put his calligraphy to use and wrote some poetic tracts about Beijing's scenic wonders. His *Morning Moon Over Lugou Bridge* is now engraved into stone tablets and placed on steles next to the bridge. On the opposite bank is a monument to Qianlong's inspection of the Yongding River.

Despite the publicity campaign by Marco and Qianlong, the bridge wouldn't rate more than a footnote in Chinese history were it not for the famed 'Marco Polo Bridge Incident' which ignited a full-scale war with Japan. On the night of 7 July 1937, Japanese troops illegally occupied a railway junction outside Wanping, which prompted Japanese and Chinese soldiers to start shooting at each other, and that gave Japan enough of an excuse to attack and occupy Beijing. The Chinese were more than a little displeased, especially since Japan had already occupied Manchuria and Taiwan. The Marco Polo Bridge Incident is considered by many as the date of China's entry into WW II.

A relatively recent addition to this ancient site is the Memorial Hall of the War of Resistance Against Japan, built in 1987. Besides Qianlong's Morning Moon stele, there is also a stele commemorating his inspection of the Yongding River. Also on the site is the Wanping Castle, the Daiwang Temple and a tourist hotel.

You can get to the bridge by taking bus No 109 to Guang'anmen and then catching bus No 339. By bicycle it's about a 16-km trip one way.

PEKING MAN SITE 周口店

Site of those primeval Chinese, the Peking Men, Zhoukoudian Village (*zhōukǒudiàn*; Map 16) is 50 km south-west of Beijing. There's an 'Apeman Cave' here on

---

Peking Man Skull

There is an interesting story attached to the Peking Man skull. Early this century, villagers around Zhoukoudian found fossils in a local quarry and took them to the local medicine shop for sale as 'dragon bones'. This got back to Beijing, and archaeologists – foreign and Chinese – poured in for a dig.

Many years later, a molar was extracted from the earth, and the hunt for a skull was on. They found him in the late afternoon on a day in December 1929, *Sinanthropus Pekinensis* – a complete skull-cap. The cap was believed to be over half a million years old – if so, then it rates as one of the missing links in the evolutionary chain.

Research on the skull was never carried out. When the Japanese invaded in 1937 the skull-cap was packed away with other dig results and the whole lot vanished. The Chinese accused the Americans, the Americans accused the Japanese, and the mystery remains. Other fragments surfaced from the site after 1949, but no comparable treasure was found. ■

a hill above the village, several lesser caves and some dig sites. There is also a fossil exhibition hall (☎ 931-0278) – though you'd have to be a fossil to stay here for more than 15 minutes. There are three sections to the exhibition hall: pre-human history, the life and times of Peking Man, and one dealing with recent anthropological research. There are ceramic models, stone tools and the skeletons of prehistoric creatures. The exhibition hall is open daily from 9 am to 4 pm, but check before you go.

You could get a suburban train from Yongdingmen station (Map 23) and get off at Zhoukoudian. Another possibility is a bus from the Haihutun bus station (on the corner of Nansanhuan Zhonglu and Nanyuan Lu). If combined with a trip to Tanzhe Temple and Marco Polo Bridge, approaching the site by taxi is not unreasonable. Pricey CITS or CTS tours to the site are available according to demand.

There is a guesthouse on the site, though it seems to be intended more for locals than foreign tourists.

SHIDU 十渡

This is Beijing's answer to Guilin. The pinnacle-shaped rock formations, small rivers and general beauty of the place make it a favourite spot with expatriate students, diplomats and business people.

Situated 110 km south-west of central Beijing, Shidu (*shídù*; Map 15) means 'Ten Ferries' or 'Ten Crossings'. At least before the new road and bridges were built, it was necessary to cross the Juma River 10 times while travelling along the gorge between Zhangfang and Shidu village.

Places to Stay

The *Longshan Hotel (lóngshān fàndiàn)* is opposite the railway station and is the one place that takes foreigners.

Down near Jiudu (Ninth Ferry) there is a camp site, conveniently located on a flood-plain.

Getting There & Away

This is one of the few scenic areas outside of Beijing which can be easily reached by train. Departures are from the south railway station (Yongdingmen), not to be confused with the main Beijing railway station. If you take the morning train, the trip can be done in one day. The schedule is as follows:

No	From	To	Depart	Arrive
Train times to/from Shidu				
595	Yongdingmen	Shidu	6.07 am	8.40 am
597	Yongdingmen	Shidu	5.40 pm	8.00 pm
596	Shidu	Yongdingmen	6.41 pm	9.03 pm
598	Shidu	Yongdingmen	10.41 am	1.05 pm

YUNSHUI CAVES 云水洞

The Yunshui Caves (*yúnshuǐ dòng*; Map 8) are in the Shangfang mountains, not far north of the highway between the Peking Man Site and Shidu. Don't expect to be the first human to explore these depths because you'll find coloured lights, souvenir shops and snack bars.

About one km to the east of the cave entrance is the Doulü Temple, a large monastery complex in the foothills.

KANGXI GRASSLANDS 慷西草园

The grasslands (*kǎngxī cǎoyuán*; Map 8) are actually in a beautiful hilly region 80 km north-west of the city. This is considered the best place in Beijing municipality for horseback riding. It is also possible to spend the night here in a Mongolian yurt.

Unfortunately, the area is being dressed up for tourism and is rapidly developing a carnival atmosphere. There is already the City of the Three Kingdoms, the Folklore Holiday Village plus camel rides and a roller skating rink.

LONGQING GORGE 龙庆峡

About 90 km north-west of Beijing is Longqing Gorge (*lóngqìngxiá*; Map 9), a canyon in Yanqing County. The gorge was probably more scenic before the dam and consequent reservoir flooded out the area. Rowing and hiking are the big attractions during summer. From mid-December to the end of January this is the site of Beijing's Ice Lantern Festival (*bīngdōng jié*). The 'lanterns' are huge ice carvings into which coloured electric lights are inserted. The effect (at least during the night) is stunning. Children (including adult children) can amuse themselves on the ice slide.

The ride from Beijing takes two hours one way. There are currently three hotels in Longqing Gorge and more are on the drawing boards.

MIYUN RESERVOIR 密云水库

Some 90 km north-east of Beijing is Miyun Reservoir (*miyún shuǐkù*; Map 10), the city's water supply and largest lake in Beijing municipality. Since this is drinking water, swimming is prohibited, but the lake is impressive for its scenery.

Chinese entrepreneurs know a good thing when they see it, and Miyun Reservoir has now acquired a number of commercial recreation sites. Most important is the Miyun International Amusement Park (*miyún guójì yóulè cháng*), not on the lake itself but 20 km to the south-east, about seven km outside of Miyun town. Facilities include a merry-go-round, monorail, automobile race track, souvenir shops – just about everything you could possibly want in life.

If the carnival atmosphere gets to be too much, there are less touristy scenic sites around the reservoir. On the east side of the lake is White Dragon Pool (*bái lóng tán*). While also being developed for tourism, it retains much of its former charm. During the Qing Dynasty, emperors on their way to Chengde would drop in for a visit, so the area is dotted with temples and pavilions which recently have been renovated.

Right in front of the dam is the In Front of the Dam Park (*bàqián gōngyuán*), though this is mainly just a place for Chinese tourists to get their pictures taken. On the shores of the reservoir itself is the *Yunhu Holiday Resort* (☎ 994-4587) (*yúnhú dùjiàcūn*) where you can stay for Y300.

North-west of Miyun Reservoir are less visited scenic spots, including Black Dragon Pool (*hēi lóng tán*), Beijing First Waterfall (*jīngdū dìyī pùbù*), Tianxian Waterfall (*tiānxiān pùbù*); due north is Cloud Peak (*yúnfēng shān*).

Trains running to Chengde stop at Miyun. Buses to Miyun depart from the car park of the Workers' Stadium on Gongren Tiyuguan Beilu near the Dongsishitiao subway station (Map 21).

YANQI LAKE 雁栖湖

A small reservoir 60 km north-east of Beijing (near Huairou), Yanqi Lake (*yànqi hú*; Map 8) is primarily a good place to go swimming. There is also a campground here.

Take a bus from Dongzhimen bus station to Huairou, then change to a bus (or taxi) to Yanqi Lake.

HAIZI RESERVOIR 海子水库

At the far eastern end of Beijing municipality is Haizi Reservoir *(hǎizi shuǐkù;* Map 8), a relatively recent artificial creation hardly ever visited by tourists. Not that there is all that much to see here. The reservoir is distinguished by the fact that it was the site of the aquatic sports (waterskiing, etc) during the 1990 Asian Games.

Due to the games (which were poorly attended), the area has decent recreation facilities, though it's hard to say if everything will be kept in good nick or be allowed to become dilapidated. At the present time, modern amenities include the *Jinhai Hotel (jīnhǎi bīnguǎn)* and *Jinhai Restaurant (jīnhǎi cāntīng).* There is a pier *(yóuchuán mǎtóu)* where you can sometimes catch a cruise across the lake to the aquatic sports area *(shuǐshàng yùndòng cháng).* The shore of the reservoir is dotted with a few recently-constructed pavilions to remind you that this is indeed China. Nearby is Jinghaihu (Golden Sea Lake) Park.

Not being next to any railway line, getting here requires a substantial detour for most travellers. It would be conceivable for tour groups heading out to the Eastern Qing Tombs to make a stopoff at Haizi Reservoir along the way.

TIANJIN 天津

The third largest city in China, Tianjin *(tiānjīn;* Map 19) is a major port about 2½ hours by bus to the south-east of Beijing. For centuries, it has served as Beijing's outlet to the sea and has often been referred to as 'the Shanghai of the north'.

For the sea-dog Western nations of the 19th century, Tianjin was a trading bottleneck too good to be passed up. British gunboats persuaded the Chinese to sign the Treaty of Tianjin (1858) which opened the port up to foreign trade. The Brits were soon joined by the French, Japanese, Germans, Austro-Hungarians, Italians and Belgians. The era of foreign concessions has left Tianjin with much old European architecture, though recently-built architectural abominations litter the skyline.

Since 1949 Tianjin has been a focus for major industrialisation and a hot destination for business travellers. For tourists, Tianjin is also worth at least a day trip. Spending the night is certainly possible, but hotels in Tianjin are expensive.

ROBERT STOREY

Tianjin antique market is one of the best places in North China to buy genuine antiques.

Information

CITS (☎ 835-8349; fax 835-2619) is at 22 Youyi Lu (just opposite the Friendship Store) as is their competitor, Tianjin Overseas Tourism Corporation (☎ 835-0821; fax 835-2619). The PSB is at 30 Tangshan Dao, and the Bank of China (☎ 331-1559) is at 80 Jiefang Beilu.

The international post office, known as Dongzhan Post Office, is next to the main railway station. Overseas parcels can be sent here, and long-distance phone calls made. For letters, there is another post office conveniently located on Jiefang Beilu, a short walk north of the Astor Hotel. A private courier, DHL (☎ 331-4483; fax 332-3932) is at 195 Machang Dao, Hexi District. TNT Skypak (☎ 332-5462; fax 311-2367) is at 2 Zhejiang Lu, Heping District.

The International Medical Centre (☎ 331-8888 ext 416), located in Room 416 of the Hyatt Hotel, caters for the medical needs of the foreign community.

Antique Market 古玩市场

Just the sheer size and variety of the Antique Market (gǔwán shìcháng) makes it fascinating to stroll through. Amongst the many items on sale include stamps, silver coins, silverware, porcelain, clocks, photos of Mao, Cultural Revolution exotica and old books.

The market runs seven days a week, on weekdays only occupying a section of Shenyang Dao in the centre of town. On weekends it expands enormously, spilling out into side streets in every direction. Operating hours are from 7.30 am until around 3 pm – it's best to arrive around 8 am for the widest selection. Sunday morning is best.

Ancient Culture Street 古文化街

The Ancient Culture Street (gǔ wénhuà jiē) is an attempt to recreate the appearance of an ancient Chinese city. Besides the traditional buildings, the street is lined with vendors plugging every imaginable type of cultural memento from Chinese scrolls, paintings and chops to the latest heavy metal sounds on CD. During certain public holidays, street operas are staged here.

Within the confines of the street is the small Tianhou Temple (tiānhòu gōng). Tianhou (Heaven Queen) is the goddess of the sea, and is known by various names (Matsu in Taiwan, Tin Hau in Hong Kong). It is claimed that Tianjin's Tianhou Temple was built in 1326, but it has seen a bit of renovation work since then.

The Ancient Culture Street is a major drawcard for tourists, both foreigners and Chinese. The street is in the north-west part of town.

Confucius Temple 文庙

On the north side of Dongmennei Dajie, one block west of the Ancient Culture Street, is Tianjin's Confucius Temple (wén miào). It was originally built in 1463 during the Ming Dynasty. The temple, and Confucianists in general, took a beating during the Cultural Revolution. By 1993 the buildings had been restored and opened to the public.

Grand Mosque 清真大寺

Although it has a distinctly Chinese look, the Grand Mosque (qīngzhēn sì) is an active place of worship for Tianjin's Muslims. The mosque is on Dafeng Lu, not far south of the west railway station.

Dabeiyuan Monastery 大悲院

This is one of the largest and best-preserved temples in the city. Dabeiyuan (dàbēiyuàn) was built between 1611 and 1644, was expanded in 1940, battered during the Cultural Revolution and finally restored in 1980. The temple is on Tianwei Lu in the northern part of the city.

Catholic Church 西开教堂

This is one of the most bizarre looking churches you'll ever see. Situated on the southern end of Binjiang Dao, the twin onion domes of the cathedral, also known as the Xikai Church (xīkāi jiāotáng), form a dramatic back-drop to the 'Coca-Cola Bridge' (a pedestrian overpass crossing Nanjing Lu). It's definitely worth a look. Church services are now being permitted again on Sunday, which is about the only time you'll have a chance to view the inside.

Earthquake Memorial 抗震纪念碑

Just opposite the Friendship Hotel on Nanjing Lu is a curious pyramid-shaped memorial. Though there's not much to see here, the Earthquake Memorial (kàngzhèn jìniànbēi) is a pointed reminder of the horrific events of 28 July 1976, when an earthquake registering eight on the Richter scale struck north-east China.

It was the greatest natural disaster of the decade. Tianjin was severely affected and the city was closed to tourists for two years. The epicentre was at Tangshan – that city basically disappeared in a few minutes.

Hai River Park 海河公园

Stroll along the banks of the Hai River (a popular pastime with the locals) and see photo booths, fishing, early-morning taiji, opera-singing practice and old men toting bird cages. The esplanades of the Hai River Park (hǎihé gōngyuán) have a peculiarly Parisian feel, in part due to the fact that some of the railing and bridge work is French.

Tianjin's sewerage has to go somewhere and the river water isn't so pure that you'd want to drink it. It's not

Venice, but there are tourist boat cruises on the Hai River which start not far from the Astor Hotel.

TV Tower 电视塔

In an attempt to whip the masses into patriotic fervour and prove that Tianjin is a modern metropolis, the TV Tower (diànshì tái) has been declared the great wonder of the city. Indeed, it's proven to be a major drawcard for domestic tourists. You can visit the summit for a whopping Y120 fee and enjoy the warm feeling you get being atop the pride and joy of Tianjin. Views from the top aren't spectacular in the daytime, but things get better at

ROBERT STOREY

Tianjin is a bustling commercial centre that retains traces of its colonial history.

night. The tower is also topped by a revolving restaurant.

You won't have any trouble locating the TV Tower – it dominates the skyline on the south side of town.

Shuishang Park 水上公园

The large Shuishang Park (shuǐshàng gōngyuán) is in the south-west corner of town, not far from the TV Tower. The name in Chinese means 'Water Park' and over half the surface area is a lake. The major activity here is renting rowing boats and pedal boats.

It's one of the more relaxed places in busy Tianjin, except on weekends when the locals descend on the place like cadres at a banquet. The park features a Japanese-style floating garden and a decent zoo.

Getting to the park from the railway station requires two buses. Take bus No 8 to the terminus and from there hop onto bus No 54, also to the terminus which is just outside the park entrance.

Art Museum 艺术博物馆

The Art Museum (yìshù bówùguǎn) is easy to get to and is pleasant to stroll around. It's at 77 Jiefang Beilu, one stop from the main railway station.

Zhou Enlai Memorial Hall
周恩来纪念馆

Zhou Enlai is perhaps China's most respected revolutionary, in part because he tried to keep Mao's chaotic Cultural Revolution in check. Zhou grew up in Shaoxing in Zhejiang Province but attended school in Tianjin, so his classroom is enshrined and there are photos and other memorabilia from his time there (1913-17). His memorial hall (zhōu ēnlái jìniàn guǎn) is on the western side of the city in the Nankai District, occupying the eastern building of Nankai School.

Yongyang Ancient Gardens 雍阳古园

The latest addition to Tianjin's tourist potpourri, the Yongyang Ancient Gardens (yōngyáng gǔyuán) are a recreated Han Dynasty village of the sort now become popular in kitschy eastern China. Everything a tourist could want from costume jewellery to sedan chair rides are available here, for a fee.

Perhaps the most interesting exhibit is a palace based on a Chinese classic novel, *Canonisation of the Gods*. Inside the palace are 18 scenes from ancient Han times. A variety of modern sound and lighting techniques are used to create a sense of realism so you won't mistake this for a bad amusement park ride.

Yongyang Ancient Gardens is in the village of Yangcun, about 30 km north of central Tianjin and just off the Beijing-Tianjin expressway.

Places to Stay

There are heaps of decent hotels of high standard which have been placed off-limits to foreigners. Those which do permit foreigners charge ridiculous prices. So unless you've got a Chinese ID card, real or fake, and heaps of money, or ingratiate yourself into one of the university residences, you'll probably end up back at the station.

The only budget place that accepts foreigners is the *Guomin Hotel* (☎ 711-3353) (*guómín fàndiàn*), at the corner of Heping Lu and Chifeng Dao. Acceptable doubles cost Y164.

The *Bohai Hotel* (☎ 712-3391), at 277 Heping Lu, has suitable rooms for Y328.

Also on the cheaper end by Tianjin standards is the *Furama Hotel* (☎ 431-0961; fax 431-1751) (*fùlìhuá dàjiǔdiàn*), at 104 Qiwei Lu. It's on the east bank of the Hai River not far from the pricey Astor Hotel. Standard/deluxe rooms cost Y280/370, and suites are Y400 to Y500.

The *Tianjin Grand Hotel* (☎ 835-9000; fax 835-9822) (*tiānjīn bīnguǎn*) is on Youyi Lu, Hexi District. And grand it is: 1000 beds in two high-rise blocks built in 1960. Once a well-known cheapie, it's been fully renovated and prices have been ramped up. The budget rooms are Y340, but otherwise it's Y620.

The *Tianjin No 1 Hotel* (☎ 331-0707; fax 331-3341) (*tiānjīn dìyī fàndiàn*) is at 158 Jiefang Beilu opposite the Hyatt. The place boasts a bit of old world charm, which perhaps will make you feel better about having to fork out Y439 for a double. Take bus No 13 three stops from the main railway station and walk south.

If you've got money to burn, why not stroll across the street to the *Hyatt Hotel* (☎ 331-8888; fax 331-0021) (*kǎiyuè fàndiàn*), at 219 Jiefang Beilu. Superior/deluxe rooms cost Y1370/1495 and suites begin at Y1825.

Coming back down to earth, there's the *Park Hotel* (☎ 830-9815; fax 830-2042) (*lèyuán fàndiàn*) at 1 Leyuan Lu. Doubles cost Y510.

The *Friendship Hotel* (☎ 831-0372; fax 831-0616) *(yǒuyí bīnguǎn)* charges rather unfriendly prices – doubles are Y700. The hotel is at 94 Nanjing Lu.

The *Astor Hotel* (☎ 331-1688; fax 331-6282) *(lìshùndé fàndiàn)*, at 33 Tai'erzhuang Lu, dates from early this century but has been completely refurbished. Doubles cost from Y1037 to Y1328, suites are Y1411 to Y4714, or rent a cottage for a mere Y7370.

One of the most glamorous places in town is the 346-room *Crystal Palace Hotel* (☎ 835-6888; fax 835-8886) *(shuǐjīnggōng fàndiàn)*, at 28 Youyi Lu. Facilities include a swimming pool, tennis court, health club and French restaurant. A standard room is Y1062 and suites are Y1892 to Y5544, to which you must add a 15% surcharge.

Also in the neighbourhood is the *Geneva Hotel* (☎ 835-2222; fax 835-9855) *(jīnlìhuá dàjiǔdiàn)*, 30 Youyi Lu, where doubles cost Y670 to Y1340. The hotel is in the rear; the front side of the building is the World Economy & Trade Exhibition Centre, one of the most perverse architectural nightmares in China.

The *Sheraton Hotel* (☎ 334-3388; fax 335-8740) *(xǐláidēng dàjiǔdiàn)* is on Zijinshan Lu in the south of Tianjin. The hotel dishes up 281 rooms priced between Y1200 and Y1400, plus 49 suites ranging from Y2500 to Y5000. To that add another 15% surcharge, but if it helps the buffet breakfast is thrown in free. Another freebie for guests is a copy of the *China Daily*.

Places to Eat

Tianjin specialities are mostly in the seasonal seafood line and include crab, prawns, cuttlefish soup and fried carp.

The place to go is *Food Street (shípǐn jiē)*, a covered alley with two levels of restaurants. Old places close and new ones open all the time here, but there are approximately 40 to 50 restaurants on each level. You need to check prices – some of the food stalls are dirt cheap but a few upmarket restaurants are almost absurdly expensive. You can find some real exotica here, like snake (expensive), dog meat (cheap) and eels (mid-range). Food Street is a couple of blocks south of Nanma Lu, about one km west of the centre.

Rongji Dajie is an alley just one block north of Food Street and also boasts a fair share of restaurants. The *Quanjude* (☎ 735-0046) is at 53 Rongji Dajie. Upstairs are banquet rooms with moderate to expensive prices. Seafood is expensive (like sea cucumber, a delicacy that chefs love to foist on foreigners).

Kiessling's Bakery (qīshìlín cāntīng), built by the Austrians back in foreign concession days (1911), is a Tianjin institution. It's at 33 Zhejiang Lu, west of the Astor Hotel. From the railway station it's the fourth stop on the No 13 bus route.

The *Hyatt Hotel* does a memorable breakfast buffet costing Y60 which can fill you up for the rest of the day.

Should you wish to fortify a main meal, an ice cream or a coffee, Tianjin produces a variety of liquid substances. There's *kafeijiu* which approximates to Kahlua, and *sekijiu*, which is halfway between vodka and aviation fuel.

Getting There & Away

Air CAAC (☎ 730-4045, 730-5888) is at 242 Heping Lu. Dragonair and CAAC both offer direct flights between Hong Kong and Tianjin for HK$2270. Dragonair (☎ 330-1234) has a booking office in the Hyatt Hotel. CITS is also a booking agent for Dragonair.

Bus Buses to Beijing depart from in front of the main railway station. Costs depend on bus size, but average around Y25. In Beijing, catch the bus to Tianjin from the west side of the car park in front of the Beijing main railway station. The great advantage the bus has over the train is that there are no hassles in buying a ticket and you are guaranteed a seat.

Train For Beijing trains you'll want the main station in Tianjin. Some trains stop at both main and west, and some go only through the west station (particularly those originating in Beijing and heading south). Through trains to north-east China often stop at the north station.

Foreigners can avoid the horrible queues by purchasing tickets on the 2nd floor at the soft-seat ticket office.

Express trains take just under two hours for the trip between Tianjin and Beijing. Local trains take about 2½ hours.

Boat Tianjin's harbour is Tanggu, 50 km (30 minutes by train) from Tianjin proper. This is one of China's major ports, offering a number of possibilities for arriving and departing by boat. For further details, see the Boat section in the Getting There & Away chapter.

Glossary

Beiping – literally 'Northern Peace', the official name of the capital from 1368 to 1403 before changing to Beijing ('Northern Capital')

CAAC – China Aviation Administration of China, which controls most of China's domestic and foreign airlines
catty – Chinese unit of weight, one catty *(jīn)* equals 0.6 kg (1.32 pounds)
CITS – China International Travel Service
Concessions – small foreign colonies in all but name, commonly found in big eastern cities like Shanghai and Tianjin; all Concessions were abolished when the Communists came to power in 1949
CTS – China Travel Service
Cultural Revolution – a mass movement started by Mao Zedong which lasted from 1966 to 1970, causing enormous chaos and perhaps a million deaths

Dadu – the 'Great Capital', Beijing's ancient name during the Mongol period, or Yuan Dynasty (1215-1368)

fengshui – an ancient form of divination studying the influence of geographical features

gongfu – a form of Chinese martial arts, usually called *kung fu* in the West; see also *taijiquan*

hutong – a narrow backstreet or alleyway

jie – the commonest word for a street; *dajie* is an avenue

Kuomintang – the Nationalist Party which controlled mainland China from 1911 to 1949, and still controls Taiwan

laobaixing – common people, the masses
little red book – the name commonly used in the West for the *Quotations of Chairman Mao Zedong*, the book universally read and studied in China before and during the Cultural Revolution

Manchus – a non-Chinese ethnic group from Manchuria (present-day north-east China) which took over China and established the Qing Dynasty (1644-1911)

Overseas Chinese – those Chinese who have left China permanently and now live abroad

Peking – the spelling of 'Beijing' before the Communists adopted the Pinyin romanisation system in 1958
ping – Chinese unit of area, one ping equals 1.82 sq metres (5.97 sq feet)
Pinyin – the phonetic romanisation system adopted by the Communist Party in 1958
PLA – People's Liberation Army
PRC – People's Republic of China, China's official name
PSB – Public Security Bureau, the police
putonghua – the standard form of the Chinese language used since the beginning of this century, based on the Beijing dialect

qigong – a variation of *gongfu* (see above) claimed to be capable of causing miracle cures

Red Guards – fanatical devotees of Mao Zedong during the Cultural Revolution
RMB – Renminbi (or 'people's money'), China's currency
ROC – Republic of China, the nation's official name from 1911 to 1949; the Kuomintang in Taiwan still uses this name

tael – Chinese unit of weight, one tael *(liǎng)* equals 37.5 grams (1.32 ounces) and there are 16 taels to the *catty* (see above)
taijiquan – slow motion shadow boxing, a form of exercise; commonly shortened to *taiji* (called *tai chi* in the West)

Yanjing – the 'Capital of Yan', Beijing's ancient name during the Liao Dynasty (907-1125 AD)
yuan – the main unit of Chinese currency

Index

Maps

Eastern China

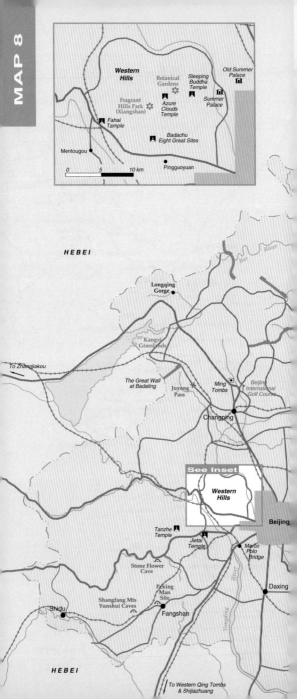

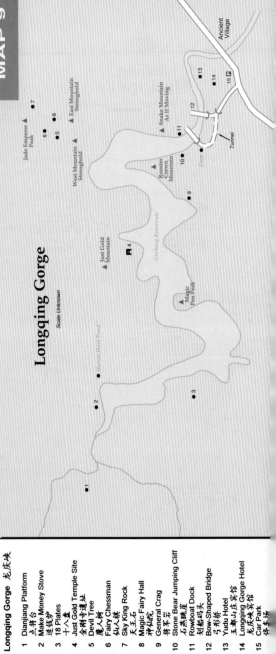

Longqing Gorge

Scale Unknown

Longqing Gorge 龙庆峡

1 Dianjiang Platform
   点将台
2 Make Money Stove
   造钱炉
3 18 Plates
   十八盘
4 Just Gold Temple Site
   全刚寺遗址
5 Devil Tree
   魔人树
6 Fairy Chessman
   仙人棋
7 Sky King Rock
   天王石
8 Magic Fairy Hall
   神仙院
9 General Crag
   将军岩
10 Stone Bear Jumping Cliff
   石熊跳崖
11 Rowboat Dock
   划船码头
12 Bow-Shaped Bridge
   弓形桥
13 Yudu Hotel
   玉都山庄宾馆
14 Longqing Gorge Hotel
   龙庆峡宾馆
15 Car Park
   停车场

Jade Emperor Peak ▲

East Mountain Stronghold ▲

West Mountain Stronghold ▲

Horse Hoof Pond

Just Gold Mountain ▲

Gucheng Reservoir

Magic Pen Peak ▲

Rooster Crown Mountain ▲

Snake Mountain As If Moving ▲

Dam

Tunnel

Ancient Village

MAP 10

Tianxian
Waterfall

Beijing First
Waterfall &
Black Dragon
Pool

1

Cloud Peak
(Yunfengshan)

2

To
Simatai Great
Wall (10 km) &
Tongliao

3

Lupi Pass

4

Miyun
Reservoir

5

White Dragon Pool
(Bailongtan)

6

7

8

To Chengde

Baihe Outskirts
Park

10

Chaobu

9

11

Miyun

eijing
km)

Miyun
Reservoir

0   4   8 km

Miyun Reservoir 密云水库

1 Fengjiayu
   冯家峪
2 Banchengzi
   半诚子
3 Bulaotun
   不老屯
4 Taishitun
   太师屯
5 Yunhu Holiday Resort
   云湖渡假村
6 Park on the Dam
   坝前公园
7 Xiwengzhuang
   溪翁庄
8 Miyun International
   Amusement Park
   密云国际游乐场
9 Miyun Railway Station
   密云火车站
10 Mujiayu
   穆家峪
11 Dachengzi
   大城子

ROBERT STOREY

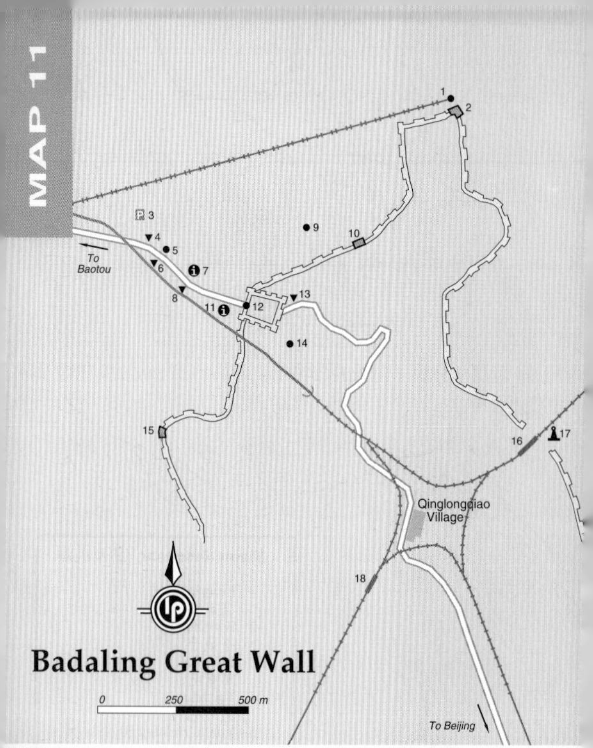

MAP 11

1
2
3
4
5
6
7
8
9
10
11
12
13
14
15
16
17
18

To Baotou

Qinglongqiao Village

Badaling Great Wall

0   250   500 m

To Beijing

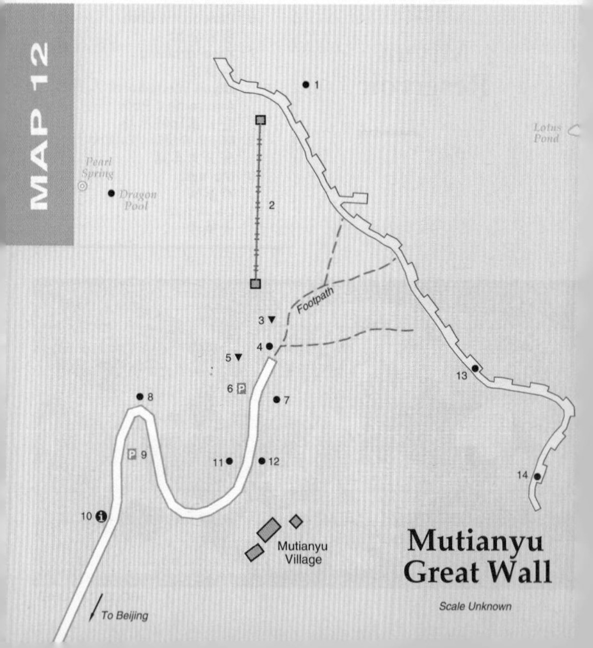

MAP 12

1
2
3
4
5
6
7
8
9
10
11
12
13
14

Pearl Spring

Dragon Pool

Lotus Pond

Footpath

Mutianyu Village

Mutianyu Great Wall

To Beijing

Scale Unknown

MAP 11 Badaling Great Wall 八达岭长城

1 Cable Car
缆车
2 North No 8 Tower
北八楼
3 Car Park
停车场
4 Yanshan Restaurant
燕山餐厅
5 Circle Vision Theatre
长城全周影院
6 Reclining Dragon
Restaurant
卧龙餐厅
7 Tourist Shop
商店
8 Restaurant
餐厅
9 Fort
炮台

10 North No 4 Tower
北四楼
11 Tourist Shop
商店
12 North Gate Lock & Key
北门锁钥
13 Foreigners' Restaurant
外宾餐厅
14 Former Outpost of Juyong
Pass
居庸外镇
15 South Fourth Tower
南四楼
16 Qinglongqiao Station
青龙桥站
17 Zhan Tianyou Statue
詹天佑像
18 Qinglongqiao New Station
青龙桥新站

GLENN BEANLAND

The Wall at Mutianyu is often less crowded than at Badaling.

MAP 12 Mutianyu Great Wall 慕田峪长城

1 Beacon Tower
烽火台
2 Cable Car
缆车
3 Foreigners' Restaurant
外宾餐厅
4 Yanjing Studio
燕京书画社
5 Locals' Restaurant
内宾餐厅
6 No 1 Car Park
第一停车场
7 Ticket Office
售票处

8 Ticket Office
售票处
9 No 2 Car Park
第二停车场
10 Tourist Office
旅游区办事处
11 Mandarin Duck Pine Tree
鸳鸯松
12 Guest-Welcoming Pine
Tree
迎宾松
13 Zhengguan Tower
正关台
14 Stone Mortar
石臼

MAP 13

Ming Tombs 十三陵

1 Tailing Tomb
  泰陵
2 Kangling Tomb
  康陵
3 Maoling Tomb
  茂陵
4 Yuling Tomb
  裕陵
5 Qingling Tomb
  庆陵
6 Xianling Tomb
  献陵
7 Changling Tomb
  长陵
8 Jingling Tomb
  景陵
9 Dingling Tomb
  定陵
10 Zhaoling Tomb
   昭陵
11 International Friendship Forest
   国际友谊林
12 Heliport
   空中旅游机场
13 Yongling Tomb
   永陵

14 Deling Tomb
   德陵
15 Golf Course
   北京国际高尔夫球场
16 Seven Arch Bridge
   七孔桥
17 Siling Tomb
   思陵
18 Small Palace Gate
   小宫门
19 Lingxing Gate
   棂星门
20 Stone Statues
   石像生
21 Great Palace Gate
   大宫门
22 Fairy Cave
   仙人洞
23 Shisanling Reservoir Memorial
   十三陵水库纪念碑
24 Stone Arch
   石牌坊
25 Changping North Railway
   Station
   昌平北火车站

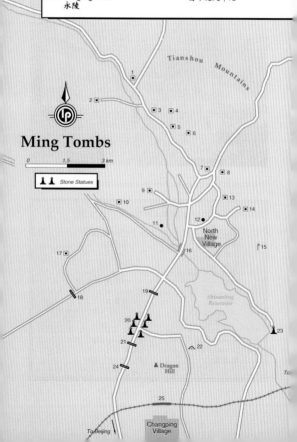

Ming Tombs

Stone Statues

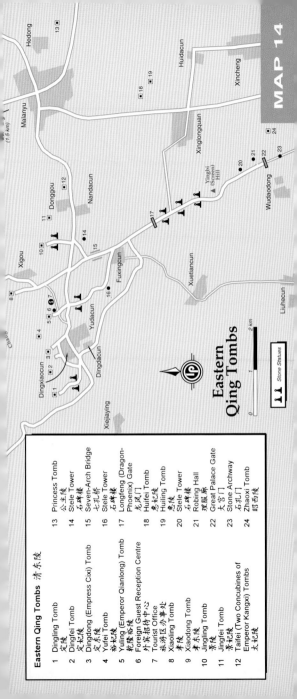

MAP 14

Eastern Qing Tombs 清东陵

1. Dingling Tomb
   定陵
2. Dingfei Tomb
   定妃陵
3. Dingdong (Empress Cixi) Tomb
   定东陵
4. Yufei Tomb
   裕妃陵
5. Yuling (Emperor Qianlong) Tomb
   裕陵玫陵
6. Foreign Guest Reception Centre
   外宾招待中心
7. Tourist Office
   旅游区办事处
8. Xiaoling Tomb
   孝陵
9. Xiaodong Tomb
   孝东陵
10. Jingling Tomb
    景陵
11. Jingfei Tomb
    景妃陵
12. Taifei (Two Concubines of
    Emperor Kangxi) Tombs
    大妃陵

13. Princess Tomb
    公主陵
14. Stele Tower
    石碑楼
15. Seven-Arch Bridge
    七孔桥
16. Stele Tower
    石碑楼
17. Longfeng (Dragon-
    Phoenix) Gate
    龙凤门
18. Huifei Tomb
    慧妃陵
19. Huiling Tomb
    惠陵
20. Stele Tower
    石碑楼
21. Robing Hall
    更服殿
22. Great Palace Gate
    大宫门
23. Stone Archway
    石坊门
24. Zhaoxi Tomb
    昭西陵

Eastern
Qing Tombs

0 _____ 2 km

Stone Statues

MAP 15

Shidu

Shidu 十渡

1 Shidu Railway Station
   十渡火车站
2 Longshan Hotel
   龙山饭店
3 Dragon Mountain
   Buddhist Character
   龙山佛字
4 Anti-Japanese War
   Memorial
   平西抗日烈士纪念馆
5 Rowboat Rentals &
   Swimming Area
   划船场
6 Viewing Buddhas Pavilion
   望佛亭
7 Xiaoyao Restaurant
   逍遥菜厅
8 Campground
   帐逢村
9 Wangyu Pavilion
   望浴亭
10 Liudu Hotel
   六渡旅馆

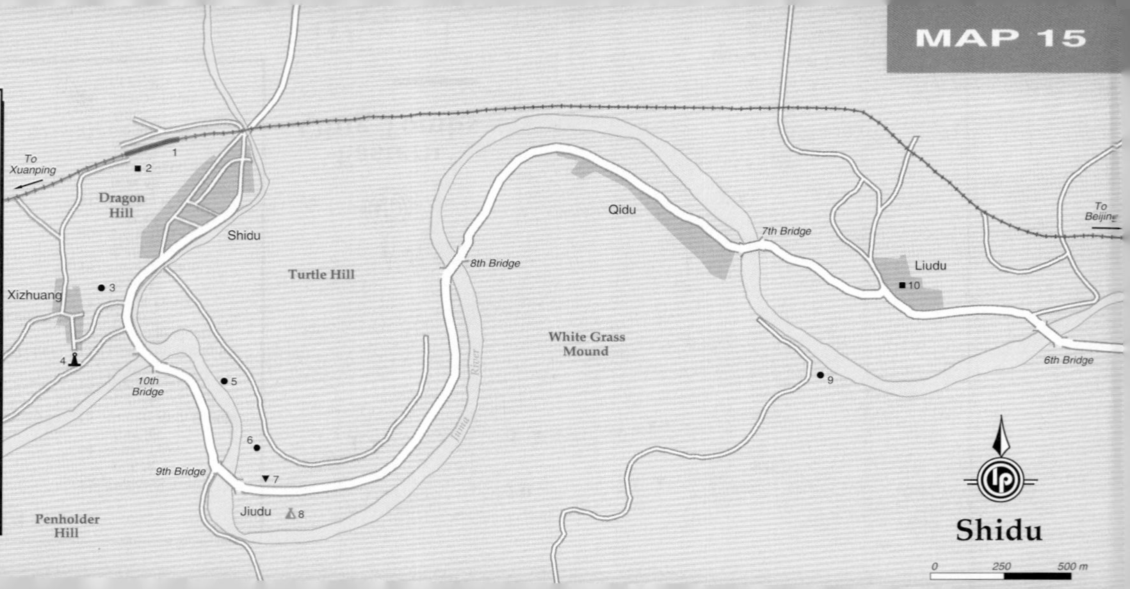

Faces of old and new China.

MAP 16

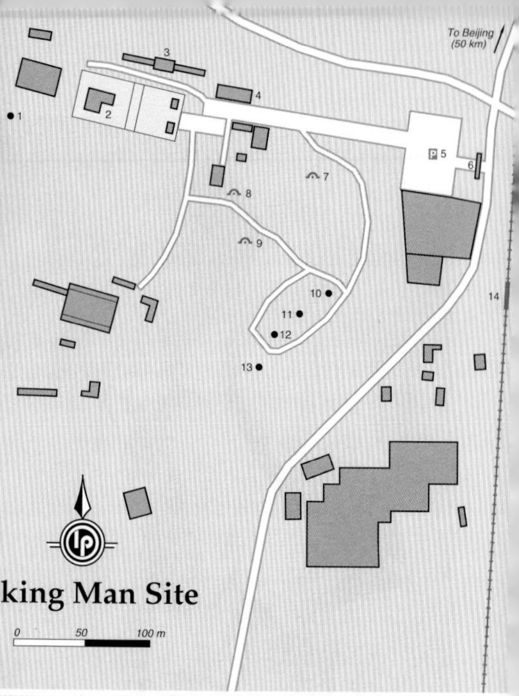

To Beijing
(50 km)

• 1

2

3

4

P 5

6

7

8

9

10

11

12

13

14

Peking Man Site

0   50   100 m

MAP 17

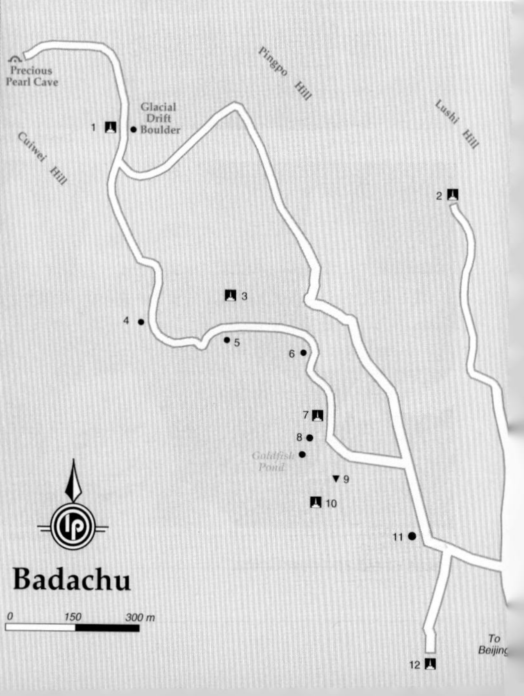

Pingpo Hill

Precious
Pearl Cave

Cuiwei Hill

Glacial
Drift
Boulder

1

Lushi Hill

2

3

4

5

6

7

8

Goldfish
Pond

9

10

11

12

To
Beijing

Badachu

0   150   300 m

MAP 16 Peking Man Site 周口店

1 No 2 Dig Site
   第二地点
2 Peking Man Exhibition
   Hall
   北京猿人展览馆
3 Hostel
   招待所
4 Foreigners' Reception
   Room
   外宾接待室
5 Car Park
   停车场
6 Front Gate
   大门
7 Pigeon Hall Cave
   鸽子堂洞

8 Apeman Cave
   猿人洞
9 Upper Cave
   山顶洞
10 No 15 Dig Site
    第十五地点
11 No 4 Dig Site
    第四地点
12 No 12 Dig Site
    第十二地点
13 No 3 Dig Site
    第三地点
14 Zhoukoudian Railway
    Station
    周口店火车站

GLENN BEANLAND

Enjoying an impromptu show at Badachu.

MAP 17 Badachu (Eight Great Sights) 八大处

1 Fragrant World Temple
   香界寺
2 Rewards Attainment
   Temple
   证果寺
3 Great Deliverance
   Temple
   大悲寺
4 Dragon Spring Nunnery
   龙泉庵
5 Badachu Villa
   八大处别墅
6 Three Hills Nunnery
   三山庵

7 Buddha's Tooth Relic
   Pagoda
   佛牙舍利塔
8 Long Corridor
   长廊
9 Restaurant
   餐厅
10 Divine Light Temple
    灵光寺
11 Ticket Office
    售票处
12 Eternal Peace Temple
    长安寺

MAP 18

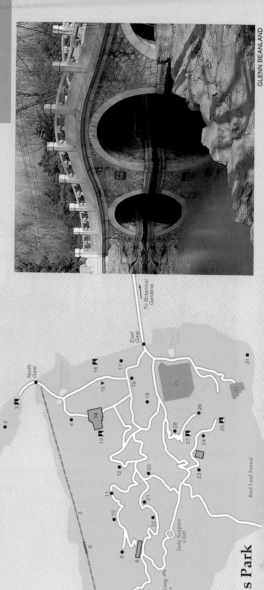

GLENN BEANLAND

Fragrant Hills Park

To Botanical Gardens

East Gate

North Gate

Red Leaf Forest

Jade Sceptre Cliff

Sun Facing Cave

MAP 18 Fragrant Hills Park 香山公园

1 Diamond Throne Pagoda
金刚宝座塔
2 Sun Yatsen Memorial Hall
孙中山纪念堂
3 Azure Clouds Temple
碧云寺
4 Unbosoming Chamber
见心斋
5 Chairlift
游览索道
6 Middle Station
中站
7 Incense Burner Peak
香炉峰
8 Platform
平台
9 Stele of Western Hills
Shimmering in Snow
西山晴雪
10 Tiered Cloud Villa
梯云山馆
11 Fourth Jade Flower Villa
玉花四院
12 Hibiscus Hall
芙蓉馆
13 Glazed Tile Pagoda
琉璃塔
14 Brilliance Temple
昭庙
15 Pine Forest Restaurant
松林餐厅
16 Xiangshan Villa
香山别墅

17 Administrative Office
管理处
18 Peak Viewing Pavilion
望峰亭
19 Scattered Clouds
Pavilion
多云亭
20 Jade Flower Villa
玉花山庄
21 Varied Scenery Pavilion
多景亭
22 Moonlight Villa
栖月山庄
23 Jade Fragrance Hall
玉香馆
24 White Pine Pavilion
白松亭
25 Xiangshan Temple Site
香山寺遗址
26 Halfway Pavilion
半山亭
27 Red Glow Temple
洪光寺
28 Eighteen Turns
十八盘
29 Xiangshan Hotel
香山宾馆
30 Twin Lakes Villa
双清别墅
31 See Clouds Rise
看云起

CHRIS TAYLOR

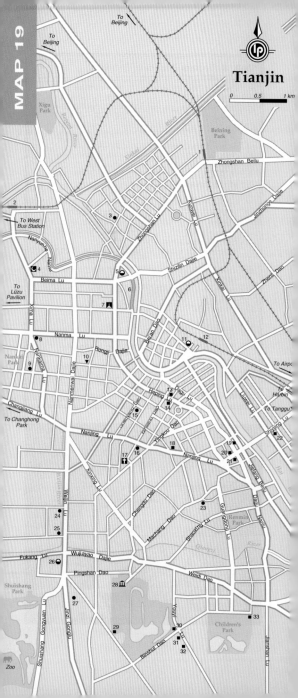

MAP 19

Tianjin

0   0.5   1 km

To Beijing
To Beijing

Xigu
Park

Beining
Park

1

Zhongshan Beilu

Jinzhong Dajie

2

To West
Bus Station

3

Zhongshan Lu

Nanwuma   Nanlu

4

Beima   Lu

5

To
Lüzu
Pavilion

6

Xima   Lu

7

Shizilin Dajie

Xinan   Lu

Zhen   Dao

Nanma   Lu

8

Beian   Dao

11   12

To Airp

Nanjing   Dajie

Rongji   Dajie

To
Harbin

Nankai
Park

9

10

Hoping   Lu

Liuwei   Lu

To Tanggu

Changjiang   Lu

13

To Changhong
Park

Chengyang   Dao

15

14

Binjiang   Dao

Nanjing   Lu

18

19

22

16

Yingkou   Dao

17

Nanjing   Lu

20

Weijin   Road

Xingou   Lu

Chengdu   Dao

23

Machang   Dao

Shaoxing   Lu

Guangdong   Lu

Renmin
Park

Jianjiao   Beilu

Diani   Nanlu

24

25

Fukang   Lu

Wujiayao   Dajie

Qiang   Ji

River

26

Pingshan   Dao

Weidi   Dao

Shuishang
Park

Gongyuan   Lu

Jinzi   Gongju

27

28

Binshui   Dao

29

30

33

Children's
Park

31

32

Jianshan   Lu

Shuishang   Lu

Zoo

MAP 19 Tianjin 天津

PLACES TO STAY

13	Bohai Hotel 渤海饭店
14	Guomin Hotel 国民大酒店
18	Friendship Hotel 友谊宾馆
19	Astor Hotel 利顺德大饭店
20	Tianjin No 1 Hotel 天津第一饭店
21	Hyatt Hotel 凯悦饭店
22	Furama Hotel 富丽华大酒店
29	Sheraton Hotel 喜来登大酒店
30	Crystal Palace Hotel 水晶宫饭店
31	Tianjin Grand Hotel 天津宾馆
32	Geneva Hotel 津利华大酒店
33	Park Hotel 乐园饭店

OTHER

1	North Railway Station 北火车站
2	West Railway Station 西火车站
3	Dabeiyuan Monastery 大悲院
4	Grand Mosque 清真寺
5	North East Bus Station 东北角发车站
6	Ancient Culture Street 古文化街
7	Confucius Temple 文庙
8	5th Subway Exit 地下铁第五站
9	Zhou Enlai Memorial Hall 周恩来记念馆
10	Food St 食品街
11	Buses to Beijing 往北京汽车站
12	Main Railway Station 天津火车站
15	Antique Market 古玩市场
16	International Market 国际商场
17	Catholic Church 西开教堂
23	Foreign Languages Bookstore 外文书店
24	Tianjin University 天津大学
25	Nankai University 南开大学
26	South Bus Station 八里台发车站
27	TV Tower 电视台
28	Natural History Museum & Cadre Club 自然博物馆, 干部俱乐部

ROBERT STOREY

Food Street: *the* place for food in Tianjin.

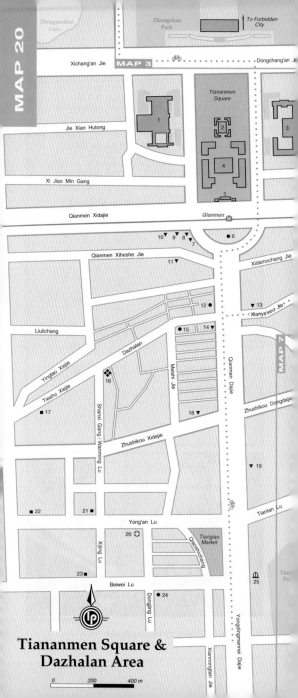

MAP 20

To Forbidden City

Zhongnanhai Lake

Zhongshan Park

Xichang'an Jie

Dongchang'an J

MAP 3

Tiananmen Square

Jie Xian Hutong

1

2

3

Xi Jiao Min Gang

4

5

Qianmen Xidajie

Qianmen

6

10 9 8 7

Qianmen Xiheshe Jie

11

Xidamochang Jie

13

Xianyu'kou Jie

12

Liulichang

15 14

Dazhalan

Meishi Jie

16

Tieshu Xiejie

Yingtao Xiejie

17

18

Zhushikou Dongdajie

MAP 7

Qianmen Dajie

Shaml Gang / Wanming Lu

Zhushikou Xidajie

19

22

21

Tiantan Lu

Yong'an Lu

20

Tiangiao Market

Qiaoshichang

Xijing Lu

23

25

Beiwei Lu

24

Dongling Lu

Xianrongtian Jie

Yongdingmennei Dajie

Tia
Pa

Tiananmen Square &
Dazhalan Area

0   200   400 m

MAP 20 Tiananmen Square & Dazhalan Area
天安门广场, 大栅栏附近

PLACES TO STAY

17 Far East Hotel
   远东饭店
21 Dongfang Hotel
   东方饭店
22 Qianmen Hotel
   前门饭店
23 Rainbow & Beiwei Hotels
   天桥宾馆, 北纬饭店

PLACES TO EAT

7 McDonald's
   麦当劳
8 Sichuan Restaurant
   四川饭店
9 Vie de France Bakery
   大磨坊面包
10 Kentucky Fried Chicken
   肯德基家乡鸡
11 Zuihong Chaozhou Food
   City
   醉红潮州城, 正阳市场
13 Qianmen Quanjude
   Roast Duck Restaurant
   前门全聚德烤鸭店
14 Liubiju
   六必居
18 Pizza Hut
   必胜客
19 Gongdelin Vegetarian
   Restaurant
   功德林素菜馆

OTHER

1 Great Hall of the People
   人民大会堂
2 Monument of the
   People's Heroes
   人民英雄纪念碑
3 Chinese Revolution
   History Museum
   中国革命历史博物馆
4 Mao Zedong Mausoleum
   毛主席纪念堂
5 Qianmen
   前门
6 Arrow Tower
   箭楼
12 Bicycle Park
15 Tongrentang Drugstore
   同仁堂药店
16 Sun City Department
   Store
   太阳城商场
20 Friendship Hospital
   友谊医院
24 Tianqiao Theatre
   天桥剧场
25 Natural History Museum
   自然博物馆

GLENN BEANLAND

Snakes in a pickle in Dazhalan.

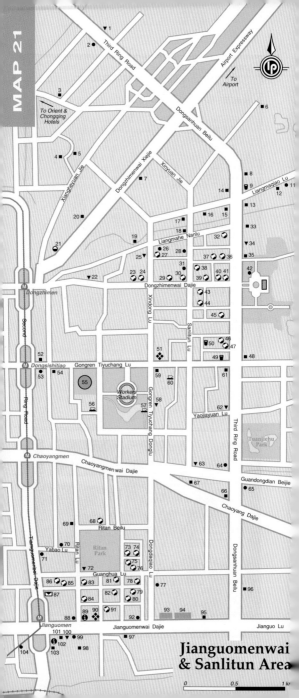

MAP 21

To Orient &
Chongqing
Hotels

Third Ring Road

Airport Expressway

To
Airport

Dongsanhuan Beilu

Xiangheyuan Jie

Dongzhimenwai Xiejie

Xinyuan Jie

Liangmaqiao Lu

Dongzhimen

Second

Ring Road

Liangmahe Nanlu

Dongzhimenwai Dajie

Xindong Lu

Sanlitun Lu

Dongsishitiao

Gongren Tiyuchang Lu

Workers'
Stadium

Gongren Tiyuchang Donglu

Yaojiayuan Lu

Third Ring Road

Tuanjiehu
Park

Chaoyangmen

Chaoyangmen wai Dajie

Guandongdian Beijie

Chaoyang Dajie

Ritan Beilu

Ritan Lu

Ritan
Park

Yabao Lu

Guanghua Lu

Dongdaqiao Lu

Dongsanhuan Beilu

Tiananmenwai Dajie

Jianguomen

Jianguomenwai Dajie

Jianguo Lu

Jianguomenwai
& Sanlitun Area

0   0.5   1 km

MAP 21 Jianguomenwai & Sanlitun Area
三里屯, 建国门外附近

PLACES TO STAY

3 SAS Royal Hotel &
   Nightman Disco
   皇家大饭店
4 Bailing Hotel
   百灵饭店
5 Jing'an Hotel
   静安宾馆
6 Huayuan Hotel
   华园饭店
7 Royal Inn
8 Hilton Hotel
   希尔顿饭店
10 21st Century Hotel
   二十一世纪饭店
12 Guangming Hotel
   光明饭店
13 Lufthansa Centre &
   Kempinski Hotel
   燕沙商城,
   凯宾斯基饭店
14 Fuhao Hotel
   富豪宾馆
15 Kunlun Hotel
   昆仑饭店
16 Huadu Hotel
   华都饭店
17 Capital Mansion
   京城大厦
19 Yuyang Hotel
   渔阳饭店
20 Sanyuan Hotel
   三元宾馆
33 Landmark Towers
   & Hotel
   亮马河大厦
35 Great Wall Sheraton
   长城饭店
48 Yongan Hotel
   永安
52 Poly Plaza
   保利大厦
54 Beijing Asia Hotel
   北京亚洲大酒店
59 Chains City Hotel
   城市宾馆
61 Zhaolong Hotel
   兆龙饭店
66 Jingguang New World
   Hotel
   京广斯世界饭店
67 Guoan Hotel
   国安宾馆
69 Ritan Hotel
   日坛宾馆

93 Jianguo Hotel
    建国饭店
94 Beijing Toronto Hotel
    京伦饭店
95 China World Trade Centre
    & Trader's Hotel
    国际贸易中心, 国贸饭店
96 Guanghua Hotel
    光华饭店
97 Guotai Hotel & Local Joint
    国泰饭店
98 CVIK Hotel & Scite Tower
    赛特饭店
101 Hotel New Otani
    长富宫饭店
103 Gloria Plaza Hotel
    凯莱大酒店

PLACES TO EAT

1   Johnny's Coffee
    咖啡店
9   Schiller's Pub
    酒吧
22 Pizza Hut
    必胜客
25 Xanadu Bar & Grill
    上都酒吧
34 Hard Rock Cafe
    硬石餐厅
49 Redwood Bar
    红杉吧
    (三里屯外交公寓)
56 Metro Cafe
    意大利咖啡店
57 Carella Cafe (Car Wash)
    洗车酒吧
58 Frank's Place &
    Berena's Bistro
    万龙酒吧
60 Cafe Cafe
    咖啡店
62 Asian Star Restaurant
    亚州之星新马印餐厅
63 Parati Restaurant
    八拉地娱乐城
71 Omar Khayyam
    Restaurant
72 Shenxian Douhua Cun
    神仙豆花村
100 Uncle Sam's Fastfood
    山姆叔叔快餐店

*Key continued on
next page*

Key continued from
previous page

OTHER

2 China International
Exhibition Centre
中国国际展览馆

10 Sino-Japanese Youth
Exchange Centre
中日青年交流中心

18 Rasput-Inn
拉斯布丁

21 Dongzhimen Bus Station
长途东直门中心站

23 Australian Embassy
澳大利亚大使馆

24 Canadian Embassy
加拿大大使馆

26 Tayuan Diplomatic
Building
塔园外交办公楼

27 Nepali Embassy
尼泊尔大使馆

28 International Store
北京国际商店

29 Malaysian Embassy
马来西亚大使馆

30 Spanish Embassy
西班牙大使馆

31 Friendship Supermarket
友谊超级商场

32 Singaporean Embassy
新加坡大使馆

36 Danish Embassy
丹麦大使馆

37 Swiss Embassy
瑞士大使馆

38 Belgium Embassy
比利时大使馆

39 German Embassy
德国大使馆

40 Swedish Embassy
瑞典大使馆

41 Pakistani Embassy
巴基斯坦大使馆

42 Agricultural Exhibition
Centre
农业展览馆

43 Hungarian Embassy
匈牙利大使馆

44 Laotian Embassy
老挝大使馆

45 French Embassy
法国大使馆

46 Italian Embassy
意大利大使馆

47 Norwegian Embassy
挪威大使馆

50 Jazz Ya & City Pub
House
爵士酒吧

51 Sanlitun Department
Store
三里屯百货商场

53 Hong Kong-Macau
Centre & Swissôtel
北京港澳中心

55 Workers' Gymnasium
工人体育馆

64 Hof Brauhaus
德国酒吧

65 Chaoyang Theatre
朝阳剧场

68 North Korean Embassy
北朝鲜大使馆

70 Yabao Lu
(clothing market)
雅宝路

71 Asia Pacific Building
亚太大厦

73 Romanian Embassy
罗马尼亚大使馆

74 New Zealand Embassy
新西兰大使馆

75 Indian Embassy
印度大使馆

76 British Embassy
英国大使馆

77 Mexican Wave &
Water Hole
墨西哥波涛

78 US Embassy (visas)
美国大使馆 (签证处)

79 US Embassy
(commerce)
美国大使馆 (商务处)

80 Irish Embassy
爱尔兰大使馆

81 Vietnamese Embassy
越南大使馆

82 Mongolian Embassy
蒙古大使馆

83 Polish Embassy
波兰大使馆

84 Czech Embassy
捷克大使馆

85 Philippine Embassy
菲律宾大使馆

86 Thai Embassy
泰国大使馆

87 International Post Office
国际邮店局

88 International Club
国际俱乐部

89 CITIC Building
国际大厦

ROBERT STOREY

Daoist sage with Peach of Immortality.

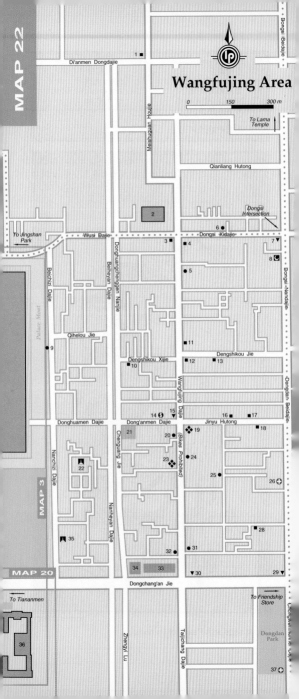

MAP 22 Wangfujing Area 王府井地区

PLACES TO STAY

1 Lüsongyuan Hotel
侣松圆宾馆
3 Wangfujing Grand Hotel
王府井大酒店
4 Guangdong Regency
Hotel
粤海皇都酒店
10 Fangyuan Hotel
芳园宾馆
11 Holiday Inn Crowne Plaza
国际艺苑皇冠假日饭店
12 Tianlun Dynasty Hotel
天伦王朝饭店
13 Novotel Hotel
松鹤大酒店
16 Taiwan Hotel
台湾饭店
17 Peace Hotel
和平宾馆
18 Palace Hotel
王府饭店
28 Xiehe Hotel
协和宾馆
33 Beijing Hotel
北京饭店
34 Grand Hotel
贵宝楼饭店
38 Jinlang Hotel
金朗大酒店

PLACES TO EAT

7 Kentucky Fried Chicken
肯德基家乡鸡
15 Dumpling King
饺子大王
21 Dong'anmen Night
Market
东安门夜市
29 Dongdan Fastfood
东单快餐厅
30 McDonald's
麦当劳

OTHER

2 China Art Gallery
中国美术馆
5 Capital Theatre
首都剧场
6 CAAC Booking Office
中国民航售票处
8 Dongsi Mosque
东四清真寺
9 PSB (Visa Extensions)
公安局外事科
14 Bank of China
中国银行
19 Xindong'an Shopping
Centre
新东安市场
20 Foreign Languages
Bookstore
外文书店
22 Pudu Temple
普渡寺
23 Beijing Department
Store
北京百货大楼
24 Dong'an Bazaar
东安市场
25 Central Fine Arts
Institute
中央美术学院
26 Beijing Union Hospital
协和医院
27 Dahua Cinema
大华电影院
31 Xinhua Bookstore
新华书店
32 China Photo Studio
中国照相
35 Huangshicheng Temple
皇史成
36 Chinese Revolution
History Museum
中国历史革命博物馆
37 Tongren Hospital
同仁医院

CHRIS TAYLOR

MAP 23 Central Beijing 北京市中心
(Map on following pages)

PLACES TO STAY

1	Longdu Hotel 龙都饭店	59	Yanjing Hotel 燕京饭店
3	Yanshan Hotel 燕山大酒店	61	Media Centre Hotel 梅地亚中心
4	Friendship Hotel 友谊宾馆	63	Xinxing Hotel 新兴宾馆
6	Big Bell Hotel 大钟寺饭店	66	Feixia Hotel 飞霞饭店
7	Jimen Hotel & NASA Disco 蓟门饭店	68	Minzu Hotel 民族饭店
8	Yuanwanglou Hotel 远望楼宾馆	78	Yuexiu Hotel 越秀大饭店
9	Desheng Hotel 德胜饭店	81	Grand View Garden Hotel
11	Grand Hotel Beijing 圆山大酒店	82	Beijing Commercial Business Complex 北京商务会馆
12	Huabei Hotel 华北大酒店	83	Qiaoyuan Hotel 侨园饭店
13	Orient Hotel 远东饭店	85	Capital Hotel 首都宾馆
14	Chongqing Hotel 重庆饭店	86	Xinqiao Hotel 新桥饭店
17	Overseas Chinese Hotel 华桥饭店	87	Chongwenmen Hotel 崇文门饭店
21	Hebei Hotel 河北饭店	88	Hademen Hotel 哈德门饭店
22	Bamboo Garden Hotel 竹园宾馆	91	International Hotel 国际饭店
29	Beihai Hotel 北海宾馆	95	Tiantan Sports Hotel 天坛体育宾馆
35	Shangyuan Hotel 上园饭店	96	Traffic Hotel 交通饭店
36	Exhibition Hotel & Exhibition Centre 北京展览饭店, 展览馆	97	Tiantan Hotel 天坛饭店
38	Olympic Hotel 奥林匹克饭店	99	Leyou & Hua Thai Hotels 乐游饭店, 华泰饭店
40	Zhongyuan Hotel 中苑宾馆	100	Longtan Hotel 龙潭饭店
43	Evergreen Hotel 万年青宾馆		
44	Shangri-La Hotel 香格里拉饭店		**PLACES TO EAT**
45	New Century Hotel 新世纪饭店	15	Shaoshan Mao's Restaurant 韶山毛家菜馆
46	Xiyuan Hotel 西苑饭店	20	Confucius Restaurant 孔子餐厅
47	Mandarin Hotel 新大都饭店	24	Li Family Restaurant 历家菜
49	Holiday Inn Downtown 金都假日饭店	27	Kaorouji Restaurant 北京烤肉季
		30	Mei Lanfang Memorial Hall 梅兰芳纪念馆

Map on following pages

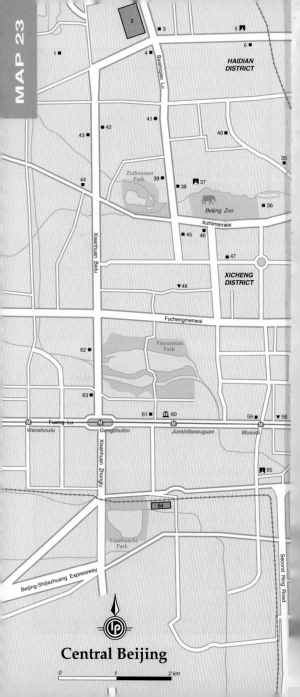

MAP 23

2

■ 3

5 ⚑

6 ■

HAIDIAN DISTRICT

1 ■

4 ■

Baishiqiao Lu

41 ●

● 42

43 ■

40 ■

35 ■

44 ■

Zizhuyuan Park

39 ●

⚑ 37

38 ■

Beijing Zoo

■ 36

Xizhimenwai

■ 45

46

● 47

XICHENG DISTRICT

▼48

Fuchengmenwai

62 ●

Yuyuantan Park

Xisanhuan Beilu

63 ■

61 ● 🏛 60

59 ■ ▼ 58

Ⓜ Fuxing Lu

Wanshoulu

Ⓜ Gongzhufen

Junshibowuguan

Muxudi Ⓜ

Xisanhuan Zhonglu

⚑ 65

64

Lianhuachi Park

Beijing-Shijiazhuang Expressway

Second Ring Road

Ⓛⓟ

Central Beijing

0   1   2 km